MANAGING EMPLOYEE WELL-BE

DONALD CURRIE

First published in 2003 by
Spiro Press
17–19 Rochester Row
London
SW1P 1LA
Telephone: +44 (0)870 400 1000

ISBN 1 904298 30 3

Reprinted June 2003
Ref 6308.JC.5.03

British Library Cataloguing-in-Publication Data.
A catalogue record for this book is available from the British Library.

Disclaimer: This publication is intended to assist you in identifying issues which
you should know about and about which you may need to seek specific advice. It
is not intended to be an exhaustive statement of the law or a substitute for seeking
specific advice.

Spiro Press USA
3 Front Street, Suite 331
PO Box 338
Rollinsford NH 03869
USA

Typeset by: Turn-Around Typesetting
Printed in Great Britain by: Biddles, UK
Cover design by: REAL451

For my wife
Sue Currie

Contents

List of figures and tables   xiii

Introduction   xv

About the author   xxv

....

1   Employee well-being   1

Introduction   1

Benefits and facilities   2

Four categories of welfare   3

Human resource management   4

Managers' perceptions of employees   5

Management and leadership   9

Employee well-being   11

Employee survival strategies   15

The effects of change   18

Emotional intelligence   19

Conclusion   22

References   22

2	**Understanding stress**	**23**
	Introduction	23
	Definition	23
	The cost of stress	24
	Stress as a commuter	26
	Types of stress	27
	Type A and Type B personalities	29
	Individual reactions to stress	30
	Sources and causes of stress	31
	Stress and change	32
	The mental effects of stress	34
	The physical effects of stress	35
	Positive stress	37
	The behavioural effects of stress	39
	Levels of stress	40
	The human function curve	41
	Managing and coping with stress	44
	Stress reduction strategies	45
	The manager as a counsellor	47
	Danger, heroes at work	49
	Coping with stress	50
	Managing lifestyle	52
	Conclusion	54
	References	56
3	**The healthy organisation**	**57**
	Introduction	57
	Work and individual differences	58
	Employment and health	60

Healthy workplace initiatives   63

The organisational perspective   68

Strategies for the long term   69

Managing change   70

Introducing policies   71

The role of culture   73

The importance of structure   74

The matrix process   78

Conclusion   80

References   82

4   Human resource management (HRM)   83

Introduction   83

Unitary and pluralistic perspectives   86

Descriptions of HRM   87

Central features of HRM   88

HRM and employee well-being   91

Human resource responsibility   92

Human resource planning   93

Human resource development   94

Teamworking   95

The psychological contract   97

Flexible working practices   98

Conclusion   102

References   103

5   Job satisfaction, involvement and motivation   105

Introduction   105

Job satisfaction and job involvement   106

Work motivation   110

Motivation theories   110

The human relations approach   122

Job enrichment, enlargement and redesign   123

Organisation Development   123

Conclusion   126

References   127

6   Managing diversity   129

Introduction   129

Discrimination   130

Equality and fairness   137

Individual differences   137

Minority groups   138

Political correctness   147

Equal opportunities policy   148

Major discriminatory factors   151

Impact on well-being   153

Conclusion   154

References   154

7   Managing individual differences   157

Introduction   157

Socialisation   158

Why we are all different   158

Perception   160

Coping vs expression   164

Attitudes   167

Measuring attitudes   167

Changing attitudes   171

Persuasive information   173

Training for change   173

Group exercises   174

Managerial attitudes   174

Implications for well-being   177

Conclusion   179

References   180

8   Legal aspects of employee well-being   181

Introduction   181

Legal aspects   183

Sex and marital status   183

Related legislation   185

Sex discrimination   187

Racial discrimination   190

Disability discrimination   191

The European situation   193

European and American approaches   194

Litigation   196

The internal justice system   201

Disciplinary rules and procedures   203

Grievance procedures   206

Administering organisational justice   208

Employee well-being   209

Conclusion   209

9   Technology in society   **211**

    Introduction   211

    Technology as an agent of change   211

    Hunter-gatherer to agrarian   212

    Agrarian to industrial   213

    Industrial to information   213

    Rate of advancement   216

    Definitions of new technology   217

    Technology and lifestyle   219

    Present and future technology   220

    The class system   224

    Effects of technology on people   225

    Conclusion   227

    References   228

10   Managing organisational change   **229**

    Introduction   229

    The nature of change   230

    Managing change   235

    Change and stress   245

    Conclusion   247

    References   248

References   **249**

Index   **253**

List of figures and tables

Figures

2.1	The social adjustment scale	33
2.2	General adaptation syndrome	36
2.3	Stress management scale	40
2.4	The human function curve	41
2.5	The job-person unit	43
2.6	Some typical symptoms of stress	46
3.1	A matrix organisation	79
5.1	Extrinsic and intrinsic job factors	108
5.2	The hierarchy of needs	112
7.1	A semantic differential scale	168
7.2	Example of a Thurstone scale	170
7.3	The managerial grid	175

Tables

2.1	Extrinsic and intrinsic stressors	43
5.1	The work environment	107
6.1	Common assumptions among managers	139

Introduction

This book is written from a general management perspective. The focus throughout is on employees, with the emphasis upon the ways in which the management of modern organisations affects employee well-being. Employee well-being is a subject that has been neglected until recent years, but significant changes in managerial style, and in employees' attitudes towards the way they are treated at work, have forced it rapidly up the managerial agenda. The education and training of managers has been modified to reflect current changes, particularly the need for organisations to survive in a fiercely competitive global market, the shift away from traditional management and the resultant adoption of the techniques and principles of Human Resource Management (HRM).

An additional preoccupation of managers has been the relentless advance of technology that has increased the rate at which organisations meet their targets in the production of their goods and services and carry out their administrative processes. New technology has also altered the nature of the work that people do and the kinds of skills they need in order to do it. Until the early to mid 1980s, people were promoted into managerial positions because they had a good track record along some specialised line or profession, such as engineering or accountancy, but there was little or nothing in their background or training to indicate that they knew how to handle the kinds of change that have taken place; nor indeed was there any evidence of their ability to manage and lead people through that change.

When competition in the 'global market' became fierce, great emphasis was placed upon the importance of the appropriateness of the organisation's design and how to manage within it. As a result, new structures changed the responsibilities of managers to become much more orientated towards eliciting commitment and involvement from employees as individuals. The 'boss–subordinate' relationship became redundant and was replaced with more of a 'colleague' relationship. The programmes that were designed to educate and train managers were redrafted and, as a result, a new generation of managers has now emerged.

It is still the case, however, that despite these changes knowledge and skills relating to employee well-being are rarely found in the background and training of most managers. References to the subject have crept into the curricula of long-term management training programmes, and one may find it as a short chapter, or as part of a chapter, in some management text books, but it is clear that those who design management training programmes, and those who write the recommended books, are yet to catch up with the fact that what is going on in organisations has conferred significant importance upon this subject. For one reason or another, organisations have perceived internally the need to pay attention to the well-being of their employees, and it is that, rather than insight on the part of academics, that has raised the importance of the subject.

While in the humanitarian sense there is an ethical and moral case for the formulation of workable policies and practices in this area of managing the human resource, there is a sound business case too. Employees who work in a culture which is free from the stress induced by prejudice, bullying, rumours of impending change and the consequent threat of redundancy are able to focus clearly on their tasks and improve their performance. Staff turnover and absenteeism reduce, and the overall effect represents significant cost savings for the employer. Inevitably, however, the well-being of some employees will be adversely affected by change, and they may experience minor ailments, perhaps associated with stress symptoms. If this happens, one should expect the absence and leaving rates to rise, and productivity to fall. Failure to recognise the importance of taking action designed to eliminate, or at least moderate, the causes can prove costly.

It is also worth mentioning that satisfied and involved employees are less likely to leave the organisation and take legal action against the employer in search of compensation for the effects of stress and loss of earnings. This kind of litigation has grown rapidly in recent years and organisations find themselves paying out compensatory sums, which in the UK can vary up to several hundred thousand pounds.

Enlightened organisations already have realistic policies in place, and with ever advancing technology, an increasing number of employers have adopted family friendly policies as part of the drive to retain employees who possess valuable skills upon which the organisation depends for its survival. In the European Union (EU), the move towards family friendliness has been consolidated with the issue of EU Directives that have led to the enactment of matching legislation in the member states, so that there is a legal obligation for organisations to reflect at least the minimum standards set by the legislative provisions. Maternity leave has been extended, and fathers now have the right to time off to be present during the newborn's early nursing weeks.

In this book, the reader will encounter such issues as how employees are affected by technological advancement, restructuring and cultural factors, and shown how changes may be introduced and implemented in ways that reduce the likelihood of a negative impact on the employee relationship. The emphasis here, however, is not a negative one of avoidance in the 'how can we get away with it' context, but a positive one that shows how humane and ethical policies can be integrated with policies that drive the organisation's strategies towards the achievement of its objectives, leading to greater productivity and profitability.

Bearing in mind that organisational change has now become a continuous process, employee well-being is already a serious problem. In this book, managers are presented with appropriate information so that they will know precisely what they are dealing with, and what steps can be taken to protect the organisation and its people.

We have moved on from the traditional paradigm of organisational life: the grimey scenario that defined the Industrial Revolution has almost disappeared, and a cleaner information-based set-up has emerged. Large organisations have flattened and widened their structures, and cultures have changed, so that 'what it's like to work here' has taken on a new meaning. In many areas, this has meant a rapid and exponential rate of change, and since it will continue, it would be foolish to try to predict future organisational cultures, or indeed the nature of organisations themselves.

Chapter 1 introduces the concept of employee well-being and takes a retrospective look at how employee well-being was handled in the past. Then it examines the employee benefits and facilities that are provided by an increasing number of today's organisations, which include provision for non-occupational matters such as those related to financial problems, HIV/AIDS and sexual health generally, and drug and alcohol abuse. In this chapter, distinctions are drawn between the 'well-being attitudes' of managers who have committed themselves to all aspects of HRM, and those who have eclectically adapted HRM to the critical needs of their organisations. Under the heading of 'pressure and well-being', managers' perceptions of occupational stress are discussed, and there are descriptive references to stress. The chapter also explains how the way in which motivation, performance, management and leadership are handled can affect well-being. The employee well-being theme is continued in respect of career opportunities, and the importance of equal opportunities in that respect. Finally, the chapter explores the strategies that are used by employees as they attempt to survive the boredom of repetitive tasks and try to show themselves to be more intelligent and capable than the nature of the work they do implies.

Chapter 2 defines and describes stress and explains the related costs sustained by industry, including those incurred through sickness absence, staff turnover, reduced performance and litigation. The main concepts and theories of stress are included, on the grounds that if managers are going to tackle stress-related problems in the workplace, they first need to acquire an understanding of what they are dealing with. How stress affects people mentally, physically and behaviourally is explained, as are the signs and symptoms of stress that managers need to be able to identify. The idea of the manager as a counsellor is also explored.

Chapter 3 deals with the overall health of employees, managers and the organisation itself. It begins with an explanation of how different people perceive their jobs and the organisations that employ them. Why people work and their attitudes towards employment and unemployment are discussed, along with explanations of the policies and procedures that govern the management of employee well-being. The business case, as well as the humane case, is made for the provision of benefits and services which, although primarily aimed at employee well-being, are coupled with the need to enhance performance and, thereby, the survival and further development of the organisation. Examples of 'healthy workplace' initiatives are given, which include the provision of occupational support schemes and employee assistance programmes. Strategies and policies for the future, including management and leadership styles, climate, culture and structure are also explored.

Chapter 4 is about human resource management (HRM). Nobody would deny that the economic rise of Asian industry in the 1980s and its penetration into US and European markets triggered the development of HRM – something had to be done if the West was to compete effectively. In 1990, it was suggested by the Japanese that the US and Britain were still locked into the early twentieth-century principles of 'Taylorism' (scientific management) but in fact on both sides of the Atlantic management theory and practice had moved on considerably since then, although reflecting upon the market activity that followed it seems that the progress that had been achieved in the West had been insufficient. While the management systems that had emerged in the middle and late twentieth century were more sophisticated than their predecessors, they still held on to overt managerial control; and even those who were regarded as the management 'gurus' of the day reasserted the need for a conspicuous managerial command structure. After introducing the concept of HRM, and some of the misconceptions surrounding it, the chapter moves on to explain how its continuing influence is affecting employee well-being.

Chapter 5 is concerned with the ways in which some fairly commonplace but central management subjects, such as job satisfaction, job involvement and motivation now feature in the spectrum of employee well-being. People need to derive satisfaction from their work and feel involved in what they are doing. If people feel that what they are doing is worthwhile, they themselves will feel valued and will be motivated to do their jobs to the best of their ability. The chapter explains how the managers, who are responsible for the determination and control of the physical and psychological aspects of the work environment, can through their activities have a significant impact on the attitudes of their staff towards the work, the managers themselves, the organisation and the degree to which they feel satisfied, involved and motivated to work. The main theories of work motivation are discussed, along with the role of reward in the motivation process.

Chapter 6 moves to the issues of equality of opportunity and explores possible outcomes for organisations that attempt to adopt an internally oriented attitude towards the provision of equality. A distinction is drawn between organisations that regard the need to provide equal opportunities as purely an externally imposed, legal requirement which is not related to the main purposes of the organisation, and those that integrate the policies that advance the main purposes of the undertaking with those that provide equality. In the latter case, the organisation is not merely complying with the law, but is also taking advantage of the diversity of knowledge and skills that exists in the community from which they recruit their staff, in the belief that the organisation can thereby benefit. The chapter does not over-emphasise the detail of the law, since legislation varies considerably from one country to the next, although among democracies that are advanced in the industrial sense, the main purposes of legislation on equality are similar.

Chapter 7 explores the differences between and among individuals regardless of their background, including their sex, race, age and so forth. Personal differences have a profound effect on the manager's ability to manage, especially when the groups are large, as they are inclined to be when the organisation has adopted HRM principles and techniques. It is well known, of course, that all individuals are different from each other in terms of their genetic inheritance, but in this chapter we are concerned with the psychological differences that people acquire through their encounters with the environment, and as their personalities develop through experiences in childhood, through adolescence and into adulthood. The chapter also explores ways in which people are alike, examining similarities that develop within them as they are socialised into the communities and cultures into which they are born, which is a process that continues throughout life.

Chapter 8 takes a closer look at the legal aspects of employee well-being. While there are variations in legislative measures between one country and another, in general the types, patterns and provisions of such legislation have been drafted with very similar objectives in mind. Examples of differences in specific legislative provisions in particular countries are given when making comparisons. Otherwise, the chapter addresses the law in general and discusses the overall objectives, although managers are advised to apprise themselves of the detail of the law in their own states, and may find it interesting to observe similarities and differences in other states. The chapter also discusses the issue of litigation in which employees take legal action against their employers because their well-being has been affected by the way they have been treated in the organisation. Examples are included to illustrate how the circumstances that lead to such litigation can affect the well-being of employees, as well as the health of the organisation in terms of cost, efficiency, effectiveness and reputation as an employer. Finally, the chapter includes reference to internal legislation, in which we examine the policies and procedures that are formulated by organisations to ensure that on the one hand the organisation has a formal means of regulating and controlling behaviour, while on the other the individual employees have access to a system of justice without necessarily having to seek redress externally.

Chapter 9 has the main purpose of demonstrating the effects that the introduction of new technology may have upon the well-being of individual employees. Arguments that support the introduction of new technology in terms of how it may promote and favour employee well-being and arguments that imply a negative impact are presented. Technology is defined in several ways: (a) as a human quality in that it is a combination of knowledge and skills; (b) as a reference to machinery, equipment and devices such as computers and mobile telephones; and (c) as 'a way of doing things' in which, for example, it is the means by which the organisation converts its inputs into outputs. It is pointed out that human beings have, since time immemorial, been interested in devising new technology, or new 'ways of doing things', and in its glance at the history of technology, the chapter goes back to the early days of man when he first began to create settlements and cultivate the land. Progress in this respect is seen as a series of three successive lifestyle paradigms in which we began as hunters and gatherers, moved on to the agrarian age, and then to the industrial revolution. Where we see ourselves now in terms of our long-term development is discussed, concluding that we are about to leave the industrial revolution behind, and move on into the technological, information-based paradigm.

Chapter 10 is about managing change. Of all the causes of workplace stress, change is one of the most significant. No one would argue with the suggestion that one of the most important managerial skills that will be required in the twenty-first century is the ability to manage change effectively. While managing change always has been an essential managerial skill, it has to be accepted that it is a skill that is being used now more than ever before. In the past, the pace of change was comparatively moderate and changes were made slowly, and usually with great caution. In today's organisations, however, change occurs rapidly, and its exponential character has turned it into a continuous process, so that change has become an integral part of organisational life. For a variety of reasons, organisations are forced to make changes, implying that the alternative could be their demise. People who wish to succeed, and wish their organisations to succeed, therefore, have to be willing to accept and adapt to change.

About the author

Donald Currie is HR Consultant to the Southampton Business School where he teaches Human Resource Management.

He has extensive experience of personnel management, having been a personnel manager for twelve years and a lecturer in personnel management at the Southampton Institute.

In 1990–2 he carried out a survey on stress on 26,000 NHS employees, the result of which was a report entitled 'Stress in the Health Service'. His other publications include *Personnel in Practice* published in 1977.

Donald Currie's principal interest is in employee well-being and he writes, lectures and broadcasts on that subject.

The author may be contacted via the publishers.

CHAPTER 1

Employee well-being

Introduction

This chapter introduces the concept of employee well-being, and the advantages to the organisation of having a healthy workforce. The term 'employee well-being' refers to the physical and mental health of the workforce. This means that employees should be working in a stress-free and physically safe environment, a situation which is more easily achieved in some organisations than others. The reader will be aware that most industrialised nations have introduced legislation that regulates how organisations should operate in these respects. Here, we are also examining the effects that social reform movements have had on the corporate conscience, and on the policies of organisations as they increasingly lean towards the ethical and moral dimensions. Concurrently, however, organisations are also beginning to understand the business case for promoting employee well-being, in that they perceive it as a prime contributor to the achievement of success.

A retrospective look

The introduction of the subject of employee well-being into business and public sector organisations is a relatively innovative move. Although historically employers have paid little attention to employee well-being, there have been some notable exceptions. In the UK, the Quaker Cadbury family are famous for providing housing and sick pay for their employees at Bourneville in the late nineteenth century. Lever Bros. at Port Sunlight in Merseyside and Rowntree at York are two further UK examples. But these were exceptions, and the employer as someone who regarded employees as a necessary but burdensome financial evil was a far more frequent phenomenon than the employer as someone who genuinely cared about their well-being. Social and economic history shows that most employees have had to wait a long time – in fact centuries – to experience an employment relationship in which in part their well-being has been recognised as an organisational responsibility. Many, of course, are still waiting.

Benefits and facilities

It was said above that employee well-being refers to the physical and mental health of the workforce, but the term 'well-being' can incorporate many issues. Among the benefits and facilities that employers might provide are: a pension scheme; access to medical care; a healthy and safe working environment; help with long-term sickness; assistance with family matters, such as bereavement, creche facilities, paternal leave for fathers, help with schooling and transport for families of employees who are moved around geographically; counselling; access to employee support schemes, such as an internal Occupational Support Scheme (OSS), or an Employee Assistance Programme (EAP); staff restaurants and social and recreational facilities; preparation for redundancy and retirement; advisory policies for contemporary welfare issues, such as HIV/AIDS and sexual health generally, alcohol and drug abuse, and the formulation of policies such as those on smoking in the workplace.

Four categories of welfare

Torrington and Hall (1995) suggest that there are four main categories within the bounds of what they refer to as 'welfare' at work: physical, emotional, intellectual and material, which to some degree are interdependent.

Physical well-being can be provided by attending to health and safety matters, such as ensuring that risks of accident and injury are reduced as far as is possible and practicable, providing reasonable working hours and providing paid holiday time. In Europe there are legislated *Working Time Regulations* under which particular categories of employee are permitted to work a limited number of hours a week. Also there are regulations relating to risk assessment that has to be carried out and recorded regularly. Many organisations provide physical recreational facilities, in some cases a fully equipped gymnasium, a swimming pool and playing fields, and sports teams represent their organisations in formal leagues.

Emotional concerns can be ameliorated by treating individual stress as a serious issue, regardless of where it was induced, and offering counselling services, communicating openly with employees, showing employees that they and their work are valued by the organisation and implementing an equal opportunities policy.

Intellectual well-being can be principally addressed through job design and appropriate education, training and further development. Many jobs can be redesigned to offer an intellectual challenge to employees, while consulting the work team about methods and other problems generates increased motivation and commitment. Delegating tasks which are more complex than the job a person is doing can also provide intellectual stimulation and consolidate feelings of job security.

Material welfare can be provided through a fair reward management system, including non-cash benefits. Materialistic concerns are also related to promotion, since more responsibility usually carries with it an increased reward and it should be made visibly clear to employees that opportunities for promotion are there for everyone. A policy and organisation-wide procedure for appraising employees' *potential* carries with it a very positive message, so long as the system does not become confused with, or included in, the *performance* appraisal system.

Organisations can be criticised equally for doing too much or too little in the way of employee well-being. Some HR managers take the view that they should not appear to be 'too soft' with the staff, although much of this attitude has its roots in the origins of the personnel management function, the related professional institution of which in the UK started life in the 1920s as the Industrial Welfare Society, with welfare as its main concern. As history has demonstrated, that institution was well ahead of its time, and besides, organisations that fully provide for employee well-being are likely to subscribe to the view that the implementation of policies on employee well-being will be rewarded by increased levels of commitment and productivity and reduced absenteeism and staff turnover.

Human resource management

The approach to well-being that an organisation prefers to adopt will be informed by its interpretations of human resource management (HRM). If, as is the case for some HRM advocates, organisations essentially see employees as disposable resources that can be engaged and replaced as and when necessary, then they are likely to regard expenditure on the provision of employee well-being as ill-focused. Those who believe that it is the human factor that makes the difference, however, and gives the organisation its competitive edge, will tend to regard such expenditure as a worthwhile investment to support key assets. Current trends in the recruitment market tend to demand the latter view. Attending to employees' physical and emotional needs will free them from handicaps which could serve to impede their contribution. It is in this way that, beyond the issue of conscience and humane morality, the business case for providing for employee well-being is made.

In recent years, comparatively new issues such as HIV/AIDS, smoking and alcohol have occupied the attention of personnel specialists concerned with employee well-being. Many organisations have formulated policies and practices in relation to these matters. The alcohol issue in the workplace, for example, illustrates how many employers have become determined to seek all means available of taking up slack in the organisation. For many years, most employers would ignore the matter of employees drinking at lunchtime, so long as no embarrassing incidents occurred. Some businesses saw social and recreational benefits in lunchtime drinking, while others viewed alcohol as an essential element in securing contracts and maintaining customer relations. While many organisations still hold these views, others are discouraging or prohibiting lunchtime drinking. Their rationale for doing so is primarily that alcohol impedes individual performance in many respects. Someone who has been drinking does not perform as well as they would otherwise; they may produce a safety risk if they operate a machine; and the whole idea runs counter to the organisation's main efforts to *improve* performance and *reduce* danger through training and developing employees, which is expensive.

Managers' perceptions of employees

There are two main perceptions of people in the workplace. The first implies that the employment of staff is a financial burden on the organisation, and it is true that the cost of employment does represent a significant proportion of the organisation's total expenditure. When business becomes economically tough, perhaps because of a recession, senior managers tend to reach first for the staffing list to see if the wages and salaries bill can be reduced. The view that staff are 'a necessary nuisance' and 'a financial burden' on the organisation has tended, by association, to generate among many senior managers a disparaging attitude towards employees in a more generalised and broad way, and they behave towards employees as if they are somehow inferior. Obviously, this attitude is communicated to employees, mostly in a non-verbal way; as a result, a cultural rift develops, and an 'us' and 'them' culture emerges.

It is perhaps ironic that the second view is the HRM perception of the role of people at work, since HRM has so far had little to say about employee well-being. Its proponents regard people as a resource in which the organisation has invested, and of course when an organisation invests, whether it be a short-, medium- or long-term investment, it wants to see a return on its capital. HRM is a set of beliefs and techniques through which the organisation is managed. One of its significant features is the recognition of the relationship between human performance and organisational success. It sees survival and development as a 'mutuality of interest' between the organisation and its employees. HRM is not, as some would have it, another name for personnel management; it is, where it has been adopted, the influence that determines how the whole organisation is managed, and all managers, therefore, in every department and function are human resource managers.

Pressure and well-being

The main alternative to workplace health is workplace stress. Managers vary considerably in their perceptions of stress. At one end of the dimension there are those who totally reject the existence of stress. They claim that individuals have weaknesses, which they refer to as stress, and which come to light when they are asked to do something they do not like doing, or a weakness because they '… do not work well under pressure'. At the other end of the dimension, there are managers who recognise stress and claim that workers' performance increases significantly when they are under pressure: 'push 'em 'til the pips squeak and you'll get high productivity'. The truth is that they are both wrong.

The fact is that nobody ever suffers from stress per se, but it certainly does exist. Stress is a perfectly natural mental and physical reaction to an unfamiliar and uncomfortable or threatening situation. Obviously, the individual in such a situation perceives the unfamiliarity, discomfort or threat, and there is a mental and physiological reaction that is designed to prepare the individual to adapt to the situation. This is an internal reaction that has developed within us over millions of years. It evolved to enable us to deal effectively with threatening situations which, normally, would be short in duration, and when it occurs the body and brain are in an abnormal condition. On the other hand, if the pressure of the situation is sustained, and the abnormal condition continues with it, then ultimately there will be adverse mental, physical and behavioural consequences. It is not, therefore, stress itself from which we suffer, but the *effects* of stress. These effects can produce ailments that range from the slight to the severe, and may even be life-threatening, since they include severe mental problems that may lead to suicide, and physical conditions such as serious digestive ailments and heart disease, either of which can cause death. Whether or not stress exists, therefore, is not a matter for discussion – it is a fact of life, and sadly we manufacture most of today's causes ourselves.

Motivation and performance

Since the manager plans and allocates the work while the staff physically carry it out, the manager should be principally interested in their work performance; without the staff's active cooperation, which includes the application of their knowledge and skills, the manager cannot achieve his or her objectives. Performance is dependent on two main factors: ability and motivation. Until the 1920s, it was believed that productivity was determined by combining two factors: the employees' skills and managerial exhortation to get the work done. Since then, however, research by motivation analysts has shown that employees who possess knowledge and skills may not readily apply them on your behalf – they need to be motivated. You may, for example, have two workers whom you know to be equally skilled, yet one does a better job than the other. The reason for this is that the better performer is more motivated than the other; and the more motivated a person is, the more they will use their knowledge and skills in their work.

Seen in this way, an individual's ability may be enhanced through training and experience, but the degree to which he or she will then apply the results of the training and experience depends on the level of motivation. It is also true that an individual who lacks the ability or self-confidence to carry out a particular task, or set of tasks, may appear to lack motivation. It is possible to solve this problem through training, since when an individual has been exposed to appropriate training, his or her self-confidence and motivation to perform will increase.

The manager who wishes to implement these ideas would be wise to assess the trainability of staff before embarking on an expensive programme designed to enhance motivation through training. At any one time, an individual's actual ability should be seen as a constant factor; that is to say, a person's capabilities are limited to what he or she can do now. It is true that with further training it is possible to broaden and deepen the individual's range of abilities, but only if they are intellectually capable of assimilating the necessary knowledge and able to develop the related skills; otherwise, the manager could be wasting the organisation's money. An individual's amenability to training is also determined by his or her motivation to learn, but the enhancement of motivation is a possibility, whereas intelligence levels are inaccessible to the manager (see Chapter 7).

Management and leadership

Good leadership ability is undoubtedly the most important of all personal qualities possessed by a manager. Leadership is generally regarded as important since the performance of any organisation in terms of its success or failure is usually attributed to those who lead it. In this sense, those who lead may be in a precarious position. The leadership style that is adopted by the organisation's managers is also regarded as important since it is one of the most influential components of the organisation's culture. Ideally, the leadership style will be cascaded throughout the organisation from the top. To a considerable extent, leadership style is a reflection of the personality of the individual manager, but broad indications of a particular style should be communicated to the managers from the top. Those who manage the departments and functions are the media through which the leadership style of the whole organisation is interpreted and passed through to the employees.

A manager is someone who has been given responsibility for achieving the objectives of a particular function or department. To meet his or her objectives, the manager is given the authority and the resources that will enable him or her to get things done. Of all the resources at the manager's disposal, the human resource is the only one that can advance and further develop its capacity to serve the organisation. Resources, such as money, machinery, hardware, software, furniture and so forth, depreciate in value, but the human resource with appropriate training and experience can add value progressively. As the employee develops and length of service increases, he or she experiences feelings of security and becomes more stable, which enables him or her to adopt greater responsibility.

Some say that 'leaders are born and not made' while others say that it is possible to train leadership skills into people. To some extent, both are right. In fact, leadership is defined as the ability of one individual to influence the behaviour of others towards the achievement of a particular task or set of tasks. Good leaders are those who can get things done in the way they wish them to be done. There are some exceptional people who seem naturally to be able to influence the behaviour of others, but leadership training should help them to become even more skilful. Anyone who has directed leadership studies will tell you that it is much easier to develop leadership skills within those who have at least a fragment of natural ability to begin with, than to produce a 'leader' who is purely the product of training.

Leadership is not something that can be found on the organisational chart – those are merely managerial positions. Good leaders are those who inspire mutual trust and confidence in people. To get things done they do not issue orders; they consult their employees and use the work group as a problem-solving and decision-making unit. When staff are consulted about problems they use their knowledge, skills and experience to help solve them. In this way, the planning and the doing of the work is integrated and because staff have been given an input into, say, how some item of work should be carried out, they become committed to the achievement of a successful outcome. Managers who separate the planning and doing of work, issuing orders as and when the work needs to be done, are usually authoritarian in attitude, and regarded as untrustworthy by their staff; giving orders through the use of hierarchical authority is the last resort of the failed manager.

There is no evidence to support the view that the democratic or consultative leader raises individual performance or the general productivity of the workplace, but there is a wealth of evidence to suggest that the democratic leadership style reduces absenteeism and staff turnover. Where the leadership style is democratic and consultative, employees look forward to coming into the workplace, they experience feelings of attachment, and feel not only that their work effort is appreciated and understood, but that they themselves are valued and trusted. This is the kind of leadership that fosters feelings of, as well as actual, well-being.

Employee well-being

Employee relations and well-being

It would be reasonable to assume that most organisations, and certainly the large commercial undertakings, would have an employee relations policy that demonstrated commitment to the employees, but in fact most do not. It seems absurd, therefore, that they expect unrequited commitment from their employees. If commitment is not a two-way affair then eventually there will be no commitment at all, from either side. The top managers in large organisations express a naive surprise at employees' lack of commitment; it seems not to occur to them that commitment is a reciprocal concept. The managerial attitude here is that by employing a person, they have somehow done them a favour.

That is not the way things are at present. Talented employees are in great demand, and the organisation relies on their knowledge and skills for its success, and for this reason employee retention policies have become critically important. Until recent times, most organisations did not have a retention plan, and those that did had one because they had found it was cheaper to encourage the talented

---

staff to stay by looking after them and demonstrating a caring attitude. While this is still the case, there are now further good reasons to have a retention plan. The recruitment market is such that employees who are not satisfied with their employer's attitude do not have to withstand the stress of being poorly treated, feeling under-valued, and made to feel relatively unimportant. They can simply go elsewhere – and they do.

Equal opportunities and well-being

The recommendation that organisations should formulate and implement an equal opportunities policy is made on several grounds. First, while having such a policy is not a legal requirement in all industrialised countries, compliance with the law is, and patently this can best be achieved through the implementation of a relevant and appropriate policy.

Secondly, it is morally and ethically appropriate to demonstrate commitment to the provision of equal opportunities to *all* employees, regardless of their status. Thirdly, it makes good business sense in today's economic climate to take advantage of the knowledge, skills and attitudes from wherever they are available in the community.

Even if we put aside the moral and ethical dimensions of equal opportunities, as well as the organisation's obligations under the law, experience has shown that an organisation that is overtly committed to the provision of equal opportunities has an enhanced reputation as an employer, not only among women and minority groups, but among all potential employees. The truth is that organisations today can no longer afford to turn away the kind of talent for which others are prepared to compete.

Failing to provide equal opportunities to women and minority groups by rejecting their job applications or holding them down in inferior and menial positions does not produce any positive results for the organisation. It does, however, have two main negative effects. First, it causes frustration and stress among the affected individuals; and secondly, it deprives the organisation of the opportunity to maximise on talent that has either gone elsewhere for employment, or is left lying fallow at the bottom end of your workplace.

Career opportunities and well-being

The degree to which HRM has penetrated organisations seems to have produced two management attitudes towards the duration of an employee's tenancy in the workplace. One view is that we employ a person for their skills and ultimately, perhaps because of advancing technology, our need to access those skills either diminishes or disappears, in which case we discharge the individuals with the redundant skills. When other employees witness the manifestation of this attitude, a high degree of *job insecurity* becomes evident among them.

The senior managers who take this view think that there must come a time when the individual and the organisation are no longer compatible and, therefore, they separate. Apparently they think that this can all be done pleasantly, by mutual consent and agreement, without the slightest hint of conflict or animosity on either side. People are not expected to anticipate a career with any one particular organisation or, indeed, in any one particular craft or profession. This attitude is predominently typical of managers in HRM organisations.

The second attitude is more conducive to the development of a career in an organisation. Here, managers take the view that change is inevitable, and that a willingness to adapt to change and even proactively create change wherever possible is the most essential ingredient to organisational and individual success. Hence, managers in this situation adopt a developmental approach to their employees. They formulate and implement career management policies, and employee and management development policies through which their employees are trained, developed and promoted through systems that provide access to knowledge of the implications of change, along with the opportunity to keep pace through training, coaching and counselling. Clearly, employees who are treated in this way will develop a high degree of *job security*. The implementation of such policies will carry the 'commitment' message to the employees, and they are very likely to reciprocate. In such an organisation, the three main developmental objectives are:

1. To ensure that the performance, satisfaction and involvement of all employees are kept up to standard through monitoring and appraisal processes.

2. To offer employees the opportunity to develop the kinds of knowledge and skills that will become the task demands of the future. This is likely to lead to the continued employability of the employees, and increases the likelihood that the organisation's and the individual's mutual expectancies will be met.

3. To encourage employees to structure and implement a flexible self-development plan, and to offer assistance and support in this.

It should be borne in mind, however, that not all employees are motivated to develop themselves, nor are they all intellectually capable of assimilating the knowledge and skills required to meet the demands of a working society that is increasingly involved in using new technology. Such people need to work, of course, because they have to make a living and to that end they are prepared to suffer the tedium of low level jobs; and even though they are capable of experiencing involvement and satisfaction, they are unlikely to achieve those experiences in the workplace.

Employee survival strategies

Managers should be aware, therefore, that for many employees work fails to provide the sense of fulfilment and satisfaction to which many texts on management and organisational behaviour refer. Low level work, as we know, can often be repetitive to the extent that it becomes a set of tasks each involving a habit-forming work cycle of just a few seconds, inducing soul-destroying boredom. Employees at the bottom of the pile or engaged in peripheral work can become locked into work of this nature, which to them is nothing more than a means to an end. 'High tech' is not yet everywhere, and even if it was such employees could not become involved in it because they lack the experience and qualifications that would enable them to escape into more challenging and satisfying work roles.

When faced with drudgery, boredom, monotony and powerlessness, employees become resourceful and creative in developing strategies that allow them to assert some control over, and construct meanings for, the work activities they are instructed by managers to undertake. It is believed that such strategies are the means by which they maintain their mental stability and can continue to perform work tasks which evoke essentially negative feelings.

To the industrial sociologist, such workers are 'alienated' from their work and they see their tasks as meaningless. Such workers are alienated because they lack control over work processes and conditions – they are merely implementing work that was planned by someone else. The work is seen as meaningless because the workers are unable to see the relevance of their work roles; in a sense, they feel isolated because they cannot relate to the ideology of their employers and they gain no sense of identity through their work.

Such workers, however, do not lack the normal human need for interest and excitement. Some 'get their kicks' outside the workplace by directing their meaningful efforts towards charity work, hobbies, sporting interests and so forth. Others attempt to reduce the boredom of their day-to-day drudgery by trying to 'beat the system' by finding ways of getting around the formal rules and practices, and exploiting loopholes in the systems that govern what they are supposed to be doing. First, this might be done for financial advantage by manipulating the bonus or overtime system, or by frustrating attempts by managers to exercise controls. This should not be regarded as a serious threat to managerial control. It has been argued that these 'games' actually amount to consent, which is to say that employees are prepared to pursue managerial objectives, but use these games to demonstrate to themselves, each other and the managers that they cannot be totally dominated. Some managers turn a blind eye to these 'illicit' activities in the belief that it may enable the employees to derive some elements of self-respect that they cannot obtain from the kind of work tasks they carry out.

A second strategy is fiddling. Research has demonstrated that a high proportion of workers fiddle time, money, or goods and services from their employers. A well publicised book by Gerald Mars in 1982 categorised the various ways in which cheating at work took place. For many employees, fiddling represents a means of expressing their workplace-related frustrations. Alternatively, it might provide a means of injecting excitement into an otherwise monotonous and tedious shift. Most employers are aware that fiddling takes place and some are prepared to accept it and recognise the function it serves. However, most will take steps to 'clamp down' if the level of fiddling becomes excessive.

Humour is a third strategy, and has long been used as a coping device at work as well as in other areas of life. In addition to providing an amusing distraction from boredom, joking around also reduces animosity and heads off the likelihood that frustrations will be expressed in a more sinister way. Pranks and banter can be used to establish and confirm the relative status of employees among their peers; it can consolidate group identity and role and provide welcome relief from the alienating aspects of work.

A fourth strategy is sabotage when it is used as a reaction to employees' experience of alienation. Modern-day Luddites may corrupt computer records, introduce 'bugs' into the systems, or anonymously publicise harmful information about their employer's activities. However, identifying the motivation behind acts of sabotage can be difficult. In some instances the reason may be just a temporary feeling of frustration, whereas at other times it may be a determined desire to undermine management objectives. It is likely that whatever the reason, managers will take acts of sabotage far more seriously than any of the other survival strategies discussed here.

Finally, employees may escape the tedium of work by absenting themselves. This can include mental as well as physical absence. Clearly, physical absence is taking time away from work, whereas mental absence is a failure to concentrate one's thoughts on work tasks. The latter variant is a passive form of 'escapism' which is particularly difficult for employers to detect as employees drift into daydreams while ostensibly carrying out their work. However, in an age where organisations are keen to elicit commitment and take up all the slack within their operations, mental withdrawal presents the employer with a difficult challenge. It is, however, something for which managers should keep a vigilant watch, since daydreaming is one of the principal causes of accidents at work.

For managers, the key issue here is how they should interpret these survival strategies. Do they represent consent to managerial control, or resistance to it? If they are perceived as a sign of consent managers may be happy to continue to use their blind eye, and only take measures to reduce the incidence of them when a notional line of what is acceptable is crossed. However, if they are considered to be a sign of active resistance more resources may be deputed to attempt to eliminate them.

The effects of change

Much has been written and discussed about organisational change. Undoubtedly it is one of the major causes of stress in an organisation; and yet, the idea of an unchanging world of work seems unthinkable. Change, of course, is inevitable and we live in a time of rapid and exponentially advancing changes. Today, there are two main causes of organisational change. The first is related to the ways in which organisations are managed, and the second is related to advancing technology, in which change has now become continuous.

The past twenty years has seen a severe increase in the fierceness of global competition and organisations have had to 'downsize', 'rightsize' and delayer, and generally reorganise their structures in order to remain competitive and survive. This process created a reduction in human resource demands in terms of numbers and an increase in terms of knowledge and skills, especially on the part of managers and specialists whose jobs changed markedly. Managers had to learn (or re-learn) how to manage and specialists had to adapt to new standards and ways of working. The education, training and development of managers and specialists, therefore, also had to change to meet industry's new demands.

Employees who were made redundant in this process had no alternative but to stand and watch. Those who kept their jobs became demoralised and anxious as their obvious insecurity increased. The psychological contract was destroyed, and managers making the changes destroyed a considerable amount of trust and goodwill in the process. Goodwill was also destroyed by incorporating into new contracts work that previously had been carried out on a goodwill basis. Obviously the more an organisation regulates in this way, the more goodwill disappears. As a result of the ways in which these changes were handled, cases of workplace stress with consequent litigation burgeoned, and many organisations found themselves paying out large compensatory sums. In human resource terms, most managers still do not understand the full implications of mishandling the introduction of workplace changes, despite the amount of literature and advice on the subject that has been available since around 1990.

It was said above that the introduction of new technology into the workplace was the second of the two main reasons for organisational change in recent years. In fact, technological change has become a continuous process and while some employees have welcomed it, others have come to regard it as a stress-inducing threat to their job security. We return to this complex subject in Chapter 9.

Emotional intelligence

This has been defined as: *the ability to sense, understand and effectively apply the power and acumen of emotions as a source of human energy, information, trust, creativity, connection and influence* (Cooper, 1998). Most managers find themselves preoccupied with good quality output and believe that this is best achieved through knowledgeable, skilled and motivated people who have been set attainable, timebound objectives which are measureable. Such managers believe that results are critically important … and, of course, they are right.

When a manager, therefore, employs a person, presumably he or she does so because that person possesses the required knowledge, skills, and experience that are demanded by the job. However, there is much more to the individual than that. After all, when they come in to the workplace, it is not just the bits for which the manager employed them that come in, it is the whole person. Admittedly, this means that they bring with them all of their personal prejudices and preferences, attitudes, motivations and so forth, but they also bring knowledge and skills which are not related to the job for which they were employed, which implies that there is much more that they will be able to contribute now, and at a later stage.

Additionally, they will bring in their emotions. Typically, most managers do not regard themselves as utilisers of human emotions, but they should take a second look at what they actually do, since the use of emotions has a long history in management techniques. For example, all five of the human needs that make up Abraham Maslow's famous 'hierarchy of needs' refer to emotions (Maslow, 1987). His so-called 'lower order needs' are made up of physiological factors such as thirst, hunger and fear; 'safety and security' refer to the need to satisfy related emotions. Further up the scale, where his 'higher order needs' are located, he uses expressions such as love and belongingness, esteem and ego needs, and finally 'self-actualisation'. Maslow first suggested this hierarchy in the 1940s, and certainly it became (and still remains) a familiar sight in management training rooms all over the world.

Maslow's theory, however, is based upon what psychologists refer to as our primary emotions, which means emotions with which we are born and which relate to our physical and mental survival. As we begin to mature we develop secondary or acquired emotions, which are related more to our experiences of life, likings and dislikings of particular things, and relationships with others. It is these secondary emotions that have entered the management scenario in recent years.

Many of the demands that HRM makes of employees are designed to exploit secondary emotions, which are very powerful determinants of behaviour. One of the chief aims of HRM, for example, is to elicit *commitment* from employees, and commitment is a secondary emotion. It is true that some HRM advocates claim that commitment improves work performance, although this is very doubtful – that is to say commitment *alone* cannot enhance performance in any way, since performance is determined entirely by the possession of skills, the application of which is regulated by the degree to which an individual is motivated. As we shall see later, 'Performance = Ability × Motivation'. On the other hand, if an individual is committed to the organisation's purposes and objectives, then clearly there is a likelihood that he or she will be motivated to develop themselves further, and broaden and deepen their skills, so that an enhanced performance may result. Individuals then may be committed and loyal, and they may trust the organisation and its managers, but there are several further steps to take before performance will be positively affected.

It has been postulated, by those who promote the exploitation of human emotions as a management technique, that conventional thinking is wrong and that emotions are inherently neither positive nor negative. This can be misleading. The truth is that they can be either, or both, but never 'neither'. Emotions are positive when they create exhilaration and feelings of great satisfaction within people, for example when a long-term and difficult task has been completed successfully, such as winning a sporting trophy, or turning a new company into profitability for the first time. On the other hand, emotions can be negative when stress causes an individual to become depressed, fretful and filled with anxiety, perhaps over the threat of redundancy, or being bypassed for promotion. Anyone who has encountered an individual who has been suffering from the effects of severe stress for an amount of time that has caused it to be more than they can bear would never say that emotions are neither positive nor negative. Emotions can be both positive and negative when they create an energy which initially is used to experience negative feelings, but can be turned into something positive. For example, depression induced by, say, redundancy can be turned into elation when a new and better job is acquired.

Commitment, trust and loyalty are the main emotions that are said to drive creativity, successful innovation and individual success. They are said to be the prominent personality characteristics of those who can take an idea and develop it into some kind of profitable reality for the organisation. In other words, these emotions drive intrapreneurship. It is for these reasons that organisations today claim that they have had value added, and they talk about 'emotional intelligence' and the 'emotional capital' of the organisation.

Conclusion

Managers vary considerably in their perceptions of stress. One view is that stress is a myth, and that it does not exist. Another view is that stress is a good and healthy thing that managers can use to crank up performance, while a third view is that stress is to be avoided at all costs, that managers should keep a keen eye on vulnerable employees. This last view is taken in the belief that employees who work for a caring employer who has created a stress-free environment are able to focus more sharply on their work and, thereby, become more highly productive.

While the issue of employee well-being has reached a new level of importance in the minds of managers, there are still too many organisations that pay limited attention to it. Such organisations are depriving themselves of the opportunity of reaping the benefits of a healthy workforce, and some still hang on to the outdated belief that organisations should not appear to be 'too soft' with their employees.

Advocates of human resource management (HRM) are divided in their approach to employment; while some regard employees as a resource whose skills can be accessed whenever required and then discarded when they are no longer needed, others regard employees as a resource in which the organisation has invested and seeks a return on its investment by developing people further so that the value of their contribution is increased. Retention plans are developed to increase the likelihood that such skilled and valued staff remain on the books.

References

Cooper, R. (1998) 'Sentimental Value', in *People Management*. London: Institute of Personnel and Development.

Maslow, A.H. (1987) 'A Theory of Growth Motivation', in A.H. Maslow, *Motivation and Personality*. New York: Harper & Row.

CHAPTER 2

Understanding stress

Introduction

This chapter defines and describes stress. It explains the related costs sustained by industry, including those caused by sickness absence, reduced performance and litigation. The main theories and concepts are outlined, along with the results of research that has identified the most frequently reported causes of stress in the workplace and elsewhere. When and how stress may occur are explored, and how it affects people mentally, physically and behaviourally. The typical signs and symptoms of stress that managers should look for among their staff – and themselves – are listed and the idea of the manager as a counsellor is explored.

Definition

Definitions of stress vary depending on who has drafted them and why. Engineers define stress in terms of its effects upon metals and other materials, and medical experts define it in terms of how it affects our mentality and the functioning of our bodily systems. The word itself is derived from the Latin *stringere* meaning to pull something tight or taut.

For our purposes, it is sufficient to say that *stress occurs when an individual is pushed or pressurised into situations which are beyond his or her normal coping capacity, or when a person's perception of a situation induces tension and anxiety at a level that is outside of that of his or her normal experience.*

The cost of stress

Estimates of cost vary only slightly but overall, research suggests that in the UK alone between 90 and 100 million potentially productive working days a year are lost through unapproved and sickness absence and reduced performance caused by the effects of stress. Managers will be interested to learn that this is by far the greatest cause of lost productivity. For example, the working days lost that are attributable to the effects of stress are approximately 30 times greater than the current annual number of working days lost through employee relations problems.

If we were to summarise the cost of the resources that government, trade unions and employers provide for the maintenance of industrial peace, and compare them with the resources they dedicate to the elimination, or at least moderation, of workplace stress, a clear incongruity comes to light. This is not to suggest that the resources allocated for employee relations should be reduced or switched to something else; clearly, recent history shows that the legislation and codes governing the conduct of industrial relations, and the organisations and institutions set up to solve problems and dispense justice in that field, are working very well and should be left in place, but there is a sound argument in favour of allocating resources to address a problem that is costing industry 30 times as much, which is roughly £7 billion a year, in addition to costs paid by stress sufferers themselves.

A further cost is that of litigation. The number of employees taking legal action against their employers has been growing steadily since about 1990. Typically, an employee who is suffering too much pressure at work becomes ill, and on medical grounds eventually leaves the organisation. He or she then takes action against the organisation, seeking compensation for loss of earnings, physical or mental limitations imposed by their illness affecting their future employment prospects, plus medical and other costs.

In an increasing number of cases, the ex-employee receives compensation, the amounts of which in the UK have varied between £500 and £500,000. It is difficult to estimate what this kind of litigation is costing industry, since most cases are settled before they reach the courts, but in three fairly recent cases the amounts were £450,000, £150,000 and £67,000; this, of course, is in addition to the legal charges, which can equal the amount of compensation paid.

When cases of this nature do reach the courts, they usually receive comprehensive news coverage, especially when the amounts are high. In terms of the organisation's reputation such publicity can be disastrous, particularly if it is a public limited company, or if at the time it is undergoing some kind of large-scale change, such as an acquisition or merger. Also, in the wake of such an action, an organisation that is dependent on highly skilled workers for creative product innovation and/or the smooth internal running of the place will experience great difficulty when attempting to recruit such personnel.

Yet another cost is that of management time, in which senior managers' attentions are focused on the case and away from their normal duties; time has to be spent with the organisation's lawyers, making statements, checking company policies, preparing documents for the defence, and potential witnesses within the organisation have to be interviewed. Obviously, while all this is going on, people are not doing their jobs.

Stress as a commuter

We often hear people say, when I get home I switch off. I shut the gate on work, relax and think about something else. For many reasons, this is impossible. Work and home are large and important parts of most people's lives, and clearly the two are tied together. They are interdependent in many ways, and it is unrealistic to claim that one never thinks or talks about work when one is at home, and vice versa. We have only one brain and the fact that in that brain we carry about with us, *inter alia*, the stresses and strains that occur at home and at work is irrefutable. The stress effects that are produced at work are carried home by the individual, where they may cause further stress-inducing problems. This kind of situation can deteriorate, since as stress commutes with the person, it snowballs and becomes more intense, and since the effects of stress are added at both ends, victims find themselves treading the *stress mill*.

Some say that they never suffer from stress, and regard individuals' reactions to situations as an inability to cope, a personality weakness that surfaces when they are under pressure. In fact, what happens is precisely the reverse. Stress is a perfectly natural human reaction that has developed within us as we have adapted to the environment across the millions of years of our existence on earth. Far from being an inability to cope, our natural reaction to pressure is the very factor that *enables* us to cope, especially with emergencies and other complex or fearful situations.

The truth is that at some time in their lives everyone experiences at least a little stress. It can happen as a result of a personal misfortune, such as the loss of a loved one, redundancy, divorce, long-term caring for a sick or elderly relative, or it may be caused when a testing or intimidating experience is imminent, such as a court appearance or job interview that is expected to be difficult. In such ways, stress is imposed upon us by environmental factors.

Conversely, some people have the kind of personality that causes them to worry unnecessarily; they sit around and brood about their current situation, and after asking themselves several 'what if' types of question, begin to imagine all kinds of negative outcomes. Others harbour unfounded and, sometimes, irrational fears, while yet others suffer anxieties about a whole range of improbable situations. Stress, therefore, is not always something that is inflicted upon us by external, environmental pressures; it may be self-induced. On the other hand, when it is clear that an employee is experiencing stress, managers are strongly advised to examine the employee's work situation thoroughly before concluding that his or her stress is self-induced. In any case, the employee should be referred for treatment.

Stress may also result from a combination of situational and personality factors. Indeed, it is the personality that causes a person's perception of a situation to be different from that of another person. The situation, therefore, may be stressful to one person and not to another. Some people have the kind of personality that makes them more vulnerable to external pressures. It is for these reasons that different people attempt to cope with or adapt to situations in their own individual ways.

Types of stress

Causes of stress are referred to as *stressors*. There are several approaches to classifying stress, and at this point we will classify it in terms of the *type* of stressor and *when* it takes its effect. In this way, we can identify three categories of stress.

Transient stress occurs at the same time as the stressor and is a short-term experience. For example, it may be of the kind experienced by emergency service workers when they are dealing with events such as public disorder, accidents, fires and a variety of other types of incident. These situations often involve people working at speed and perhaps using particular skills to head off a potentially disastrous situation, such as attempting to save someone's life. Also, individuals reacting to emergency situations at work, such as meeting deadlines or restoring crucial systems that have gone down, may experience transient stress. In these kinds of example, however, the emergency aspects soon leave the situation, and as the urgency diminishes, so those involved will start to 'come down' and return to normal.

Post traumatic stress disorders (PTSD) occur *after* a shock owing to some critical life event, such as involvement in a serious traffic accident, personal injury, divorce or redundancy. PTSD may succeed transient stress when, for instance, after someone has done all they can to deal with an emergency and the cause of their transient stress is no longer present, they believe, rightly or wrongly, that the aftermath of the incident holds personal implications for them with which they will have difficulty coping. This also may happen when the effects of shock emerge, having been suppressed beforehand by the need to concentrate on taking urgent action.

Chronic stress occurs as a result of pressures being felt by the individual for an amount of time that is too long for the person to endure. Those who experience this kind of stress perceive themselves to be in situations in which things are getting on top of them, causing them to feel anxious and frustrated; they feel that the pressures will never go away and that there is no escape. Often the pressures are small but numerous, having accumulated over many months or years, causing feelings of futility and despair. Ultimately the person feels that his or her efforts are meaningless, that the future is hopeless and that they cannot go on any more. This is a very dangerous kind of stress, which can lead to serious physical ill-health, mental breakdown or even suicide. It is worth mentioning here that chronic stress is the type that is most frequently related to the workplace.

Type A and Type B personalities

Academics have long been interested in the relationship between personality and stress. Two researchers in the USA carried out an exploratory study of the relationship between stress and coronary heart disease. In addition to their central findings, the research results indicated two extreme personality types, Type A, and its opposite, Type B (Friedman and Rosenman, 1974). According to the research, the personality characteristics that typify the two types are:

Type A	Type B
Competitiveness	Leisurely
High need for achievement	Not concerned about achievement
Aggressiveness	Placid and easygoing
Working at speed	Steady worker
Impatience	Seldom impatient
Restlessness	Calm
Extreme alertness	Relaxed
Tenseness	Normal or slow movement and speech
Feeling pressurised	Takes things in stride
Time consciousness	Always has time to do things

Each of the pairs of characteristics listed above, i.e. competitiveness – leisurely, etc., should be seen as the extremes of a dimension, rather than as a pure dichotomy with nothing in between. It is the behaviour of individuals that helps observers to place them somewhere on each dimension, through assessing the degree to which they possess the characteristics that categorise them as Types A or B. For example, Type A people get through a large amount of work and set themselves tight deadlines to meet objectives that are only barely attainable in terms of time and skill. To the organisation, being a high achiever, getting through a high workload and being competitive are welcome personal qualities, but as we shall see, there is a price for the organisation and the individual to pay.

Type Bs, on the other hand, rarely set themselves deadlines and objectives. They work at a steady pace, are not particularly concerned about high achievement, and they attach considerable importance to their holidays and other leisure pursuits. They tend to be thorough in their work, and they get the job done because they allow themselves sufficient time. Type Bs usually make moderate career progress, and they are never going to produce scintillating ideas or suggest exciting changes, but they are reliable and enjoy good relationships with colleagues, although an extreme Type B character can sometimes annoy an extreme Type A. The research shows that people with Type A personalities are three times more likely than those with Type B personalities to experience stress-related illnesses, including coronary heart disease, high blood pressure, digestive problems and depression.

Individual reactions to stress

Stress is a relative thing. Mentally, physically and behaviourally, no two individuals are exactly alike. People perceive things selectively so that no two individuals perceive the same thing in precisely the same way; and for the same reason, no two individuals react in the same way to the same stressor. Furthermore, any single individual may or may not be stressed by an event or situation, depending upon *when* it occurs and what else is going on in the person's life at the time. These variations in perception may cause a social or work-related event to be seen by one person as pleasurable and by another as a cause of misery and apprehension. Retirement, or extensive organisational change, for example, may be eagerly anticipated by one person and viewed by another with extreme anxiety and misgivings. Also, there are stressors that affect almost everyone, but this does not mean that they are all affected in the same way. Whether it is externally imposed or self-induced, the effect that stress has, and the degree of its severity, are determined by the nature of the situation in which it has arisen, when it has arisen, and the degree of seriousness with which each different individual perceives it and feels capable of coping with it.

Sources and causes of stress

We can distinguish between *sources* and *causes* of stress and spotlight the main causes which, according to research, are the most frequently reported in responses to questionnaires and interviews. Field research and a literature search ranging from 1970 to 1998 revealed that the six main *sources* of stress are the places in which we spend most of our time and/or the issues that are of the greatest importance to us (Currie, 1990):

1. the workplace;

2. one's marriage;

3. home and family;

4. finance;

5. living accommodation;

6. social and leisure pursuits.

Causes of stress, or *stressors*, are the concerns, situations and relationships that reside within the sources and which impose pressures upon us. Sources of stress are interrelated and interdependent. For example, financial difficulties might be caused by being underpaid at work; marriage problems might be caused by the extra time that one of the partners spends at work. Being caught in the 'bed-to-work trap', or the 'long hours culture' as it is sometimes called, may also deprive us of opportunities to follow our social and leisure pursuits. When a stress audit is carried out in an organisation, it usually shows that the workplace is not the only source of stress. The source could be at home, or in any of the other sources listed in the previous paragraph, but since stress commutes with the individual it will affect his or her work performance, regardless of the source. From this an interesting question arises: *should employers become involved if the well-being of employees is being adversely affected by stress, when the stress is attributable to sources outside of the workplace?* To employers who are interested in employees' work performance, the answer is 'yes', since in addition to the organisation's humanitarian motive, there are sound business reasons for this answer.

Stress and change

One of the most frequently cited causes of stress is change. When changes improve our situations they are welcome, but when they are unwelcome, depending on their perceived severity, they can be disastrous. In a very general context, life events that bring about what individuals may perceive as significant change were studied by two American researchers in 1967, and as a result they drew up a rating scale. The tabulation lists 43 commonly occurring positive and negative life events, each of which carries a score, so that the more stressful the event, the higher one scores (Holmes and Rahe, 1967). Figure 2.1 lists the 43 items on a scale of 11 to 100, in order of the severity of the stress experienced. (Less than 11 was regarded as insignificant.) Note than even the positive changes can be stressful.

The items on the scale are life events that were found to cause stress among most people, although when examining these items we should be careful to remember that they arise from research that investigated stress in a general way, and that the individuals who experience stress as a result of these events do not all experience it in the same way, or at the same level. This research was carried out in the USA, and it is interesting to note that most of the sources and causes are similar to those found in the UK and the rest of Europe.

Figure 2.1 The social adjustment scale (Holmes and Rahe, 1967).

Event	Measure of impact
Death of spouse	100
Divorce	75
Marital separation	65
Jail term	63
Death of close family member	63
Personal injury or illness	53
Marriage	50
Dismissal from work	47
Marital reconciliation	45
Retirement	45
Change in health of family member	44
Pregnancy	40
Sex difficulties	39
Gain of new family member	39
Business readjustment	39
Change in financial state	38
Death of a close friend	37
Change to different line of work	36
Change in number of arguments with spouse	35
Major mortgage	31
Foreclosure of mortgage or loan	30
Change in responsibilities at work	29
Son or daughter leaving home	29
Trouble with in-laws	29
Outstanding personal achievement	28
Partner begins or stops work	26
Begin or end school	26
Change in living conditions	25
Revision of personal habits	24
Trouble with boss	23
Change in work hours or conditions	20

Change in residence	20
Change in schools	20
Change in recreation	19
Change in church activities	19
Change in social activities	18
Small mortgage or loan	17
Change in sleeping habits	16
Change in number of family get-togethers	15
Change in eating habits	15
Vacation	13
Christmas	12
Minor violations of the law	11

Note While the structure of this scale may tempt one who has recently experienced one or more of the above events to try to calculate a personal 'score', it should be pointed out that the figures related to the events are there purely to indicate their *relative* impact, and that a 'score', therefore, would be meaningless.

The mental effects of stress

Either chronic stress or PTSD may cause mental illness. When anxiety levels are raised, people feel tense and uneasy; in severe situations they may feel fretful, distressed or highly alarmed, depending on their perceptions of the situation and the degree to which they feel capable of responding to it. In cases of chronic stress, where the individual has been under continuous pressure for a long time, feelings of being alone (deserted/isolated) set in, the individual becomes depressed, and all or any of the emotions and ailments related to chronic stress may be experienced. A person who is stressed to this extent is mentally ill and should be seen by a medical practitioner. Society, however, has stigmatised mental illness which has reduced the likelihood that the affected individual will present himself or herself to the manager to state the problem. In the work situation, for example, an ambitious person who is working hard for promotion and fearful of being overlooked, or even working hard in the hope of avoiding redundancy or being bullied by the boss, will also be keen to avoid being thought of as stressed. The most frequently found fear is that they may be seen as a weak or ineffective employee.

Employees who do go to see their doctor almost always find that the visit results in being prescribed drugs that are designed to reduce their symptoms. Most doctors today, however, are well aware of the kinds of cultural environment in which their patients work and may ask questions and offer advice about the person's lifestyle. In severe cases of stress, the doctor may think it appropriate for the patient to be examined by a specialist, such as a professional counsellor or behaviour therapist, to assess the gravity of his or her condition and carry out or prescribe treatment. Doctors' awareness of the culture in their local organisations and their natural protectiveness towards their patients may, when issuing sick notes for example, make them reluctant to indicate an ailment that could be interpreted as even the slightest form of mental illness.

The physical effects of stress

Stress is experienced through the mental thought processes and perceptions, but there are consequent physical effects, and whatever the cause, whatever type of stress is experienced, and whether it is externally imposed or self-induced, the bodily reactions to it are the same. We all have an in-built physiological reaction to stress that has evolved within us over millions of years of environmental adaptation. One researcher referred to this as the *General Adaptation Syndrome (GAS)* (Selye, 1976). In this context, a syndrome is a group or structure of symptoms that occur in a sequence, and in this syndrome they occur in the following order: *1 alarm reaction*; *2 resistance*, and *3 exhaustion* (see Figure 2.2).

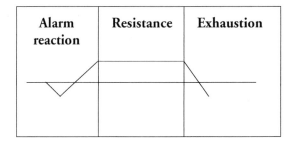

Figure 2.2 The three stages of the general adaptation syndrome (GAS) (Selye, 1976).

Phase 1: Alarm reaction

This occurs as a reaction to the stressor. If we perceive the stressor to be very severe, this initial reaction may be one of shock, and if this does happen our physical and mental responses will immediately fall below normal, and we may 'freeze'.

Phase 2: Resistance

If the stressor continues to affect us, we move on to this phase. We 'unfreeze' and our responses return to normal. Then resistance to the stressor increases, and to enable us to adapt effectively to the situation, the 'fight or flight' reaction (Cannon, 1934) occurs, in which: first, the heart rate increases, blood sugar levels and blood pressure rise, and quantities of blood are diverted from our extremities towards the main organs; secondly, the air passages expand to allow more air into the lungs and breathing becomes deeper and faster; thirdly, digestion reduces or stops altogether; fourthly, the adrenal glands secret extra adrenaline into the bloodstream, which stimulates the heart and other organs. These reactions provide an awesome example of how the body can prepare itself to adapt to and cope with a wide variety of stressors. These bodily changes occur automatically and are capable of rapid adjustment, so that the level at which their effect plateaus off is commensurate with our perceptions of the gravity of the situation and a reflection of how perceptions of 'grave situations' vary from one individual to the next.

Phase 3: Exhaustion

This is the third and final phase. The human body does not have an infinite capacity to withstand these internal changes, nor does it have an inexhaustable supply of hormones and other resources, and if stress is continuous they become depleted and eventually peter out. Our inclination, however, is to continue to try to call upon those resources, even when they are no longer there, and if stress continues the consequences will be extremely serious, in the form of a heart attack, a nervous breakdown or even death. It should be borne in mind that the GAS evolved within us as a *short-term* defensive reaction, and when stress is continuous, we are concurrently trying to follow our normal routines. For example: we eat, but the digestive system is not working properly; we try to focus on our friends and families, but our minds are elsewhere; we try to sleep, but the body and mind simply will not rest adequately.

Positive stress

So far we have described stress as if it is a negative experience that should be avoided at all costs. Conversely, it is claimed by some that a little stress is good for you. This claim is made in the context of so-called *positive stress* which we can refer to as *eustress* (a term coined by Seyle; *eu* from the Greek, meaning 'good'), which enhances our performance. It helps us to achieve our goals and promotes feelings of well-being, satisfaction and self-confidence. Truly, there are certain types of pressure that appear to have a positive effect, such as that which is experienced by a sprinter waiting for the starting pistol to go off. Surely, they say, if the fight or flight reaction occurs, he or she can run faster. If we are in a mental state that enables us to think more quickly and effectively, we should be able to pass those dreaded examinations or succeed at that important job interview.

Before agreeing with the suggestion that *a little stress is good for you*, we should, however, remind ourselves of the mental and physiological changes that enable us to enhance our performance and ask ourselves if the longer-term maintenance of those levels, in which the bodily systems are in an abnormal state, can be a good thing. The severity of stress can reach levels that are too much for most human beings to bear, but it is far more frequently the length of time over which we are stressed, rather than the amount of stress, that causes the damage. Our internal reaction as the mechanism through which we react to and attempt to cope with today's stresses and strains may seem inadequate, but it is all we have. Selye distinguished between *eustress*, which is pleasant, short-term and often self-induced stress, such as physical exercise, and what he called *distress*, which he saw as unwanted, such as a frustrating or threatening situation. In view of the foregoing it may be safer, and indeed more accurate, to say that '… a little *short-term* stress probably is not harmful'. We all remember athletic events in which, for example, we saw Linford Christie, taut as a bow string as he toed the line waiting for the starting pistol, but that is a far cry from an office manager or a shopfloor worker struggling to meet never ending deadlines.

In this light, it is important to note that transient stress that is caused by attempting to meet a short-term deadline in the workplace may, depending on the circumstances, be regarded as '… not harmful', since the pressure will ease when the deadline has been met. In many work situations, however, employees are faced with continuous end-to-end deadlines, which is when transient stress becomes chronic stress. Where this is happening, managers should review their systems of work allocation and, perhaps, even the whole work system.

Also, we have to be careful to draw a distinction between stress and something that motivation analysts call *arousal*, which is a natural mental condition that stimulates our actions and, depending upon the degree to which we are motivated, also influences our behaviour in the form of performance standards. But in the context in which this is said, the degree of arousal, and hence the degree of motivation, is determined by individually perceived rewards as the outcome of the person's performance and the extent to which the person desires and can predict the type and value of the rewards available.

The behavioural effects of stress

The bodily effects mean that when stressed the person is in an abnormal physiological condition. As we know, this can be slight or severe, short term or long term. If it is severe and long term, so that the individual's internal physical resources are depleted, he or she will feel less able to cope – indeed, for very clear physiological reasons, he or she *will be* less able to cope. Also, it is pretty obvious that if the abnormal physiological condition is prolonged, the individual will begin to suffer from digestive, cardiovascular and nervous disorders, since prolonged stress affects the blood pressure, inhibits the actions of the digestive system and induces depression. All of this will exacerbate the feelings of hopelessness and misery. It becomes a vicious circle.

Across an extended period of stress, an individual's behaviour changes. Those who smoke tend to smoke more, some turn to alcohol as an escape mechanism, while others become dependent on drugs, prescribed or otherwise obtained. People have their own individual ways of attempting to reduce the feelings that arise through stress. The total situation that has been described so far renders the individual incapable of behaving as they would normally. The standard of their work performance reduces, they may become irritable and lose their temper, which is behaviour that those who have known them for a long time would describe as 'out of character'. Chronically stressed people also may experience a number of minor ailments, such as aches in the neck and jaw muscles, recurring headaches, migraine, skin rashes, high blood pressure, impotence or frigidity, minor heart and prolonged digestive irregularities and sleeplessness. Sometimes these ailments precede the onset of a serious stress-related illness. Psychologically, people who are so affected also may feel a dread of going to work or experience inexplicable panic attacks and depression.

Levels of stress

While it is clear that stress may occur at different levels of intensity within an individual, it is difficult to devise a precise and objective means of measuring it, since the level at which it is experienced is determined by the personality of the individual and his or her capacity to cope with the pressure caused by the perceived nature and gravity of the stressor. In self-report questionnaires, respondents are asked to tick boxes, which are set against a semantic differential scale, which is a scale that places numerical weightings against statements about the severity of the stress. A five-point semantic differential scale may be used (see Figure 2.3). In the questionnaire the respondent is asked to circle the number that most closely reflects the degree of stress that he or she experiences as a result of some particular cause.

Slight or none	Moderate	Extra	Severe	Very severe
0	1	2	3	4

Figure 2.3 Stress measurement scale.

The human function curve

Dr Peter Nixon, a senior consultant cardiologist at Charing Cross Hospital in London, studied the physiological effects of stress and produced the *human function curve* (see Figure 2.4).

According to the human function curve, work performance increases with pressure, but there comes a point at which the pressure begins to take its toll and the employee becomes fatigued. If the pressure continues, exhaustion, ill health and eventual breakdown will be the result. The point at which fatigue appears on the curve will vary from one individual to the next, but the general principle is the same for everyone. The 'curve of intended work performance' provides an indication of the employee's unfulfilled intentions. The standard of an employee's work performance is determined by ability, multiplied by the degree to which he or she is motivated to do the work: *Performance = Ability × Motivation*. But the curve shows that no matter how highly motivated an employee might be, there comes a point when, in

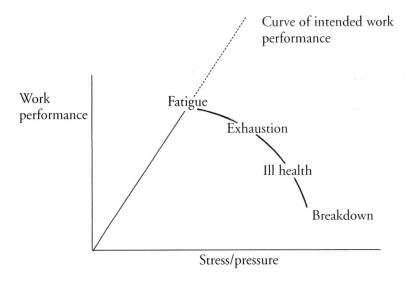

Figure 2.4 The human function curve.

physical and psychological terms, a limit is reached and performance standards fall; the ability factor can no longer be applied. This change in behaviour should interest the manager and influence his or her decision over what to do about it.

The human function curve provides an explanation of what can happen when an individual is expected to cope with end-to-end emergencies, a continuous high workload or an excessive amount of time spent in the workplace. It may be that the wrong person has been selected for a job, in that someone with a low tolerance for pressure is put in a high-pressure situation. Or it may be that the demands of the job itself would put anyone under pressure, which could indicate poor job design, ineffective work systems, inadequate planning or inefficient work allocation. On the other hand, some jobs, just by their very nature, are stressful. Cooper (1991) says that mining, piloting, police work, advertising and acting are believed to produce the highest stress levels.

Earlier, we saw categories of stress expressed in terms of type and time, but we may also see stress as *extrinsic* and *intrinsic*. This concept is similar to that proposed by *content* theorists of work motivation (Maslow, 1972; Herzberg, 1957), when they identify and categorise job factors as motivators and non-motivators. Most managers and management students will be familiar with this concept. Table 2.1 gives examples of extrinsic and intrinsic stressors.

As a source of stress, the workplace accounts for more than 50 per cent of all reported causes (Currie, 1990), and it is clear that a manager who wishes to address the stress issue would benefit from a structured framework through which he or she might identify the types and locations of workplace stressors.

The framework is one in which a *job-person unit (JPU)* is set within the total context of the work environment; potential stressors may be identified within the broader work environment and within the JPU itself. The stressors are classified as extrinsic and intrinsic, the

Table 2.1 Extrinsic and intrinsic stressors

Extrinsic stressors	Intrinsic stressors
• Company policy, including employment, welfare, equal opportunity, health and safety, etc. • Organisation's stability • Wage and salary levels • Training opportunities • Promotion opportunities • Internal politics • Bullying • Managerial style – leadership • Lack of planning • Time spent in the workplace • Working climate and culture • State of infrastructure	• Nature of the job • Status of the job • Level of continuous workload • Level of job satisfaction • Degree of job involvement • Amount of responsibility • Extent of authority • Amount of autonomy • Recognition for work carried out • Opportunity to use knowledge and skills • Relationship with immediate boss

former being environmental, since they are in the workplace but external to the actual job itself, and the latter being within the cocoon of the JPU (see Figure 2.5).

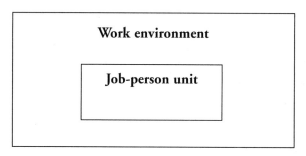

Figure 2.5 The job-person unit (JPU).

Viewed in this way, we can see that all employees may be affected by the common influence of the extrinsic stressors, while additionally, each individual employee may be affected by his or her own particular intrinsic stressors.

The employee unconsciously separates the intrinsic job content from the content of the broader work situation, and establishes intrinsic orders of priority within the job itself, first by perceiving some parts of it to be more important than others, and secondly by developing preferences in that he or she regards some parts of the job as more satisfying and enjoyable than others. There are high correlations between what job-holders regard as important and what they regard as satisfying and enjoyable. The orders of priority within a job that are set by the organisation are altered by the employee as his or her experience of the job lengthens.

It is also clear that when change in the form of reorganisation is announced, individual job-holders become stressed when they feel that the 'important' parts of their jobs may be under threat. They examine any proposed changes very closely to see what implications there might be for their own situations, and as a result become more or less concerned, depending on how they interpret the changes and their possible consequences.

It has long been established that employees are predominantly interested in what is going on in their own immediate work area, and that personal interest in organisational matters reduces as one moves away from it. Matters affecting one's job and oneself, therefore, are of greater interest than those affecting others in remote parts of the organisation. Research also shows that the closer a stressor is to the *intrinsic* job situation, the higher is the level of the stress experienced.

Managing and coping with stress

A distinction is drawn between 'managing' and 'coping' with stress. This helps when we are discussing the actions that may be taken to alleviate the effects of stress. Managing stress is the term used to describe managers' decisions and actions that are designed to reduce or eliminate the effects of stress in the workplace. On the other hand, when people are actively doing something to assuage the effects of their own individual stress symptoms, we say that they are coping with stress.

Individual stress problems – what to look for

Not only do managers need to be able to recognise stress symptoms, they also need to be able to place the symptoms in context. For example, the fact that a member of staff is smoking heavily should not necessarily be regarded as a symptom of stress; it may be that the person smokes a lot anyway. It is when the employee is smoking more than usual that the manager might reflect upon why this might be. An employee who returns to work from a lunchbreak smelling of alcohol may have resorted to alcohol as a mental escape from the effects of stress. Or it could be that, while the employee was out at lunch, he or she may have met an old friend and gone for a drink to chat over old times. Managers need to get to know their staff so that they can recognise 'out of character' behaviour when it occurs. Figure 2.6 illustrates factors that are typical of the mental, physical and behavioural effects of stress.

Stress reduction strategies

Most stress management systems are part of a more comprehensive healthy workplace initiative. Organisations that have introduced such initiatives in the recent past have done so on humanitarian grounds, but now there is also the belief that a healthy workforce means a reduction in accidents, grievances and sickness absence, and an increase in job satisfaction and performance, leading to greater productivity and profit.

Physical effects		Mental effects
Lethargy		Anxiety
Insomnia		Tension
Gastric problems		Mental illness
Heart disease		Worry about the future
Headaches – migraine		Job satisfaction level
Blood pressure problems		Depression
		Boredom

Behavioural effects

Reduced work performance

Excessive smoking

Excessive drinking

Inadequate sex life

Drug abuse

Illicit affair

Figure 2.6 Some typical symptoms of stress.

Strategies that are designed to reduce stress have to tackle the problem on two fronts, the first addresses current individual stress problems, while the second addresses the organisation itself, in terms of its policies and procedures related to employee well-being, climate, managerial attitudes and leadership style (see Chapter 3).

'If you can't stand the heat ...'

Many managers believe that individuals who become stressed in particular work situations should not have put themselves in such situations to begin with. In most organisations today, however, 'normality' is represented by continuous change, in which reorganisation programmes have moved employees from one job situation to another, moves in which the only alternative is redundancy. 'If you can't stand the heat, get out of the kitchen' is a phrase used by US President Harry S. Truman when he was addressing his senior executives shortly after he had ordered the bombing of Nagasaki and Hiroshima in 1945. Amazingly, after 55 years, managers are still heard to use the expression when talking to stressed employees. Fortunately, such managers are a dying breed and methods of managing organisations has moved on considerably since Truman. 'If you can't stand the heat, then redesign the kitchen' would be a more appropriate expression for today's managers.

The manager as a counsellor

Counselling is dismissed by some as 'airy-fairy nonsense'. 'We never had anything like that in our day. We just had to get on with things.' Today, of course, there are many innovations that did not exist in 'their day', but which have proved themselves to be useful. That's progress. On the other hand, a familiar figure that has been around in organisations for many years is the so-called 'company auntie' – the self-appointed industrial agony aunt who claims that 'people always come to me with their problems'. Usually untrained, such people can do a lot of damage. They give advice that can lead to disaster, while in most cases people are looking for support rather than advice. More often than not, the individual who has the problem also has the solution and is looking for some kind of confirmation that the actions they propose to take are reasonable. In such cases, a professional counsellor will listen intently to the client while saying very little, just a guiding 'yes' or a nod now and then, until the whole story has emerged, at which time the client has usually reached the point where he or she expresses possible solutions. Counsellors do not offer advice; they are interested in the individual's well-being, they offer support and assistance and may refer the person to a colleague, who may be a clinician, financial expert, marriage guidance counsellor or lawyer, depending on the nature of the problem.

Despite what is said above about the 'company auntie', counselling is a skill that comes naturally to some people, while in others it is a skill that has to be acquired through training. Natural ability, of course, is a quality that evolves within people as they develop and gain experience through life, but no matter how gifted a person may be, the effectiveness of applying his or her natural ability can always be improved through training. Where the natural ability is counselling, one can, through training, obtain formally recognised qualifications. Occupational support schemes (OSS) and employee assistance programmes (EAP) employ counsellors who are qualified in a variety of subjects (see Chapter 3). For example, there is a vast difference between the kind of counselling that supports and assists people who have legal or financial problems and the kind that is administered in cases of post traumatic stress disorders. Where this last is identified, the manager should always, without exception, arrange for the person to be seen by a qualified professional specialist.

Managers, like any other group of individuals, vary in their ability to counsel their employees, and in all cases the nature of the counselling that is required influences the manager's ability to be effective. For example, where a manager observes a shortfall in the performance of an employee, he or she may conclude that 'job counselling' is needed; perhaps, for example, there is a gap in the individual's knowledge or skills, and it may be possible to fill that gap through on-the-job counselling. On the other hand, a glance at the employee's performance record may show that normally he or she performs well, which implies that the shortfall may be due to some other cause, a stressor perhaps. In such a case, the manager might question the person in order to discover the nature of the problem. Once the problem becomes clear, the manager then has to decide what to do, whether to continue with the counselling, or refer the person to the personnel department, the organisation's OSS or EAP. The manager should aim for a satisfactory outcome for the employee. The most important ingredient in achieving this through counselling someone is the ability and the motivation to listen. Most managers are busy people and it is sometimes against their nature to do something in which speed is not of the essence, but good staff today are hard to find, and it is worth stopping for a while to give a distressed employee 100 per cent of one's attention, especially if the ultimate outcome is to recover the person to their normal productive self. It should be borne in mind that no matter how effective the ultimate treatment might be, it will have been a total waste of time and expense if the stressed employee is returned to the situation in which the stress occurred in the first place, without addressing the cause.

Danger, heroes at work

'Heroes' are workers who think that they carry the problems of organisation on their shoulders. This kind of personality will be familiar to most managers. Regardless of the high improbability of what they think, they honestly believe it. They carry out tasks which do not appear on their job descriptions, and they remain at their desks or machines for far longer than is necessary. They do not usually seek extra financial reward for what they do, but they gain great satisfaction from their 'commitment' and work rate being noticed, which is reward enough. They like to feel important to the organisation. Employees who have this kind of personality suffer stress from their self-generated work overload, and yet they are adept at concealing the symptoms, especially in behavioural terms. Not only, therefore, are they the most difficult to track down as stress victims, they are also the least likely to come forward and admit that they have a problem. By the time it becomes obvious that they are stressed, the condition is usually well advanced.

Coping with stress

The purpose of this section is twofold. First, it is to help the manager who may experience the effects of stress him- or herself, and secondly, to provide information that may be useful for counselling purposes. There are two main approaches to coping with personal stress. The first concerns the way we perceive what we regard as stressors, which can be situations at work involving a high workload, having to meet continuous deadlines, relationships, problems at home, and so forth. The second concerns lifestyle, in which we need to examine our daily habits, including smoking, drinking, spending too much time at work and not enough with our friends and family, eating the right foods, eating at the right times and generally looking after our health. If we are fit and healthy, we are less likely to suffer adversely from the physiological effects of stress, since being fit and healthy helps us to fend off the worst effects and cope effectively.

Perceptions of stress

In the early parts of this chapter, we saw that all individuals are different from each other, and that what stresses one person may not stress another. As people develop from childhood into adulthood, they learn and internalise unique sets of values, beliefs and attitudes which are what cause people to perceive things in the way they do, and which in turn determine their actual behaviour. Here we are examining two factors: the situation and the unique personality of the individual. How the individual perceives a situation, interacts with or reacts to it, and his or her own assessment of their ability to cope, determines the level and duration of any stress that is experienced as a result. It may be, therefore, that people who regard themselves as particularly vulnerable to the effects of stress would benefit from reassessing the true extent of their stressors, and reassessing their true ability to cope.

Through their experience of work, and life in general, people develop expectations about the outcomes of particular situations. Perhaps there was a situation in the past that did not turn out very well, and now a similar situation has arisen. It is on the basis of what happened before that people feel apprehensive about outcomes from current, similar situations.

A large proportion of stress is unwarranted. That is to say, people are frequently stressed because they do not fully understand the situations in which they find themselves. Also, their fearful perceptions of particular situations are often unfounded. For example, people become anxious about visiting their doctor, or solicitor, or bank manager, yet when the visit is over they wonder why on earth they were so concerned. An employee might worry when the boss wants to 'have a word' in the office. Flashbacks of recent behaviour and work performance occur, and they become anxious about what it could be. Am I to be made redundant? Have I done something wrong? Will this be a 'first warning'? They brace themselves before entering such situations, only to find that the boss wants them to stand in for a supervisor who is going on holiday, or wants a particularly interesting project carried out.

Clearly, we need to prepare ourselves in case things do go awry – at least then we have put ourselves in a good position to cope. It is wise to analyse a situation that seems threatening, think about how important it really is and, above all, ensure that it genuinely is your problem and not someone else's. It is also a good idea to reflect upon the situations that have worried us in the past, but did not produce the expected harmful outcome. Indeed, some may even have had positive outcomes, and if there were situations that ended unsatisfactorily, at least we survived to tell the tale. Stressful events seldom occur in isolation, and even though there are many concurrent events that are not stressful at all, we have a strong tendency to focus exclusively on the worst of them.

What can be done?

The effects of stress can build up gradually, indeed almost imperceptibly, so that you may not notice the changes that you are undergoing. If, eventually, you do suspect that you might be experiencing such effects, then take time to reflect and compare how things were in the past against how they are now. Sleeplessness, for example, could be a symptom, especially if it is accompanied by inexplicable feelings of panic, loss of appetite, a dread of going to work or irritability, especially with people with whom you would not normally be irritable, such as friends or members of your family. Any single one of these symptoms might easily be explained away, but when several of them appear concurrently and are persistent, it is time to take action. Firstly, try to identify what is causing it. Is it something at work, such as having too many successive deadlines to meet, insufficient control or decision-making authority over your own work, lack of support from above, or poor relationships with colleagues or seniors? Secondly, if you have a close, trustworthy friend, talk things over with them; perhaps they have noticed changes in you but have been reluctant to mention it. Also, if it is something in the workplace, talk it over with the boss. Thirdly, try to come up with ideas that might eliminate or at least moderate the cause/s. Fourthly, analyse your lifestyle and look for areas that could stand improvement.

Managing lifestyle

Since stress can cause serious mental and physical harm to employees, it would seem natural for a caring employer to promote strategies designed to reduce stress in a direct way, yet very few do this. Instead, they try to manage stress by promoting healthy lifestyle initiatives. In fact, while there are some elementary and common-sense 'ground-rule' approaches to leading a healthy life, such as, for example, engaging in regular physical activity, lifestyle itself is regarded by many as a very personal issue, and some employees might feel that it is an unwarranted intrusion for the organisation to advise them on how they should live their lives. On the other hand, if an organisation wishes to promote a healthy workplace, such an initiative should be regarded as positive and, indeed, a clear demonstration of caring. Healthy workplace initiatives normally include:

1. Smoke-free work areas and the implementation of a comprehensive 'smoking' or 'no smoking' policy. A smoking policy is one in which areas are provided for the use of smokers, on condition that they do not smoke elsewhere on the work premises. A no smoking policy is one in which smoking is forbidden throughout the workplace.

2. Consult the workforce about the kinds of food that may be provided in the staff restaurant, and formulate and implement a food policy for the organisation.

3. Provide employees with information about healthy living, including advice on physical activity, healthy eating, generally looking after one's health, and warning about the dangers of smoking and the use and abuse of alcohol and drugs.

4. Provide all employees with the opportunity to have comprehensive annual health checks, to monitor their mental and physical conditions, including checks for coronary heart disease, obesity, blood pressure levels and respiratory problems.

5. Where possible, provide facilities for employees to engage in physical activities, and encourage them to participate in sport.

6. Create a work culture and physical environment that is physically safe and generally conducive to good health.

7. Identify causes of stress within the organisation and externally and ensure that employees are provided with appropriate and adequate

support with problems. This means conducting organisation-wide stress surveys as well as dealing with individuals who have problems.

Obviously, not all organisations will be financially sound enough to make all of these provisions, but most of them can be achieved in most organisations.

Conclusion

The definition of stress is particularly important to managers. Having seen the damage that stress can inflict, not only upon the individual but on the organisation too, one might decide to reconsider one's views on pushing or pressurising individuals in attempts to increase their productivity.

Stress within the organisation is costly. Lost productivity through stress-related sickness absence and reduced performance, replacing absent workers, managers absent from their jobs dealing with grievances, disciplinary procedures, employment tribunals and court cases all add up to a very expensive way of failing to enhance profitability through productivity. Furthermore, the amount of litigation being processed is increasing, and while much of it is settled out of court, the compensation involved is hefty. The cost of treating employees with the care and respect they deserve costs less and produces more.

Stress affects people mentally, physically and behaviourally, and it deprives them of the ability to focus on their work and do a good job. While a little stress is certainly not 'good for you', it is the duration, rather than the intensity, that is dangerous. Short-term stress probably is not harmful – it enables people to cope more effectively with emergencies, for which the internal human capabilities have evolved.

Stress results from the way in which people interact with the situations they encounter in the environment. Personality factors determine different individuals' perceptions of situations, and from their past experiences they have learned to expect particular outcomes, which, in turn, determines their perceived ability to cope. What stresses one person may not stress another, and a stressor may affect an individual at one time, but not at another, depending on what else is going on in their lives at the time.

Individual differences make stress difficult to measure; results from the use of the scale given in this chapter have to be taken in the context of the individual's work situation and his or her personality. In any case, it is best to engage the services of a professional, usually a psychologist, to administer any stress test and interpret the results.

There are typical stressors in the workplace, and in general terms their importance to the individual may be governed by the 'extrinsic' or 'intrinsic' nature of the stressors. Also, because of the strength of the context of the situations in certain categories of employment, they have been identified as particularly stressful regardless of the strength of the personalities of the job holders.

Managers need to be able to recognise stress symptoms among their staff, and the nature of these is listed. The important subtlety of this is to perceive the symptoms in the correct context.

Managers have the key role to play in how stress is handled by the organisation. There are no set techniques for training managers in stress management, but there are actions that managers could take, for example: (a) interacting with the employees to develop within them the ability to recognise situations and features in the work environment that could produce stress; (b) for managers to develop within themselves the ability to recognise stress symptoms in themselves, as well as in their staff; and (c) to practise *recommended* techniques such as relaxation and meditation. Techniques such as massage, reflexology, aromatherapy and certain other 'alternative' techniques are fine for the short term, but relaxation and meditation become lifetime habits and have a longer lasting beneficial effect. One might need instruction in the techniques, but it is well worth it. In addition to what is said above, it is important to manage one's lifestyle carefully.

References

Cannon, W.B. (1929) *Bodily Changes in Pain, Hunger, Fear, and Rage*, 2nd edn. New York: Appleton-Century-Crofts.

Cooper, C.L., Cooper, R.D. and Eaker, L.H. (1988) *Living with Stress*. Harmondsworth: Penguin.

Currie, D. (1990) *Stress in the National Health Service, Southampton* (a report for Southampton Business School). Southampton: Southampton Institute.

Friedman, M. and Rosenman, R.H. (1974) *Type A Behaviour and Your Heart*. Knopf: New York.

Herzberg, F.W., Mausner, B. and Snyderman, B. (1957) *The Motivation to Work*. New York: Wiley.

Holmes, T.H. and Rahe, R.H. (1967) 'The social readjustment rating scale', *Journal of Psychosomatic Research*, vol. 11, pp. 213–18.

Maslow, A.H. (1987) *Motivation and Personality*. New York: Harper & Row.

Selye, H. (1974) *Stress without Distress*. Philadelphia: J.P. Lippincott.

CHAPTER 3

The healthy organisation

Introduction

This chapter begins with an explanation of how different individuals perceive their jobs and the organisations that employ them. Why people work and attitudes towards employment and unemployment are discussed, along with explanations of the policies and procedures that govern the management of employee well-being. The business case as well as the humane case is made for the provision of benefits and services which, although primarily aimed at employee well-being, are coupled with the need to enhance performance, and thereby with the survival and further development of the organisation. Examples of 'healthy workplace' initiatives are given, which include the provision of occupational support schemes and employee assistance programmes. Strategies and policies for the future, including management and leadership styles, climate, culture and structure, are also explored.

For many managers, the mention of a 'healthy organisation' arouses the idea of workplace health and safety which is related to accident prevention, the safe storage and use of dangerous substances, the proper use of machines on the shop floor, such as fork-lift trucks, and so forth. The law and codes of practice in such respects have been in existence for many years in all industrialised countries, and are well known. Here, the approach to the achievement of a healthy organisation advocates, first, that to ensure physical well-being the legal provisions should be regarded by the organisation as minimum standards rather than as the norm, and second, that in going beyond those provisions, managers should systematically monitor employee well-being in terms of the staff's *mental* as well as their physical condition.

Not all organisations use internal surveys to monitor well-being, but the practice is growing. Additionally, in an increasing number of organisations the health of all staff is monitored annually, and managers are trained to observe and report any changes in their staff's general behaviour, patterns of attendance, quality of work and the standard of performance; much can be learned from changes in these areas. An examination of international examples of health and safety legislation shows that they have little to say about how the work environment and the nature of work itself affect employees' mentally, for example the dangers associated with pressurising employees causing stress. Since legal provisions barely cover such issues, responsibility has been assumed by organisations, but experience shows that they are not all motivated to do so.

Work and individual differences

Most people who go to work do so to make a living, and in the kind of society that we have made for ourselves, working for one's living is the socially acceptable way to provide for oneself and one's family; the mere fact that one has a job carries with it a positive status and there is still a stigma associated with being unemployed. Until recent times there were noticeable changes in the behaviour of people towards acquaintances who had become unemployed, treating them as if somehow it was their own fault; even today there are still traces of this.

People like to think that their talents are worthwhile and valued; it makes them feel as if they themselves are worthwhile and valued.

We have to recognise the distinctions between different individuals' perceptions of work. To some people work is not the top priority in their lives, they simply use it as a means to some other end. If a job meets their needs in terms of, *inter alia*, income, the length of the working week, the distance between work and home, etc., they are prepared to accept it. If they were to find themselves unemployed, they would seek another job in the same area, with roughly the same terms and conditions. They value the friendships and family ties that they have in their community and are not prepared to uproot themselves and move away for the sake of taking up a particular job. They belong to a large group of people who are not fulfilling their work potential; their values are such that they are prepared to content themselves with jobs that allow them to attend to what they regard as their higher priorities, which are at home in the family and in the community.

Conversely, there are people to whom work is the number one priority. Most often these are professional, managerial or those who are technical specialists in fields that demand high levels of skill and knowledge. Such people enjoy what they do and are deeply involved in the purpose and/or the technology of their work. They would readily move to another country, even to the other side of the world, if that was where their work took them.

These are, of course, very broad distinctions between individuals, and 'worker types' may be classified in much greater detail, but whichever category they belong to there is no doubt that being in the workplace and the nature of the work itself have an important effect upon employees' mental and physical well-being, an effect that can be positive or negative. While individually different perceptions of job factors and workplace situations play a significant role in this respect, there are factors which are within the control of managers, which also play an important part. Such factors include the system of payment, non-cash rewards, equal opportunities, employment policies, how diversity is managed, access to education, training and development, holiday entitlement, the length of the working week, sick pay arrangements, the nature of the work and the financial stability of the organisation. Most of these factors are there because they have been put in place by the organisation, but other factors which relate to the individual work experience, such as motivation, job involvement and job satisfaction, are natural human responses to work situations. What all of these factors have in common, however, is that they too have a significant impact on some aspect of employee well-being.

Employment and health

In the Western industrialised world, managers' perceptions of the importance of a 'healthy workplace' changed profoundly through the nineteenth and twentieth centuries. Historically, physical safety was the sole aim, although until the middle of the twentieth century, the thrust towards ensuring physical safety was an issue that was very much a secondary matter to the manager's main aims, which were to ensure that the organisation met its objectives and, thereby, survived and developed. For many years, therefore, policies related to employee well-being were tied in with health and safety at work policies, and even in many organisations today, tasks related to employee well-being are not at the top of the average manager's 'things to do' list. This lack of attention to what some writers cast as the 'welfare role of personnel' is undoubtedly due to the inherent orientation of organisations that health and safety aspects of employment can be fulfilled by complying with the law and that any related policies are externally imposed upon them and somehow isolated from the policies and strategies that drive the enterprise towards the achievement of its corporate objectives. A corollary of this traditional orientation is the continuation of the view that ensuring employee well-being is a matter of taking the steps that one can to reduce the likelihood that employees will suffer *physical* injury while in the workplace. This has resulted in more attention being paid to 'health and safety' in organisations that operate in what are seen traditionally as workplaces in which employees are most vulnerable to injury, such as coal mines, chemical plants, building sites, engineering workshops, oil rigs and gas explorations, and so forth. It is unfortunate that certain regulations and codes of practice (for example, in the UK, the Code of Practice on Risk Assessment) tend to perpetuate this attitude, since they are written in 'engineeringese', as if they are directed exclusively at such places of work, while in fact the legal provisions in most countries apply to all work environments, including offices, schools, shops and other so-called 'safer' places.

In too many organisations the drafting of employee well-being policies is still regarded as a response to external (statutory) pressures, rather than out of a genuine concern for the organisation's people. Despite this generalised view, and despite what is said above about recent regulations and codes of practice, there is growing evidence that many managers' perceptions of employee well-being are broadening, and their attitudes towards it are undergoing significant revision. The larger employers, for example, are beginning to accept that there is a sound business case for developing policies for well-being which encompass not only individuals' general health, including their mental health, but which are integrated with policies designed to drive forward the central purposes of the organisation. Also, legal action instigated by employees and ex-employees has drawn extra attention to the cost of complacency towards employee well-being. Since 1990, such litigation has increased steadily, and has pushed the well-being issue further up the manager's agenda.

It has to be accepted that in today's terms, therefore, employee well-being is a varied and diverse issue. It goes much further than what we used to accept as the traditional components of health and safety legislation, codes of practice, regulations and mandatory internal policies and procedures. Whereas earlier concerns about employee well-being centred mainly around such measures, for example, as those for the prevention of accidents, toxic inhalation and the safe storage of dangerous substances, today's approaches include techniques that extend into areas beyond the traditional physical safety aspects, and are designed to develop job involvement and job satisfaction, systems of reward, stress reduction strategies, and the commissioning of internal surveys to assess the 'health' of the organisation in general. These techniques are part of a strategy that perceives employees' physical and mental well-being as equal in importance. Furthermore, managers now recognise that there is a powerful relationship between human performance and organisational success, and they realise that human beings can perform optimally only if they are mentally free to focus exclusively on their work. This means free from the pressures of over- or under-utilisation, anxieties about job security, bullying, workplace relationships, domestic responsibilities, finance and so forth.

Managers still exist who adopt coercive managerial styles which, although still exercised in too many organisations, are long out of date in terms of modern thinking. It has been shown that bullying and blackmailing employees by threatening to obstruct their promotion, giving them poor performance appraisal reports and witholding privileges – and sometimes even entitlements – in order to get them to work harder and longer increases absence (including sickness absence), staff turnover, the frequency with which the disciplinary and grievance procedures are used and the number of times the organisation finds itself on the defensive in the courts and/or employment tribunals. For these reasons, so-called 'macho management' incurs costs to the organisation in terms of lost productivity through absence, staff turnover, reduced performance and compensation paid to employees or ex-employees who have complained to employment tribunals or the courts – all of which are avoidable.

PYTBULLS

Sadly, this kind of behaviour is still evident. It typifies insecure or failed managers and is largely the result of their lack of understanding about how best to maximise the knowledge and skills of the human resource. In many cases, such managers believe that they are demonstrating a 'strong leadership style' to their own seniors, thus protecting themselves from the axe when it comes to reorganisation. An example of this is the manager who belongs to the brigade we might call the *Pull Yourself Together Bullies*, or PYTBULLS for short. When, for example, such managers encounter distressed employees who clearly are experiencing the effects of too much pressure, they become aggressive and tell them 'pull yourself together and get on with your work'. They do this because they do not know how to manage the situation. They either fail to recognise the seriousness of the employee's plight, or they do realise what it is, but do not wish to get involved in it. The last thing they think is that such employees might be feeling the effects of the pressures that they themselves have imposed upon them. As managers, PYTBULLS are failures. They lack social skills, which is said to be an essential managerial quality; they are inadequate and they lack self-confidence. These so-called managers exercise bullying tactics in order to conceal their own shortcomings. Thankfully, in organisations that employ modern approaches to personnel management, the style that includes applying excessive pressure to employees, in the mistaken belief that 'a little stress is good for you', has been made redundant.

Healthy workplace initiatives

In the UK, these began in earnest in the early 1990s, after the publication of the Chief Medical Officer's Report, *The Health of the Nation*. The UK National Health Service (NHS) was the first to take up the initiative and launched two 'healthy workplace' campaigns. The first, *Health at Work in the NHS*, was internal and aimed at NHS employees. It was designed to address such issues as: 1. sexually transmitted diseases; 2. stress; 3. drug and alcohol abuse; 4. HIV/AIDS; and 5. poor spects of lifestyle, including smoking, poor diet and lack of physical activity. The second, *Look After Your Heart*, was internal and external, in which the aim was to involve employing organisations, largely by appealing for commitment to the initiative, offering literature and running advisory workshops and conferences on the subject.

In the United States, healthy workplace initiatives have the longest history, having been in existence for most of the twentieth century. These are positive, systematised schemes which may appear in a variety of structures, from the home-grown occupational support scheme (OSS) that is customised to meet the specific requirements of an organisation, to such external access schemes as employee assistance programmes (EAPs), which are agencies or consultancies to which a client organisation's employees are given access.

Occupational support schemes

Many public sector organisations and large private sector employers have set up their own internal occupational support schemes (OSS). Where they are permanent and comprehensive, these schemes have been successful. Their main functions are to offer training and counselling sessions that deal with the five issues itemised above, although additionally, they generally employ medically qualified staff to offer immediate support and advice, refer people to specialists, provide treatment for minor ailments and offer counselling to employees with severe problems. Advisory, support and counselling services also provide assistance with problems that employees encounter outside the workplace. Prevention and treatment are at the core of these initiatives. Prevention usually takes the form of advice on lifestyle: healthy eating, giving up smoking, controlling intake of alcohol, advice on sexual behaviour, stress avoidance techniques and providing advice on engaging in regular physical activity. Treatments vary, ranging from the direct treatment of minor ailments, referral to specialists, job counselling and stress counselling. Clearly, a national health service such as that in the UK, which employs around 750,000 people, is ideally placed to establish its own occupational support scheme.

Managers need to exercise care and be sensitive to employees' possible reactions when explaining the introduction of an OSS. It has been shown that in organisations where manager–employee relations were poor to begin with, these initiatives have proved controversial. Even where managers saw the OSS as an initiative which, in addition to its main purposes, might also be seen as a show of genuine concern for staff by offering support services could, thereby, enhance the employee relationship. But employees harboured suspicions about the organisation's underlying motives. For example, while in fact all of the OSS staff's contact with employees was conducted in strict confidence, some saw it as a possible source of information for managers about their employees' private lives and about their views on particular aspects of the organisation and its senior managers. This perception of the OSS was reinforced by the knowledge that the staff specialists working in the OSS were, in fact, fellow employees. Also, everyone knew where the OSS was located and many employees felt embarrassed to be seen entering or leaving it; perhaps their colleagues might perceive the visit as a sign of weakness or ineffectiveness in managing one's own affairs. A further objection came from managers themselves, in which they claimed that the OSS was an unnecessary and expensive luxury, especially in the light of the tight controls over their own budgets.

The OSS, however, does have the advantage of being able to perceive employees' problems within the context of an organisation with which they, as fellow employees, are familiar. There are times when counselling someone you know can be more effective than counselling a stranger, although it has been found that some employees are reluctant to disclose detailed information about their deepest personal problems to someone who is a work colleague.

Employee assistance programmes

An alternative to developing the organisation's own occupational support scheme is to engage the services of an employee assistance programme (EAP). EAPs first appeared in the USA in the 1960s as external consultants who have access to a range of specialists, including psychologists, medically qualified staff, lawyers and a variety of counsellors who specialise in stress, marriage problems, finance, careers and so forth. Now EAPs are firmly established in most industrialised countries.

The independence of the EAP is a major advantage. Their staff do not become embroiled in the internal politics of the client organisation and they do not feel threatened or inhibited by its working climate, managerial style or culture. Without an internal political axe to grind they can be objective and straightforward when they communicate with senior managers without thinking that their careers might be in jeopardy.

Employees are less likely to feel embarrassed about explaining details of their personal anxieties to someone who is not an employee of the organisation. They are likely to have more faith in the confidentiality of the process than they would if the counsellor was a member of the internal staff. It has also been shown that a non-colleague in a support and advisory role carries more credibility as a professional than a fellow-employee in a similar role, who, although equally qualified and as capable as an external consultant, is known to the client-employee (Currie, 1990). Experience shows that this familiarity can reduce the counsellor's long-term effectiveness. A further advantage is that EAPs can usually offer the services of a number of highly skilled professionals whose support, advice and assistance can, where appropriate, be applied to just one employee's problems. Periodically, EAPs report to the senior managers and, while preserving the confidentiality of the sessions they have had with employees, they summarise any repetitive or continuing problems that are related to how the organisation is managed. EAPs are very experienced at identifying organisational HR problems and many of them will offer solutions. Eventually, most senior managers come to regard this objective kind of reporting as credible and useful.

EAPs have been criticised, particularly by middle managers who, in addition to complaining about the cost, tend to regard them as 'touchy-feely do-gooders who know nothing about the organisation'. It is true that EAPs are unfamiliar with the organisation when they first encounter it, but this is compensated by their objectivity and, given time, they do acquire an understanding of the organisation, the nature of its business, the managerial style and the culture. Conversely, managers who have worked in an organisation for several years often become blind to its faults, or do not see them as important enough to justify their attention.

While EAP's fees vary, they usually charge an annual amount, based on the number of employees. Employees make their first contact with the EAP by telephone. The telephone number may be posted in conspicuous places around the workplace, and additionally, it may be included in employees' wage or salary envelopes, along with an explanation of the function of the EAP. From that point on employees can talk to the EAP in confidence, and usually their first contact is an adviser. In some cases the adviser will suggest that they should meet to talk further or, if it becomes clear that the problem is one that demands the attention of a different expert, such as a counsellor, he or she may refer the employee to a specialist who is appropriately qualified and experienced. The large majority of problems, however, are solved on the telephone.

The organisational perspective

Some managers might conclude that if they were to employ the techniques and services to which we have referred above, they would feel as if they were running a convalescent home rather than an organisation whose chief aim is to make a profit or provide a service. Managers who are concerned in this way will derive at least some comfort from the knowledge that the more effective the facilities and services are, the less they will need to be used by the staff.

Managers should not be in any doubt that there are powerful strategic as well as humane reasons for providing such facilities and services for their employees. In most industrialised countries, organisations have a legal duty of care towards their employees, which includes ensuring their *mental* as well as their physical well-being in the workplace. It is worth bearing in mind that in recent cases the courts' decisions that have favoured litigants have been made partly on the grounds that the defending organisations were unable to demonstrate that they had taken positive steps to ensure their employees' well-being, and/or that they had failed to comply with the relevant legislation. Many employers have now developed strategies, policies and procedures, the contents of which convey a clear intention to comply with the relevant legislation, and most regard the legislative provisions as minimum standards rather than as norms.

We said earlier that many managers are striving to integrate strategies to ensure employee well-being with those that are designed to further the central purposes of the organisation. This is being done in the belief that a healthy workforce is a more productive workforce. This belief is well founded, although the evidence for it is not found so much in academic research results as it is in the organisation's own sickness absence and staff turnover figures, the frequency with which the grievance and disciplinary procedures are used, and employees' general attitude to work, all of which affect the cost of maintaining the human resource.

In Chapter 2 we raised the question: 'Should employers involve themselves in the well-being of employees whose stress is attributable to sources outside the workplace?' It is clear that regardless of which area of the individual's life is producing the stress, he or she will carry their anxieties with them no matter where they go, and patently a person who is suffering from such effects is neither mentally free to concentrate on the job nor, possibly, in the best physical condition, which means that his or her productivity will suffer as a result. Indeed, the employer has a vested interest in the resolution of employees' problems.

Strategies for the long term

It will be clear to the reader that the occupational assistance and support schemes described above are generally set up to address employees' short-term problems, while strategies for the long term should be designed to reduce the likelihood that such problems will arise in the future. Formulating such strategies is no easy task, especially when they have to be implemented in the face of continuous change, which is the case in most organisations today. Nobody would disagree that several significant phenomena have coincided and combined to precipitate the kinds of change that are taking place:

1. The rapid and exponential rate at which new technology is advancing.

2. The continuous need for organisations to make internal changes, particularly structural, to accommodate new ideas in management, production and administrative processes in order to remain

competitive by responding to market demands for new or modified products.

3. The emergence of the global market, more easily exploited through advancing technology.

4. New approaches to managing and structuring the organisation, with a particular spotlight on the growth of human resource management.

Today, market demands for new products are changing continually, and to survive organisations have to ensure that they are always in a position to meet them. There is nothing new in the notion that the survival and development of the organisation is determined by its ability to continue to meet the changing demands of its customers and clients, and that this almost always dictates the nature of internal change; it is the *rate* at which change is taking place today that is new.

Managing change

Managing change is dealt with in more detail in Chapter 10, but for the purposes of this chapter, it is worth pointing out how change might affect individuals' well-being. Change has a significant impact on the well-being of the individual at work. People become worried about the security of their jobs, being moved to another work area and losing contact with their long-term work colleagues, having to work for a different manager who was previously unknown to them, fear of having to work for a manager who is known and does not have an 'employee-friendly' reputation, having to take on a job of lower status, having to suffer a reduction in income as an alternative to redundancy.

All of these concerns induce stress and emphasise the need for sensitivity when changes are being made. Organisations, for example, which are widening and flattening their structures, concurrently downsize and rightsize in terms of HR numbers, which obviously produces redundancy programmes. Supervisors and junior managers who are to be retained, maybe in different and perhaps lower status roles, should be handled carefully. They see themselves having to work alongside the people who were their subordinates and are now their equals in status, which can be very difficult in certain situations. They may need to be counselled in how to handle such situations, since on the one hand it is hard to change one's own supervisory/managerial attitudes and habits, while on the other erstwhile subordinates may continue to behave as if one is still in a senior position. Conversely, subordinates may subject the 'demoted' individual to negative comments and treatment. In larger organisations such situations can be avoided by transferring regraded employees to other departments, but those who plan such internal HR movements are not always sensitive to these issues.

Organisations undergoing these processes usually retain 'transferred down' staff on their current salaries. These 'guaranteed' salaries are excluded from peer pay rises and maintained for an agreed period of time, or until other employees' salary increases over the years level the income within the grade.

Introducing policies

If any long-term internal strategy is to succeed, commitment to it has to be open and obvious from the very top of the organisation, which will increase the likelihood that managers will actually implement it. In this way an understanding of the strategy will cascade downwards and throughout the total workplace. Also, managers will need to be educated and trained so that they acquire an exact understanding of the purposes of the strategy and are capable of implementing its policies and procedures.

Policies need to be unambiguous so that managers and the workforce share an equal appreciation of what the organisation is trying to achieve. This can present considerable difficulty, since in these respects employees tend to assess the organisation's expectations of them from their perceptions of how they themselves are treated by the managers, rather than by listening to what the managers say they want, and even less likely by referring to the organisation's policies. For example, in organisations that have strong customer care policies, managerial exhortations about the respect, courtesy and speed with which customers should be treated will fall on deaf ears if the managers themselves fail to treat their staff with normal courtesy and the respect to which they too are entitled.

Another difficulty may be presented by differences between and among the managers, who typically are not all in agreement about how employees should be treated. Douglas McGregor originated the X–Y Dimension, upon which the attitudes of all managers towards employees can be found (McGregor, 1960). Managers who assumed that employees were lazy, indolent and work-shy, in need of continuous supervision and prodding and seeking only security while avoiding responsibility, were categorised by McGregor as Theory X Managers, which meant that they used an authoritarian managerial style to get things done. On the other hand, managers who used a democratic managerial style were those who regarded employees as self-starters, to whom work came as naturally as rest or play. Such managers assumed that employees were committed to the achievement of organisational objectives and willing to apply their initiative and creativity to those ends. They do not need supervision and will seek out challenges and responsibility. The terms Theory X and Theory Y have become widespread in the field of management, and probably more readily than academics practising managers have accepted McGregor's principles.

Preparing the ground

Before making any announcements to the workforce, and certainly before taking any positive action, the ground has to be prepared. To achieve a clean and effective launch of the policies, the PYTBULLS (or Theory X managers) have to be cleared out of the place for good; organisations today cannot afford them anyway. Those who draft the policies need to be as sure as they possibly can that they stand a reasonable chance of succeeding, since failure can have disastrous results. For example, if a survey discovers that stress is widespread in the organisation, and employees are told that 'something is going to be done about it', the apparent levels of stress will reduce almost immediately. Before making such an announcement, the plans for managing the situation should be well advanced, since if subsequently too much time is taken over preparing remedial plans, stress levels will rise again, but this time the levels at which they will plateau off will be higher than they were in the first place. On a more optimistic note, successful policies and actions for the promotion of employee well-being represent the first steps to an improvement in the culture of the whole organisation.

The role of culture

Before setting out to prepare the ground for the introduction of a new approach to employee well-being, the end product should be envisioned, which will be the kind of culture that will be receptive to the overall strategy. By far the two most important factors that contribute to the culture are: 1. the style that managers adopt in the way they lead and communicate with employees, and 2. the atmosphere, or the 'climate' of the place. Clearly, much of the climate is determined by the managers' leadership styles anyway, and organisations should have a clear policy on leadership. Climate, however, is also influenced by the nature of the organisation's business, the technology it uses, the long and deeply held values, beliefs and assumptions of the employees and the historical idiosyncrasies of the organisation itself. When they are first analysed some of these factors seem to be unshakeable, as if they are embedded in the very foundation stones of the buildings; but they can, where it is desirable, be replaced. Promoting the right kind of culture involves managers making conscious and rational attempts to cultivate and subsequently manage a benign alternative to the old fashioned model in which managers control and direct, and employees comply, yet it also has to be a culture that will be conducive to the achievement of the organisation's objectives.

Here, one is not suggesting that if the 'right kind of culture' is realised, everything else that is desirable will naturally fall into place – it will not. An appropriate organisational culture, per se, will not for example produce a good performance, but a hostile, inappropriate culture will make it impossible for managers to elicit an enhanced performance. If, however, the organisation wishes to promote and implement specific strategies and policies which, it is thought, should lead to high performance and at the same time promote the well-being of employees, then the development of a culture that will be receptive to the strategies and policies should be seen as a priority, since it is an essential precursor to successful implementation. Put negatively, if the culture does not readily assimilate the strategies and policies, then it is not the right kind of culture, and performance will suffer.

The importance of structure

Rather than explain the mechanisms and dimensions of organisational structures in the conventional sense, which are pretty well known anyway, the objectives of this section are to emphasise the importance of structure in terms of how it affects:

1. the efficiency and effectiveness with which the organisation performs;

2. the performance of groups and individuals;

3. work and non-work relationships between employees;

4. the nature of the organisation's culture.

An examination of these factors will necessarily include explanations of the primary purposes of structure and the factors that need to be weighed when the structure is being designed or modified.

All organisations are unique; they vary in the nature of their business, size, scope, type of technology, geographic spread, functional demands and managerial attitudes. The structural needs, therefore, of any one organisation are also unique. Small organisations usually experience little difficulty in defining where authority resides within the structure, who does what and who reports to whom. Everyone knows everyone else, and the structure is easily altered if, for example, there is a need to improve efficiency and effectiveness. Most small organisations do not even find it necessary to draft out their structures on paper.

Larger organisations tend to have complex and varied structures, which are the dynamic forces driving towards the objectives within the strategy. Large organisations need to specify in very precise terms:

1. how responsibility within the required strategic specialisms is allocated, and which of those specialisms are needed for that particular organisation, e.g. finance, personnel, information technology, marketing and so forth;

2. how operational authority, responsibility and accountability are distributed between and among the line managers and their staff;

3. where accountability lies in terms of reporting responsibilities and working managerial relationships;

4. how key tasks are distributed among the non-managerial staff.

The components of structure

When creating the structure, the factors comprising its basic design should first be considered. Mintzberg (1979) asked nine questions related to critical areas that form the structure's basic components:

1. How many tasks should a given position in the organisation contain and how specialised should each task be?

2. To what extent should the work content of each position be standardised?

3. What skills and knowledge should be required for each position?

4. On what basis should positions be grouped into units, and units into larger units?

5. How large should each unit be – how many individuals should report to a given manager?

6. To what extent should the output of each position or unit be standardised?

7. What mechanisms should be established to facilitate mutual adjustment among positions and units?

8. How much decision-making power should be delegated to the managers of line units down the chain of authority?

9. How much decision-making power should pass from the line managers to the staff specialists and operators?

Mullins (1993), groups the nine areas to which Mintzberg's questions refer under four broad design headings: design of position; design of superstructure; design of lateral linkages; and design of the decision-making system.

Structure and culture

Most people are familiar with the hierarchical design of structure, often referred to as *pyramid,* with its lateral layers that separate the levels of authority and responsibility in terms of seniority, and its vertical lines that track the reporting responsibilities. Structure is designed primarily for business purposes, and specifically with an eye on organisational performance; it physically sets up work and non-work relationships between and among the employees. Structure, for example, allocates authority and responsibility up, down and across the organisation, thus establishing vertical subordinate–manager reporting responsibilities and lateral non-reporting relationships between employees working with each other at the same level. Clearly, people are positively and/or negatively affected by the nature of these relationships. Structure, therefore, is one of the influences that determines the culture of the organisation.

Lean and flattened structures

The conventional kind of structure that is referred to in the previous paragraphs draws a clear distinction between the positions of supervisory, middle and senior managers. It evolved from the patterns of management that were common for much of the twentieth century, in which managers planned the work, allocated it and controlled output and performance, while the workforce complied with their demands. This established a visible gap between managers and the workforce, and produced the well-known 'us-and-them' phenomenon.

Organisations today, however, seek to achieve a 'leaner, flatter, more competitive structure', which is one of the changes that has evolved with the emergence of human resource management. Through the processes of delayering, which means removing lateral tiers of management from the conventional structure, downsizing, which means reducing the number of staff at corporate level, and rightsizing, which means employing the bare minimum number of staff to do the work, the structure becomes wider and flatter. It is recommended that from shopfloor levels to the board room, there should be no more than four lateral tiers in the structure.

In its favour, the flat structure tends to blur the distinction between management and workforce; it thus enhances manager–subordinate relationships and improves communication by providing opportunities for face-to-face meetings and, because written messages have a shorter vertical distance to travel, thus reduces the risk of distortion. Those who criticise flat structures do so on similar ground, saying that closing the gap between management and workforce provides a greater opportunity for the manager to over-supervise, or bully individual workers; that not all face-to-face communication is positive and pleasant; that having fewer people on board, at any level, fails to take sufficient account of absence; that four layers not only provides ample opportunity to distort messages, but also reduces career opportunities through, for example, promotion prospects.

The matrix process

The distinction between line and staff management reputedly causes confusion. As a generalisation, line managers are those who have direct responsibility for getting the job done. Alternatively referred to as *operational managers*, their objectives are to ensure that the tasks related to achieving the organisation's objectives are actually carried out efficienctly and effectively by their subordinates. Staff managers, alternatively referred to as *functional specialists*, are the organisation's experts and work in a strategic management role. They advise and assist where the organisation needs their expertise in such matters as finance, marketing, information technology, research and development, legal and human resource issues. Organisations engage such specialists on the basis of intrinsic need, and therefore each organisation has its own unique set of functional specialists.

A conventional hierarchical structure contains both line and staff reporting responsibilities, but does little to explain the relationships between them. The *matrix organisation* provides a clear picture of these relationships. In this kind of structure, the functional specialisms are shown vertically, while the operational departments are shown horizontally (see Figure 3.1).

In, for example, a construction company, responsibility for the tasks belongs to the project managers (operational managers), seen on the left in the figure, while the provision of the advice and assistance is the responsibility of the functional specialists, who are ranged across the top of the figure. The project managers, therefore, draw laterally upon the services provided by the functional specialists' departments.

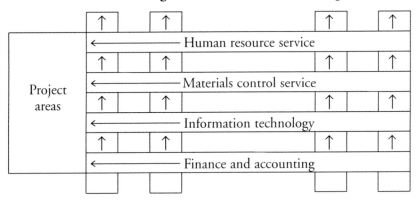

HR services IT Marketing Finance Research & Development etc…

Figure 3.1 A matrix organisation.

There is a variety of reasons for viewing the organisation through a matrix structure, and some writers produce a graphic version with the sole purpose of expressing the line and staff relationship. However, when it is used as the force that drives the organisation forward, the matrix structure can have a significant impact on the well-being of the people who operate within it, especially those who work in the staff specialisms. For example, from Figure 3.1, it can be seen that the project managers make demands upon the specialist staff by drawing upon their services and resources laterally across the structure. The specialist member of staff has to ensure that the demands, if justified, will be met. On the other hand, he or she also reports to the functional head and this 'two bosses' situation can induce stressful dissonance within the individual, and may divide his or her loyalties between the functional head and the project manager. A matrix structure also emphasises the distinction between line and staff and, like the conventional structure, separates the planning of the work from actually carrying it out. Where, for example, a manager takes the opportunity to use the work group as a problem-solving and decision-making unit, employees have a say in how the work might best be carried out, which gives them an interest in achieving a successful outcome, and thereby makes them feel as if their contribution is valued. In many of today's organisations, teamworking, in which the teams are made up of a mixture of line workers and functional specialists, has become the most popular way to ensure that the work is done.

Conclusion

To say that a healthy organisation is one that is financially sound, has a solid customer base and can afford to be optimistic about its future seems to be stating the obvious. The current belief, however, is that the organisation cannot sustain such a promising position if it fails to recognise the importance of the performance of its people. It is true that financial stability is vital and money is the lifeblood of the organisation, but the talents of its people are an integral part of its total wealth. Therefore, if an organisation wishes to succeed in the face of today's fierce competition, including global competition, it will have to recognise that a great deal will depend on the knowledge, skills and attitudes of its employees.

The degree to which employees will apply their abilities to the purposes of the organisation will depend on the circumstances in which they find themselves in the workplace. If the conditions in which they work are unnecessarily pressurised, if the work they are given fails to arouse and motivate them, if the organisation seems not to value what they do, if their potential goes unnoticed and if the general state of the employment relationship is below standard, they may leave. As many organisations have discovered, there is a price to pay for failing to recognise employees as people who have normal human failings and limitations, and for failing to take account of the provisions of legislation that outlines minimum standards for the treatment of employees.

The strongest influences on these considerations are to do with employees' responses to the way they are treated, how managers demonstrate their perceived value of their staff's work and the effects of culture and structure on the working and non-working relationships that the employees encounter every time they come into work.

Unemployment has reduced markedly in the past four years. Today's organisations find themselves competing with others for talented people and cannot therefore afford to waste them. The retention of employees depends on the ways in which the managers regard them and treat them. In this chapter we have explored the practical steps that organisations can take to ensure employee well-being and drawn attention to the business case for fostering a healthy workforce. At the same time, organisations need to preserve their day-to-day efficiency and effectiveness, and managers may feel that there are benefits to be had from exploring the possibility of integrating strategies for organisational success with those for employee well-being.

References

Currie, D. (1990) *Stress in the National Health Service, Southampton* (a report for Southampton Business School). Southampton: Southampton Institute.

McGregor, D. (1960) *The Human Side of Enterprise*. New York: McGraw-Hill.

Mintzberg, H. (1979) *The Structuring of Organisations*. Englewood Cliffs, NJ: Prentice Hall.

Mullins, L.J. (1993) *Management and Organisational Behaviour*, 3rd edn. London: Pitman.

CHAPTER 4

Human resource management (HRM)

Introduction

Nobody would deny that the economic rise of Asian industry in the 1980s and its penetration into US and European markets triggered the development of HRM – something had to be done if the West was to compete effectively. In 1990, it was suggested by the Japanese that Britain and the US were still locked into the principles of F.W. Taylor's 'scientific management', but in fact on both sides of the Atlantic management theory and practice had moved on considerably, although reflecting upon the market activity that followed, it seems that what had been achieved in the West had not progressed enough to put us into a competitive position. While the management systems that emerged in the middle and late twentieth century were more sophisticated than those that preceded them, they still held on to overt managerial control; and even those who were regarded as the management 'gurus' of the day, such as E.F.L. Brech, reasserted the need for a conspicuous managerial command structure:

[Management is] a social process entailing responsibility for the effective and economic planning and regulation of the operations of an enterprise, in fulfilment of given purposes or tasks, such responsibility involving:

(a) judgement and decision in determining plans and in using data to control performance and progress against plans

(b) the guidance, integration, motivation and supervision of the personnel composing the enterprise and carrying out its operations.

With the previous chapter in mind, the purposes here are to explain the main features of human resource management (HRM), and to show how its widespread progress has influenced changes in management education, training, development and practice, and how the implementation of its principles and techniques are affecting employee well-being. A great deal of its adverse effects may be attributed to the current misunderstanding of it among managers. Some regard HRM as simply an alternative term to describe personnel management, and undoubtedly there is enthusiasm for the terminology that has arisen from this mistaken perception, even to the extent that some personnel managers have removed the 'personnel manager' sign from their doors and replaced it with 'human resource manager', not realising that, for reasons we will encounter later, according to HRM proponents all managers are human resource managers.

While the 'personnel' and the 'human resources' (HR) of an organisation are obviously one and same thing, the employees, the sign 'personnel manager' should be taken as an indication that the incumbent of that office is in charge of the personnel department, or the personnel function, rather than in charge of the organisation's personnel or human resource. Undoubtedly, the people 'in charge' of the employees are the departmental and functional managers. On the other hand, many organisations have taken to referring to their staff as the human resource and, thereby, to the specialised function of personnel management as HR management, which could at a stretch legitimatise the new sign.

In reality, human resource management (HRM) is a unitary system of management that attempts to elicit employees' commitment to, and involvement in, the purposes and goals of the organisation. Far from being purely an alternative term for personnel management, its principles and techniques influence how the *whole organisation* is managed. The so-called 'commitment model' is said to replace the 'control and compliance model' which is usually attributed to F.W. Taylor's 'scientific management' (1911 and 1947); although it is clear that people worked under the strict control of their employers right from the beginning of the Industrial Revolution, Taylor was the first to prescribe the manager–subordinate relationship in formal terms. While elements of 'Taylorism' are still practised today in some organisations, its influence as the creator of the first organised industrial paradigm has been dwindling since the human relations model was introduced in the 1930s (Mayo et al.). Since then, a great deal of time and ingenuity have been invested in management research and practice, and this has produced several significant approaches, including 'Management by Objectives' (MbO) (Drucker, 1955), 'System Theory' (Katz and Kahn, 1978 and Trist et al., 1963) and 'Contingency Theory' (Lawrence and Lorsch, 1969; Woodward, 1980; Burns and Stalker, 1966 and Perrow, 1967).

Some of these managerial models are simply ways of looking at organisations, while others are action-orientated such as MbO, for example, which is a very direct managerial method that leads the manager towards achieving results. Other investigations alongside Taylor include the discovery of 'Bureaucracy' (Weber, 1964) and the 'Hawthorne Studies' (Mayo, 1933). All of these items of research produced information for managers that provided the basis for their endeavours to achieve good practice throughout the twentieth century. Unlike these models, however, HRM simply evolved; it may be set apart from other systems of managing organisations in that its principles and techniques cannot be attributed to any single researcher or manager.

Unitary and pluralistic perspectives

The managerial model that an organisation has decided to adopt should be one that complements the frame of reference through which the top managers prefer to regard the relationship between the organisation and its employees. The preferred frame of reference is determined by the managers' values and the strength of their beliefs about such things as managerial authority, power and control (Currie, 1997).

Alan Fox (1966) suggested that managers may adopt one of two philosophical approaches:

1. *The unitary perspective*, in which there is only one source of power in the organisation, in which managers value and protect the legitimacy of their authority. There is an assumption that all employees share the common goals of the organisation and that they will receive a portion of the rewards, which will come if, through their efforts, the organisation succeeds in its purposes and goals. Where there is conflict, the cause is attributed to failures in communication, or the foolish temperaments of those involved. Unitarists eschew trade unions and prefer to communicate directly with their staff. The managers maintain total command, regard themselves as the 'authoritative group' and assume that the employees share that perception.

2. *The pluralistic perspective*, in which managers may allow, and actively foster, freedom of expression and the development of groups which establish their own norms and elect their own informal leaders. In this way, power and control arise in several

parts of the organisation, and loyalty is commanded by leaders of groups which are often in competition with each other for resources. Within this kind of approach, the managers achieve results through joining the groups, encouraging participation, motivating employees and coordinating their work efforts. In this way, the managers are exercising good leadership, although sometimes it can be difficult to achieve the necessary balance, in which the interests of customers, suppliers, shareholders and employees have to be taken into account. However, when employees become involved in solving work-related problems and making decisions, they develop commitment to the achievement of successful outcomes.

From this, it can be seen that HRM is largely a management system that prefers to adopt a unitary frame of reference through which it manages the whole organisation. Superficially, it may appear to be pluralistic, especially when one reads about the development of groups and 'commitment to successful outcomes'. But in fact, in HRM organisations, there is only one source of power, the management group, which prefers to communicate with employees as individuals rather than through trade unions or other staff representative groups.

Descriptions of HRM

Definitions of concepts tend to draw boundaries around them and limit one's thinking range to the confined areas that the definition produces. Also, in the light of current perceptions of HRM, it would be dangerous to risk defining something which, even after its first appearance in the mid-1980s, is clearly still developing. So, rather than confine the reader to an HRM cocoon by offering a definition, it will be more productive to offer descriptions of where HRM stands at present, and it may be that the reader will recognise one of them, or at least a hybrid of a number of them, as a description of his or her current work situation. Nor would it be very enlightening to define HRM in terms of its content, since there is nothing new within it. As a system of management, it seems to have selected its content eclectically from the basic elements of earlier management models, particularly those of the human relations school, while for its processes, it attempts to foster a new attitude towards its use of the normal practices of appraisal, employee development and motivation in order to elicit commitment and, thereby, an enhanced performance.

Central features of HRM

1. *Structure*: the classical 'tall' hierarchy is replaced with a flatter, wider structure.

2. *Mutuality of interest*: managers and employees have a mutual interest in the success of the organisation; employees are frequently reminded of this in attempts to obtain their commitment to the achievement of common goals.

3. *HR responsibility*: wherever possible, this is devolved to line managers.

4. *HR planning*: this is integrated with the corporate strategy.

5. *HR development*: employees are regarded as a resource in which the organisation is willing to invest; people have potential for further development and HRM facilitates this in accordance with organisational needs.

Flatter, wider structure

This is achieved through a process of delayering, which means stripping layers of management and supervision away from the kind of hierarchical order that used to typify an organisational structure, resulting in a vertical flattening of the visible design, so that instead of seeing a tall structure in which four, five or six employees each report to one manager, one sees a kind of wide 'garden rake' structure in which a larger number of employees work to each remaining manager. The process also includes downsizing – reducing the overall number of staff at corporate level – and rightsizing – employing the bare minimum number of people to carry out the actual work.

Whereas before delayering employees each had their own specific jobs, after delayering they will have been trained to carry out a variety of tasks – multiskilling – and empowered to make minor operational decisions. The intention here is to blur the distinction between managerial and non-managerial staff, although an examination of the leaner, flatter structure on paper shows that the managers are firmly placed in the senior positions. In this way HRM overrides the Tayloristic 'control/compliance' model of management (which separated the planning of work from carrying it out), and uses the work team as a problem-solving and decision-making unit to integrate planning and performing the work, an idea originated by Rensis Likert in 1961.

Mutuality of interest

The purpose here is to reinforce employees' commitment to, and involvement in, the achievement of the goals and objectives of the organisation by generating the belief that employees will benefit from its success. By putting in an enhanced performance they are thereby investing their time and skill in their own future. This characteristic of HRM is based on the notion that there is a strong relationship between human work performance and organisational success, and that people therefore are the most important resource. This is of course perfectly obvious and is something that personnel specialists have been pointing out for many years, while HRM champions present it as something that has just been realised.

Before going any further, we have to dispel the HRM myth that commitment produces performance. It does not. There is no doubt that commitment, involvement, performance and satisfaction are linked, but there are no academic grounds to support the view that there is a relationship between commitment and performance alone, and similarly between involvement and performance alone, although assumed relationships have been postulated by eminent academics. The efficacy of strategies designed to inculcate commitment and involvement have never been formally tested in a real organisational setting, although it has been claimed that where commitment *and* involvement are evident, the motivation to perform well follows naturally. Performance is produced only by a combination of the degree to which a person is knowledgeable about, and skilled in executing, the tasks demanded by his or her job, multiplied by the degree to which he or she is motivated to employ those talents to that end: *Performance = Ability × Motivation.*

Undoubtedly there is a 'feel-good factor' that typifies employees' experiences of their organisation's successes, and clearly this has a visible, positive effect on them. However, one would suggest that this is far more frequently due to the enhanced feelings of job security that are produced when employees learn of the organisation's successes rather than to feelings of personal involvement that might include, say, endorsement of the *nature* of the organisation's goals per se, feelings of personal achievement, or that for the enterprise to have achieved its objectives is a 'good thing'. History has shown that the employees of an organisation that has won a contract that guarantees their continued employment for so many years ahead experience positive stimulation, and they overtly demonstrate their excitement and approval. When, for example, Rover Cars in the UK were saved from extinction by a financial angel, the workers came out onto the streets to express their delight and relief. However, in the period before their salvation was announced, all of the emphasis in the politicians' and trade union leaders' pronouncements was on securing continued employment for the Rover workers. Nobody mentioned commitment or involvement in the HRM context.

HRM and employee well-being

Employees in an organisation that has adopted the principles of HRM are well aware that any changes that take place are implemented for the benefit of the organisation. The change to a 'leaner, flatter structure', for example, is usually accompanied by multiskilling and a heavier *per capita* workload for those who survive the redundancy programme. This kind of change can produce considerable stress in employees who fear that they may fail to understand the new areas into which they are being directed. HRM suggests, however, that mutual interest in the organisation's success implies that if employees become committed and involved, the likelihood that their relationship with the organisation will continue is enhanced. While younger employees are likely to welcome change, the more mature workers have 'frozen' into and feel secure in the positions they occupy. Young people may perceive the changes as opportunities to develop into new fields, whereas the older, more experienced and stable employees may experience stress, and feel less inclined to employ their talents optimally for the benefit of an organisation that is making their working lives miserable.

The degree to which employees will apply their abilities to the purposes of the organisation, therefore, will depend less on managerial exhortations for commitment and more upon the circumstances in which they find themselves in the workplace. If the conditions in which they work are unnecessarily pressurised, if the work they are given fails to arouse and motivate them, if the organisation seems not to value what they do, if their potential goes unnoticed, if they do not feel valued and if the general state of the employment relationship is below standard, they may leave, or at least their performance will suffer. It is far easier now for talented people to find alternative employment than ever it was in the 1980s and 1990s. As many organisations have discovered, there is a price to pay for failing to recognise employees as people who, no matter how skilled they are, have normal human shortcomings and limitations, and for failing to take account of the provisions of legislation that outlines minimum standards for the treatment of employees.

In this light, it is worth examining the effectiveness of the investment made by the HRM organisation in its attempts to elicit employee commitment and involvement, since what seems to be required is commitment to and involvement in the achievement of corporate goals and objectives. The notion that employees are involved in corporate affairs at that level confers an elevated status upon them, but it also raises the question of what actually employees can contribute at that level. Managers really should ask themselves what it is, precisely, that they want their employees to do. After all, presumably employees have been taken on because they possess the knowledge, skills and experience that enables them to carry out specific work to predetermined standards, and the implication there is that at the operational level employees would carry out their tasks cheerfully. Realistically, there is not much more that a serious manager would wish to ask of his or her staff.

Human resource responsibility

This is quite a mysterious characteristic. Experienced managers and personnel specialists have always been well aware of each other's roles in the organisation. Managers see themselves as people who have been given responsibility for the achievement of objectives in specified areas of the organisation, such as specialist or operational departments. To this end, they are given commensurate levels of authority and autonomy, along with the necessary resources. It is the manager's responsibility to optimise the resources that he or she has been allocated, one of which is the human resource. The possession of such management skills as leadership and motivation enables the manager to maximise the talents of the staff. There are times, of course, when staff need to be recruited, inducted, trained, coached, counselled and sometimes disciplined and even dismissed. All of these are managerial responsibilities and always have been. For expert advice and assistance in these matters, however, the manager may call upon the personnel department who are expert staff specialists engaged in the provision of such services. There is, therefore, nothing new in the idea that HR responsibility belongs to the line manager. The line manager is responsible for making selection decisions, for deciding who is to be trained, when and in what, for making decisions about handling grievance and disciplinary processes and for coaching and counselling staff. So, in what way does HRM 'devolve responsibility for people management to line managers'? Clearly, line managers have had that responsibility from time immemorial – certainly long before 'personnel/HR' departments were thought of.

Human resource planning

The recommendation that human resource planning should be integrated with corporate strategy has a long history. That is not to say that before HRM the strategies were ever integrated – they were not, despite the rather obvious case in favour. Until the 1980s, those responsible for corporate strategy became renowned for drawing up the most elegant plans for the organisation's future, without considering the availability of those who would actually carry out the necessary tasks at professional and operational levels. The personnel department used to have to wait for the all-important 'corporate plan' to emerge before they could set about constructing the 'manpower plan', as it was called in those days. Personnel people have been petitioning for the integration of these strategies for many years, but historically their function has not always enjoyed the status, nor thereby the attention, it has deserved, and this suggestion, like many others also carrying advantages, had been ignored. But if it is something that HRM has at long last achieved, then considerable credit is due.

Human resource development

This is an aspect of HRM which, more than any other, emphasises the difference that HRM has made in managers' attitudes towards employees in terms of their presence in the place. The old reductionist stance was that strategic objectives were set at the top of the organisation, interpreted by middle managers in terms of the implications for their functions, and then handed on down to the operational staff for implementation. This process of cascading the duties and responsibilities down the organisation successively reduced their size until they became small enough to be carried out by one person, who thereby had a job. It was part of the personnel function to ensure that the organisation always had the right number of people in place at the right time. This was the 'headcount' philosophy, in which people were needed simply to fill vacant posts.

Employees were engaged on the grounds that they possessed the appropriate knowledge, skills and experience to carry out the tasks, but of course when they arrived on the organisational scene, it was not just the bits that the managers needed that turned up. People brought with them their personalities, with all of their prejudices and preferences, values and beliefs, attitudes and individually orientated items of behaviour. The managerial perception evolved into: 'people are a necessary and costly evil'. When senior managers wished to cut costs, the first item on the agenda was the wages and salaries bill.

HRM has altered this view. Employees are seen as a resource, in fact the only resource that can increase in terms of its potential to contribute to the organisation's objectives. With time, other resources such as money and machines lose their value, but with training and development people become more versatile through the acquisition of further knowledge and skills, and with long-term experience of the organisation they mature, become more stable and capable of adopting greater responsibility. The HRM view of people, therefore, is more akin to that of Douglas MacGregor (1960) who, when writing about managers' assumptions about workers, proposed a two-dimensional theory, X and Y, in which he suggests that Theory X managers strictly controlled their subordinates in an authoritarian way, while the Theory Y managers were more democratic in their outlook, regarded their staff as having potential and empowered them to make decisions as a team.

Teamworking

The idea of employees working as teams goes back to Elton Mayo and the Hawthorn Studies which took place in the USA between 1924 and 1936 at the Hawthorn plant of the Western Electric Company in Chicago. Elton Mayo was a Professor of Industrial Research at the Harvard Business School, and was called in by the company to investigate productivity losses. Two of the managers had begun an inquiry at the plant before Mayo had been called in but their efforts had brought nothing significant to light. Mayo studied the employees' social interactions, their values and attitudes and discovered that of their own volition they had made decisions and taken actions that had not been planned by management. He discovered that they had banded together as teams to gain some degree of control over their tasks. Mayo's discoveries ultimately led to the human relations approach to managing organisations.

Before Mayo, it had never occurred to managers that there might be organisational benefits from consulting employees at shopfloor level. Organisational studies had been confined to Taylor's ideas about structures, physical working conditions, work methods, measurement and the production of formal rules of management. The idea that employees had minds of their own and would elaborate on their relationships beyond the formally laid down productivity requirements had never been investigated. Managers became aware that there were, in fact, two organisations in one, that there was a social organisation within the formal technical organisation, and most importantly, members of the social groups valued the informal peer recognition more highly than the employer's recognition of them as skilled members of the work groups. Naturally, informal group leaders had emerged and members regarded them as leaders who were more likely to act in their best interests than were the leaders who had been appointed by the organisation to manage and supervise them.

Mayo realised that the organisation could benefit from organising the workforce into teams. This was especially the case if, for example, before any changes were made, the teams were consulted, and their views listened to and taken into account. These were the people at the interface of where the work was taking place – they operated the machinery, performed their tasks through prescribed work methods and experienced the working conditions. Clearly there would be benefits from listening to what they had to say. Taking this a step further, one might even co-opt them into solving work problems and making minor operational decisions. In 1961, Rensis Likert was to present these ideas as a direct result of his academic research.

HRM recognises the benefits from organising the workforce into teams, but in today's terms, in an increasing number of industrial situations, individual workers are shackled to computer terminals, which makes teamworking virtually impossible. The supervisors, however, are referred to as 'team leaders', even though the people for whom they are responsible work as separate individuals.

The psychological contract

In addition to the contract of employment that describes the formal relationship between the employer and the employee, there also exists a 'psychological contract', which is a tacit, informal relationship that exists at an informal, social and cultural level. Within the psychological contract, there are powerful determinants of benign workplace behaviour that are not found in the formal contract. For example, such work-related factors as job security, organisational culture, job satisfaction, motivation and morale are never mentioned in formal documents, yet nobody would contest the suggestion that they are extremely important performance-related factors. Within the psychological contract there are factors that make up those aspects of 'being at work' that are officially outside the stated requirements of the role held by the employee, but have been elaborated upon and extended to become rights and privileges, and even perceived 'duties' and 'responsibilities', that are not included in the job description.

The truth is that if everyone worked exactly according to their job descriptions, the organisation would experience a serious backlog of unattended tasks. Out of sheer goodwill, and for no other reason, people step outside their formal remit to do things that need to be done. Sometimes, this may involve them in working for several hours more than their terms and conditions require. Many managers, particularly those who regard themselves as HRM adherents, notice this and autocratically regulate the behaviour so that eventually it is 'expected', an indication of commitment or even demanded. For example, in further and higher education in the early 1980s in the UK, most lecturers used to allocate one of their rooms at home for carrying out such tasks as lecture preparation, research and even some of their administrative tasks. To this end, they used electric light, heating, the telephone and so forth, at their own expense. The quality of the work produced in such a benign situation was far higher than could be achieved in a noisy office at the college or university with students and colleagues passing in and out. Ultimately, however, regulations increasing the amount of time lecturers should spend on the work premises were produced, and as a result, the voluntary, goodwill-based time spent on home working ceased. It is obvious to any experienced manager that the more one regulates what is already happening on a voluntary basis, the more one will erode goodwill.

Flexible working practices

One of the features of HRM that seriously disturbs the mutual benefits that are derived from the psychological contract is 'flexible working'. This is a term that has been used to describe a change in the contractual arrangements made between the organisation and its employees. The change to flexible working began to develop in the early 1980s, and in recent years the practice has become widespread. Flexible working involves a variety of patterns of working in which the flexibility can take many forms. First, there is the notion of 'numerical flexibility', in which organisations seem to be preoccupied with reducing staff numbers. Much of this 'leaning up' could be attributed to the introduction of new technology, but there is also evidence that organisations have taken advantage of weaker, more cooperative trade unions, and changes in employment legislation, to intensify work among a smaller workforce.

Secondly, there has been considerable interest in 'functional flexibility'. Employees have been encouraged to become multiskilled, which enables them to carry out a variety of different tasks. This represents job enlargement, which might well lead to increased job satisfaction for employees (Herzberg, 1957). However, it also gives managers much greater freedom to deploy employees to tasks as they wish, without the need to consider demarcation arrangements.

Thirdly, 'working time flexibility' has been sought by employers through altering the hours that people work. Electronic technology has the ability to transcend time and space and it has become possible for work to take place at different times in different places. Telecommuting has proved to be particularly attractive to employers who recognise the savings on overheads that are made if the premises they occupy are smaller. There are potential problems with these arrangements in terms of communication, control and social needs. Flexibility can also be gained through annualised hours schemes, which are attractive to employers because of the control they can exercise over deployment, and the savings they can make by reducing overtime payments.

Perhaps the furthest extent to which flexibility can be taken with regard to hours of work is through zero hours contracts, which require employees to be available for work without a guarantee that they will be needed, or if they are, for how long. Zero hours contracts is a practice that takes industry back to the 1930s. One need only recall the sight of men early in the mornings, gathered around the closed dock gates in Liverpool, waiting to see if their services will be needed that day. The chargehand would come to the gate, stand on a box and point out several men, 'I'll have you and you and you …', picking out the people he wanted (or favoured), for that day. When this process was over, those not engaged would shuffle away disappointed. It is difficult to distinguish between the ignominious experience of men waiting at the dock gate and that of people under today's zero hours contracts, which, by modern standards, many managers would regard as inhuman and degrading. Still, here we are, doing it again in the twenty-first century.

Finally, there is 'reward flexibility'. Many employers have found that traditional incremental scales of pay commit them to annual pay increases as employees complete each year of service. Performance-related pay schemes (P-rP) introduce opportunities for managerial discretion and, therefore, the possibility of making savings.

While flexible working appeared before the emergence of HRM, a key aspect of the practice is that employers should regard people as they would any other resource, which patently is a feature of HRM. According to one senior manager in a large multinational organisation: 'The fact that you need to access people's skills does not necessarily mean that you have to agree a normal contract of employment with them.' Work, it seems, can be carried out not only by full-time employees, but by people who are hired through all kinds of contractual arrangement. The important issue for organisations is to identify the most financially beneficial option. Consequently, flexibility is having a stressful impact upon people's feelings of job security, while employers deliberate over alternative arrangements to standard forms of employment.

Today's employment markets have become segmented. The practice of flexible working has taught employers that not all potential employees yield readily to the employment offers they receive; some potential candidates are knowledgeable and highly skilled, the kinds of people for which other organisations are prepared to compete. In this way a class system has emerged in terms of how candidates are categorised, which may be as *core* or *peripheral* workers. The core workers are those who possess skills which are highly valued. They experience a favourable employment relationship since they are well rewarded, have opportunities to perform challenging and satisfying work and have the chance to develop a career. Peripheral workers, on the other hand, have quite a different experience of employment. The work they perform is routine and, usually, undemanding in terms of knowledge and skills. They are given little opportunity to develop or use skills, and their terms and conditions of employment are far less favourable than those of the core workers.

An important aspect of this class system is that peripheral employees tend to become 'locked in' to particular employment markets. Opportunities for them to break into alternative markets with more attractive employment conditions are very scarce. For employers, the treatment of peripheral workers poses something of a problem, especially in HRM terms, since it is difficult to accept that peripheral workers will be prepared to offer commitment and involvement when they see very little in return coming their way. Employers who proclaim their adherence to HRM principles, particularly those which state that it is the human factor that provides the competitive edge, may have difficulty in reconciling this tenet with the way they treat their peripheral workers. In the midst of a talent war in the recruitment field, no one can afford to risk their reputation as an employer and it would be naive to assume that information about an organisation's employment practices does not spread across the market.

It would be wrong to suggest that flexible working has only negative impacts. Clearly, the opportunity to work more flexible shift patterns will appeal to many employees; multiskilling relieves the boredom of repetitive work, since it means that their tasks will be more varied, and multiskilling enhances an individual's employment prospects. Telecommuting is popular with some employees, although there are potential problems such as social exclusion and lack of feedback on performance which need to be addressed. As with most working practices, the central issues are how and why flexible approaches are being used. Employers need to be clear about their motives because employees will make their own judgements about them and be quick to spot hidden agendas.

Involvement and satisfaction

The implementation of some of the techniques of HRM involve positive interaction between managers and individual employees, and since, for example, commitment and involvement could never be achieved through authoritarian managerial attitudes, the likely effect upon employee well-being could be positive.

Conclusion

As a set of principles and techniques that provide the basis for managing an organisation, human resource management has little to say about employee well-being. Managers should be aware of the weaknesses as well as the strengths of HRM, and be aware too of employees' perceptions of the way in which the organisation is managed. Today's employees are intelligent and politically aware. Their true attitudes towards the implementation of certain HRM techniques are seldom vocalised. They vote with their feet.

The principles of HRM contain demands which many practising managers regard as idealistic and not achievable in the 'real world' of management. The demand, for example, for *commitment*, in which managers attempt to elicit employees' commitment to the organisation, the furtherance of its goals and the achievement of its objectives, is made in the belief that commitment enhances employees' performance. No doubt there are some members of the workforce from whom total commitment could be elicited, but these would be few in number, especially in organisations where flexible working practices have been adopted, in which most employees are peripheral workers. Clearly, it would be easier to generate this kind of commitment among managers, although one would wonder about how genuine it would be in the light of the combined influences of internal politics, self-preservation, promotion prospects and possible redundancy. As we said in Chapter 2, most employees go to work to sustain a lifestyle, and few become evangelistic about the purposes of the organisation. According to HRM, not only should employees be committed in the way described above, they should also feel *involved* in the actions taken by the organisation in its quest for success. It is thought that through being committed and from feeling involved, employees will experience satisfaction when the organisation succeeds.

The fact that there is no functional relationship between employee commitment and performance is an example of the various claims made by proponents of HRM that are not supported by hard evidence. It seems that while the adoption of HRM reinforces the power and authority of managers, it does little to improve human performance in a way that would lead ultimately to the success and profitability of the organisation. The fact that there are fewer managers and fewer operational staff, however, does auger well for profitability, since the leaness produces a lower salaries and wages bill.

It seems that top managers who claim to run HRM organisations have selected the techniques that appeal to them in terms of their desire to save money and make a profit, while ignoring the techniques that are designed to improve staff retention and employee welfare. The same kind of senior managerial approach occurred when Taylor introduced his scientific management proposals almost a hundred years ago; they picked up on the financially appealing bits and rejected his more humane provisions. This rejection resulted in the tainting of scientific management, and opposition to it became so fierce that in 1921 he was called before a congressional committee to explain himself. Much of what Taylor provided for in scientific management is regarded now as normal managerial practice by those who still use the prescriptions of the human relations approach (which includes most managers), but the strongest implication relates to the lack of consideration given by senior managers to the more humane provisions of HRM. Nothing really changes does it?

References

Brech, E.F.L. (1975) *The Principles and Practice of Management*, 3rd edn. London: Longman.

Burns, T. and Stalker G.M. (1966) *The Management of Innovation*. London: Tavistock.

Currie, D. (1990) *Stress in the National Health Service, Southampton* (a report for Southampton Business School). Southampton: Southampton Institute.

Drucker, P. (1955) The Practice of Management. London: Heinemann.

Fox, A. (1966) *Industrial Sociology and Industrial Relations*, Royal Commission on Trade Unions and Employers' Associations Research Paper No. 3. London: HMSO.

Herzberg, F.W., Mausner, B. and Snyderman, B. (1957) *The Motivation to Work*. New York: Wiley.

Katz, D. and Kahn, R.L. (1978) *The Social Psychology of Organisations*, 2nd edn. Chichester: Wiley.

Lawrence, P.R. and Lorsch, J.W. (1969) *Organisation and Environment*. Homewood, IL: Irwin.

Likert, R. (ed.) (1961) *New Patterns of Management*. Maidenhead: McGraw-Hill.

McGregor, D. (1960) *The Human Side of Enterprise*. New York: McGraw-Hill.

Mayo, E. (1933) *The Human Problems of an Industrial Civilization*. New York: Macmillan.

Perrow, C. (1967) *Organisational Analysis – A Sociological View*. London: Tavistock.

Taylor, F.W. (1911) *The Principles of Scientific Management*. Harper & Bros.; (1947) *Scientific Management*. New York: Harper & Row.

Trist, E.L., Higgin, G., Pollock, H.E. and Murray, H.A. (1963) *Organisational Choice*. London: Tavistock.

Woodward, J. (1980) *Industrial Organisation – Theory and Practice*, 2nd edn. Oxford: Oxford University Press.

CHAPTER 5

Job satisfaction, involvement and motivation

Introduction

Most readers will be aware that these three subjects were central to management theory and practice throughout much of the twentieth century, certainly since Elton Mayo published on his work at Hawthorn, USA in 1947. Since, in modern terms, they are also the areas into which policies affecting employee well-being have been extended, it is a good idea if managers acquire a clear understanding of what is meant by *satisfaction, involvement* and *motivation*. In this chapter we will explain what each of the three terms actually mean, and discuss how modern managers and management theorists might include provision for them in their work activities.

The chapter also examines each of these phenomena as individual workplace attitudes, and shows the implications that each holds for the well-being of employees. This implies that the managers who determine and control the physical working conditions and the terms and conditions of employment can, through their activities, have a significant impact on the attitudes of their workers towards the organisation and the degree to which they *feel* satisfied, involved and motivated to work.

Some managers tend to pair each of the three phenomena with others; for example, they refer to 'satisfaction and fulfilment', 'involvement and commitment', and 'motivation and morale'. Here we attempt to dispel any assumptions that people might have about a link between the factors in these pairs. As we shall see, satisfaction, involvement and motivation are attitudes that are determined by individual differences; fulfilment and commitment are different and separate experiences; while high or low morale relate to feelings that are evident in groups.

Job satisfaction and job involvement

If we were to give this subject its full title, we would be talking about the employee's *attitudes* of job satisfaction and *attitudes* of job involvement. In this context the word satisfaction is related to the degree to which an individual is satisfied with the terms and conditions of employment and the factors that make up the physical work environment. Individuals, for example, may be satisfied with their salaries and how well they get on with their workplace peers, or are satisfied with company policy. Satisfaction has several meanings. We hear people say, for example, that they experience satisfaction from having carried out a task successfully, or that they were satisfied with the outcome of a particular situation. Here we use the word satisfaction to reflect the degree to which an individual is satisfied with what we call the *extrinsic* job situation.

In a sense, it is legitimate to pair job satisfaction with job involvement, since they are attitudes which are determined by individuals' perceptions of their total job situations, including the physical work environment, the terms and conditions of their employment and the degree to which they are given responsibility, authority and empowerment in their jobs. Individuals may be *more or less* satisfied with, and *more or less* involved in the job depending on their perceptions of the factors listed in Table 5.1. The list is not exhaustive; it contains only a few examples of the factors that employees perceive as important.

Individuals are mostly interested in their own positions in the workplace and perceive their jobs to be set within the context of the total work situation: the work environment. The factors listed in Table 5.1 under 'job satisfaction' are examples of those that affect all employees in the organisation, since everyone is subject to the same corporate strategies, policies and procedures. The factors that are listed under 'job involvement', however, affect people individually within their jobs, since they are found within the context of the individual

Table 5.1 The work environment

Job satisfaction	Job involvement
• Salaries and other benefits	• The amount of authority given
• The condition of the workplace in terms of safety, cleanliness, layout, access to tools and other necessities	• The degree of responsibility
	• The extent of autonomy allowed
• Peer relationships	• Freedom to exercise particular skills
• The boss–subordinate relationship	• The perceived relationship between the job and the
• The culture	completed product
• Corporate strategy and policy	
• The organisation's external reputation as an employer	• The degree to which the job complements the person's self-perception

and the job that he or she is doing. In this way we can separate the factors that influence the degree to which individuals are *satisfied* with their jobs from those that influence the degree to which they are *involved in* their jobs. These two different kinds of factor are often referred to as *extrinsic* and *intrinsic* job factors. The extrinsic factors are those that are experienced by all employees, and the intrinsic factors by individuals within their jobs (see Figure 5.1). To some extent, managers can control the influence of the extrinsic factors by changing working conditions to make them more likely to produce job satisfaction.

Differences between and among individual employees cause them to evaluate extrinsic factors in their own unique way. One person, for example, may think that the pension scheme is fine, while another may regard it as totally inadequate. Employees also vary in their perceptions of what is important and what is not. For example, one person may regard promotion prospects as highly important, while another is not interested in being promoted. These are individually different perceptions that apply to all extrinsic factors.

While extrinsic factors are those that produce more or less job satisfaction, intrinsic factors produce more or less job involvement, which is the degree to which the employee sees the job as

---

JOB SATISFACTION AREA

The work environment

(includes *extrinsic* job factors)

JOB INVOLVEMENT AREA

The job–person unit

(includes *intrinsic* job factors)

Figure 5.1 Extrinsic and intrinsic job factors.

complementary to the way in which he or she see themselves. The degree to which individuals are involved in and satisfied by a job may be found on dimensions ranging from:

1. *Totally dissatisfied* to *not dissatisfied*

and

2. *Totally alienated* to *totally involved*

On the first dimension, individuals may be 'totally dissatisfied' or 'not dissatisfied' with any number of the factors listed in Table 5.1 under the heading 'Job satisfaction'. The set of personality characteristics possessed by each individual is unique. People come into the workplace with different needs and expectancies, different preferences and prejudices, different values and beliefs. As an example of the effect of these individual differences, we can take the first and second of the factors listed under the heading 'job satisfaction', which relate to salary and conditions in the physical work environment. Differences in perceptions and attitudes between and among individuals cause them to regard these factors according to their own unique values and beliefs about how things should be, and such views will vary from one individual to the next which produces a situation which satisfies some employees and not others.

Some of the factors that influence where any one particular employee can be found on the second dimension, 'totally alienated' to 'totally involved', are listed in Table 5.1 under the heading 'Job involvement'. Taking the top two factors from this list, which relate to authority and responsibility, how much authority and how much responsibility employees wish to have, and indeed may expect to be given in their jobs, varies from one individual to another even though they may have similar jobs. Some people shy away completely from authority and responsibility while others cannot get enough.

Clearly, job holders should be given levels of authority and responsibility which are commensurate with the job, since it is the nature and level of the job that determines how much of each should be given. But that does not influence individuals' perceptions of the status of their own personal situations; to them, how much authority and responsibility they are given pertains to them as individuals. On the one hand, the organisation may allocate amounts of authority and responsibility to a particular job regardless of who is the job holder, while the individual who the job holder is may perceive the allocation to be too little, too great or just about right. It is also worth bearing in mind that a large number of individuals perceive 'responsibility' as a status symbol, and to be given more responsibility therefore raises the status of their jobs and, thereby, their own personal status.

Work motivation

Managers in the twentieth century were bombarded with theories about job satisfaction. Most of the theories remain current, and most claim that the level of work motivation co-varies with the level of job satisfaction, and hence productivity co-varies with the level of motivation, which is why the theories were aimed at managers. Motivation analysts have been researching this subject for about seventy years, and while collectively they have produced several dozen theories, they have produced only two main approaches to the subject: *content theories* and *process theories*.

Motivation theories

Content theories of motivation

Content theorists identify *extrinsic* and *intrinsic* job factors, and say that employees will be more or less satisfied by the degree to which their desired job factors are present or absent. In this context, an extrinsic job factor is an element that the employees experience as a result of working anywhere in the organisation, for example in the terms and conditions of employment and the circumstances in which the job is set – these include the physical work environment, factors such as pay, working hours, pension, holiday entitlements, peer relationships, job security, company policies, equal opportunities, health and safety, and so forth. While the same extrinsic factors are common to all employees, intrinsic factors are those that affect only the individual directly in relation to the job that he or she is doing. These include the status of the job within the organisation and the amounts of authority, autonomy and responsibility that go with the job (see Figure 5.1).

Clearly, the degree to which an employee is satisfied depends exclusively on his or her perception of the extrinsic factors, which are variables within the general work situation. The intrinsic job factors, however, are *individual* variables which will determine the degree to which the job holder is likely to become *involved* in the job. For example, if two individuals are doing identical work in the same work environment, it is possible for one to be satisfied with the job but not involved in it, while the other is not satisfied but totally involved. Individuals' perceptions of job factors are personality driven, so that what is highly valued by one person may be dismissed as irrelevant by another. In the light of this, it is difficult to see how a manager, through the application of these theories, can motivate the whole workforce by inducing job involvement. The intrinsic job factors are the real motivators. It is more likely that a manager will be able to influence job satisfaction through the control that he or she has over the extrinsic factors. It is true that employees' perceptions of extrinsic factors are subject to the element of individual differences, but some factors are more important than others in the perceptions of most employees. For example, pay and required working time are very important to most employees.

Content theorists, therefore, identify job factors, categorise them as extrinsic or intrinsic and say that employees are more or less motivated to work, depending upon the degree to which the job factors they perceive as important are present or absent. Probably the two most well-known theorists in this area of thought are Abraham Maslow, who proposed a *theory of growth motivation* (1987), and Frederick Herzberg, who proposed the two-factor *motivation-hygiene theory* (1957). It is important to note that theorists tend to coin their own terminology when propounding their theories. Maslow, for example, refers to extrinsic job factors as *lower-order needs* and intrinsic job factors as *higher-order needs*. Herzberg, on the other hand, refers to the same factors as *hygiene factors* and *motivators* respectively.

According to Maslow people have needs, and it is having those needs met at the most basic level that leads to their survival. Meeting the higher order, cerebral needs leads to self-actualisation. Central to his theory is a 'hierarchy of needs', which depicts and describes the needs progressively, from the basic physical needs to the higher psychological needs (see Figure 5.2).

Maslow maintains that our drive to have these needs met determines our behaviour, and that we move progressively upwards as and when each of the five needs is met. First, we make arrangements

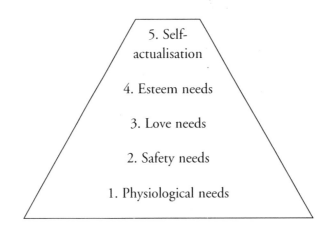

Figure 5.2 The hierarchy of needs (Maslow, 1987).

to ensure that our basic *physiological needs* are met to our satisfaction. These needs include food, drink and shelter to secure physical survival as an individual, and sex to secure the survival of the species. When we think we have done enough to ensure that the basic needs will be met, we move up to the second level, *safety needs*, and make arrangements to protect and defend ourselves against the elements and possible enemies. The third level, *love needs*, depicts us as human beings who need, for several reasons, to be with other human beings and to experience a sense of belonging. There is considerable truth in Francis Bacon's assertion that 'man is by nature a gregarious animal'. We need other people to relate to; we need to use their achievements as a yardstick by which we may measure our own performance; we are a sociable species that survives best in numbers. The fourth level, *esteem needs*, includes the need for self-esteem and the esteem of others. Finally, the fifth level, *self-actualisation*, is the level at which we feel complete: we have entered a situation in which our behaviour is a perfect reflection of our own self-concept – the way we see ourselves – and we are doing what we were born to do.

It is clear that after we have ensured that our physiological and safety needs are being met, and will continue to be met in the future, our behaviour is driven by our psychological (intellectual and spiritual) needs, rather than by our physical needs; love needs may be seen as a kind of bridge between the two. It has to be remembered that Maslow proposed the hierarchy of needs as a progressive scale containing examples of the kinds of natural human needs that determine human behaviour; initially, he did not propose it as a theory of work motivation, although it has been adopted as such. If we superimpose the idea of upward progression onto the individual's workplace situation, we can see that the extrinsic factors provide for the lower-order needs, while the intrinsic factors meet the higher-order needs.

Superficially the theory seems logical and easy to understand, but its application in the workplace has been criticised on the grounds that

---

not everyone perceives the work environment as the place where psychological stimulation or 'self-actualisation' may be achieved. To put it bluntly, most employees do not experience feelings of 'involvement' in their jobs to the extent that their psychological needs are met. Indeed, many have their higher-order needs met by participating in activities outside the workplace, such as hobbies, sports or other social, charitable or religious pursuits. It is clear, therefore, when we look at the hierarchy of needs, that the majority of employees opt out at the third level and get their psychological kicks elsewhere.

Exhibit 5.1

Ron Smith worked in the gearshop of a car factory inspecting the gears as they came off the line. He did this by running the gears against a hardened reciprocal copy and listening for knocks that indicated burrs or nodules on the teeth. If there were knocks, he would examine the gear, find the problem bump or burr, and rub it off with a bauxite stick. Obviously, a person would not have to be highly skilled or particularly intelligent to perform such a task, but Ron was an intelligent man who possessed many manual skills. So why did he do it? Why did he stand at his machine day after day carrying out this repetitive task? The simple answer is money. The wage he received from the car factory was higher than he could get elsewhere, despite his skills.

When he got home from work, and at the weekends, he could be found in his garage, which he had converted into a workshop. There he made yachts and dinghies to a very high standard, and because of the quality of his work, his boats were in great demand. Obviously, he was very skilled indeed, and totally absorbed and involved in his lucrative 'hobby'. One would have to wonder about the gearshop manager's chances of succeeding in getting Ron 'involved' in his day job!

Motivation–hygiene theory

The American motivation analyst, Frederick Herzberg, surveyed several thousand employees across a wide variety of managerial and technical professions. Principally he was interested in job satisfaction in the belief that it determined performance, and wanted to know which job factors created feelings of satisfaction within employees and which created feelings of dissatisfaction. The information upon which he based his *motivation–hygiene* theory came from responses to his survey followed by interviews with 220 accountants and engineers, who were a representational group of 'key informants' from the main survey (Herzberg et al., 1957). During the interviews the respondents were asked to recall things that had happened at work that produced feelings of satisfaction and dissatisfaction, which resulted in an analysis that showed that some job factors produced satisfaction, while others led to dissatisfaction. Herzberg labelled the factors that produced satisfaction *motivators*, and those that produced dissatisfaction, *hygiene factors*. These initial results prompted Herzberg to extend his studies even further, to manual and clerical workers, and the results were very similar to those for the accountants and engineers.

One of the interesting features of Herzberg's discoveries is that while the motivators induced positive feelings of satisfaction, the hygiene factors could only prevent dissatisfaction. He said that in this context, 'satisfaction' and 'dissatisfaction' were not opposite in meaning, in the sense that while the motivators provided satisfaction, the hygiene factors at best were capable of producing a condition that he termed 'the absence of dissatisfaction'. What Herzberg's team discovered was that people will never say that they are totally satisfied with a particular set of working conditions, '... if they are not asking for more of anything, then they are not dissatisfied with the way things are.' The motivators that feature most frequently in the responses to his questionnaires and interviews are regarded as important because they identified for managers the kinds of factors that they would find useful when trying to motivate employees to work. The 'important' motivators, therefore, were:

- achievement

- recognition

- the work itself

- responsibility

- advancement.

The most frequently occurring hygiene factors (those that can produce feelings of dissatisfaction or the absence of dissatisfaction) were:

- company policy and administration

- supervision – the technical aspects

- salary

- interpersonal relations – supervision

- working conditions.

Comparison of the two theories

The theories of Maslow and Herzberg are similar in that they both categorise extrinsic and intrinsic job factors. While Herzberg's 'hygiene' factors are different in character from Maslow's 'lower-order needs', they are still 'extrinsic' factors, since they are outside what we can call the *job-person unit* (see Figure 5.1), which contains the unique individual carrying out his or her job, and the 'intrinsic' factors that relate to that job, which equate with Herzberg's 'motivators' and Maslow's 'higher-order needs'.

From the two theories it can be seen, as we said earlier, that 'content' theorists of motivation categorise job factors as extrinsic or intrinsic and say that the degree to which people are satisfied and motivated to work is determined by their perceptions of the quality and extent, and the presence or absence of the two kinds of job factor. Herzberg does not use the term 'satisfaction' in the way that it is used by Maslow, which is to regard extrinsic factors as the source of job satisfaction, and the intrinsic factors as the source of job involvement. According to his terminology, employees may become satisfied or not dissatisfied by any or all factors within the total job situation.

Research carried out by motivation theorists is designed primarily to find out why people behave in the way they do. We often hear people say that a manager's job is to motivate people, yet people are never 'unmotivated'. Everyone, at all times, is motivated to do *something*, even if they are asleep, then that is what they are motivated to do. When people come into the workplace, therefore, they are already motivated, but to do what? Go down the line and have a chat with someone? Make themselves a cup of coffee? In fact, a manager's job is to *change* people's motivations from what they are to what he or she needs them to be. A manager's job is to motivate people to *work*.

It is important to note, therefore, that if managers understand how employees perceive the job factors that are described above, they will be in a good position to generate work motivation among their staff and, as the content theorists claim, the greater the motivation, the greater the satisfaction and, consequently, the higher the performance.

Process theories of work motivation

While content theorists study the contents of the total job situation and see motivational factors as features of the work environment within and outside of individual jobs, process theorists say that people's behaviour is driven by the individual's thought processes. As

---

people develop through the early stages of their lives, they learn that their behaviour has consequences. Sometimes the outcomes of our behaviour are welcome and pleasant experiences, and at other times they are unpleasant or even painful. Eventually, our experiences enable us to predict the kinds of behaviour that produce pleasure and those that produce pain. By the time we are old enough to go to work, we are usually experienced enough to make these predictions with a reasonable degree of accuracy, and this causes us to develop a set of expectations about the kinds of outcome that are likely to result from our actions. We learn that if we behave in a particular way, the likelihood of an expected outcome is raised and, in fact, we acquire some degree of control over the outcomes by varying our behaviour accordingly. The more experienced we become, the more accurate are our outcome predictions and, therefore, the more able we are to gain further control over them.

To a large extent, these mental processes occur without conscious thought and we develop behavioural patterns which become habitual. At another level, we are careful about our behaviour and we weigh the possible consequences of taking a particular action. While items of behaviour such as driving, dancing or carrying out the work tasks that we have been doing for a long time are formed into habits, actions that follow a thoughtful period of analysis and decision-making are the ones that cause us consciously to try to predict outcomes. These are usually the more important, sometimes even critical actions, such as taking active steps to change one's job, living accommodation or even one's total lifestyle.

The level at which we value an expected outcome determines the degree to which we are motivated to achieve it. We may expect, for example, that if we work harder or try to improve the quality of our work, we will be rewarded with bonuses or promotion. There are people, of course, to whom promotion at work occupies a lowly place in their personal order of priority, and their work performance, therefore, is modified accordingly.

The researcher and process theorist J.S. Adams (1961) said in his *equity-inequity theory* that we run a kind of mental balance sheet, in which on one hand we place a particular value upon our individual work input, and expect to be rewarded at a rate that reflects that value. If we regard the reward as inadequate, we will moderate our efforts downwards to the extent that the value we place on our work equates with the reward we receive. It may be against our nature to reduce our work effort, so instead we may ask management to increase the reward. A third alternative action might be to carry out a mini-comparability study by discovering the reactions of our peers who are putting in a similar effort and receiving similar rewards, and the result may cause us to modify our perception of the degree to which the values of the work effort and reward are equitable. If these actions do not produce a satisfactory outcome, we may seek employment elsewhere where we think the rewards will more accurately reflect the value of the work effort. It was the American, Victor H. Vroom, who in 1970 proposed the first process theory, and many of the ideas that followed were based upon his *expectancy theory*. Before politically correct terminology entered our vocabulary, Vroom described his theory as follows:

> Whenever an individual chooses between alternatives which involve uncertain outcomes, it seems clear that his behaviour is affected not only by his preferences among these outcomes but also by the degree to which he believes these outcomes to be possible. An expectancy is defined as a momentary belief concerning the likelihood that a particular act will be followed by a particular outcome. Expectancies may be described in terms of their strength. Maximal strength is indicated by subjective certainty that the act *will* be followed by the outcome, while minimal (or zero) strength is indicated by subjective certainty that the act *will not* be followed by the outcome.

It should be borne in mind that academics such as Vroom are trying to explain not only what motivates people to do what they do, but also to assess the strength of the drive behind the motivated action. The more attractive the expected outcome, the stronger the drive; and the more strongly the person *believes* that the desired outcome will follow, the stronger the motivation behind the drive.

While content theorists attempt to show that job satisfaction leads to an enhanced performance, the further development of expectancy theory by Porter and Lawler (1968) produced strong indications that it is in fact performance that produces job satisfaction. They point out that effort alone is not enough to produce a good performance; the person has to be equipped with the right skills and have the kind of personality that is attracted by the rewards. While they agree that there is a relationship between motivation, satisfaction and performance, all three are 'stand-alone' variables, so that where each of them stand in different individuals' value systems depend upon how much he or she values the expected outcome. The levels of values that people place upon rewards vary from one individual to the next.

> A senior administrator was given the task of setting up a fully equipped information service for managers and specialists. In his spare time, he collected classic and vintage cars and was very skilled at restoring them to their former glory. Often, he used them as his mode of transport to and from the office. Most people knew about his hobby and having seen the results of his work, regarded him as a 'perfectionist'. When he finally had the information service up and running, it was obvious that he had done a good job, and as a reward, the senior managers decided to give him a 'company car'!

It is just that kind of insensitivity that causes many managers to lose out on opportunities to demonstrate their gratitude for a job well done. There is no doubt at all that they meant well and honestly believed that this extra benefit would be well received. It is likely that if the management information system had been installed by a different member of staff, the 'reward' would have been more highly valued. The point, of course, is that the managers who decided on a car should have made enquiries about the kind of thing he would have preferred. Furthermore, it has been shown that it is the *promise* of a reward that motivates (Maslow, 1987), or the *expectancy* of a particular reward (Vroom, 1970), rather than just the reward itself, which implies that when managers are trying to motivate employees to carry out tasks in addition to their normal duties, they should negotiate the prospective reward before the actual work commences.

Reward as an outcome

This means that as managers we have to study the concept of reward very carefully and try to identify particular rewards with the kinds of people we employ. While reward plays an important role in the inculcation of satisfaction, motivation and enhanced performance, not all rewards are financial. While it is clear that most people go to work for the financial benefits that enable them to sustain at least an acceptable living standard, there are other aspects of the work situation which employees find rewarding. They may, for example, find that particular tasks within the work they do are rewarding because they are satisfying. For example, professional people such as doctors, nurses and teachers work at the interface of human concern in terms of their health, well-being and developmental progress. It is extremely rewarding and psychologically stimulating to achieve success in this area, even to the extent that the financial attractions of alternative employment are disregarded.

Another form of reward is the esteem we earn from others when it is related to the degree to which we are skilled, knowledgeable and conscientious in our work. Similar to this kind of experience is the satisfaction one gets from enjoying long-term personal relationships with work colleagues. Unfortunately, some employees dread going into the workplace in the mornings because of the hostile atmosphere and the negative attitudes of their bosses and co-workers. Obviously, this is a cultural issue, but where the atmosphere is businesslike but friendly, time spent in the workplace can be very rewarding and satisfying. It is well worth managers spending time exploring this kind of psychological reward, since getting it right or getting it wrong will affect the rates of 'sickness absence' and staff turnover as well as satisfaction and performance.

Non-cash rewards, in the form of time bonuses and gifts, perhaps resulting from successful participation in the organisation's suggestion scheme or as a reward for carrying out a particularly demanding project or assignment, demonstrate that one's work has been recognised, which can produce great satisfaction.

Other areas of reward include benefits and pensions, which although more formal than those mentioned above, since they carry financial value, are still subject to the element of individual difference in terms of how people perceive and value them. Many organisations conduct surveys among their employees in an attempt to discover their preferences in these respects, and when subsequent policies are based upon the outcomes of such surveys greater satisfaction will be experienced by the employees.

The human relations approach

Today's managers still have a high regard for the principles and techniques of the behavioural sciences which became prominent in managerial practice as a result of the human relations approach (1935). Theories underpinning the techniques of motivation, job satisfaction, job involvement and work performance proliferated, were widely applied in the workplace, and, with the advent of human resource management (HRM) and the application of organisational development (OD) techniques, many elements of the human relations approach are enjoying a resurgence. In HRM organisations, for example, ideas such as those of *job enrichment, job enlargement* and *job redesign* have been updated to accommodate human resource management principles (see Chapter 4).

Job enrichment, enlargement and redesign

These are empowering processes which are intended to make an individual's job more interesting. The job holder is given more responsibility and the authority to make minor operational decisions. The ideas were first used in the motor car industry in the 1960s, when research revealed a high level of boredom and low levels of job satisfaction. By providing employees with further training they became multiskilled, so that they could carry out a wider range of different tasks, thus relieving the boredom, increasing job satisfaction and enhancing work performance.

In an HRM organisation, downsizing, rightsizing and delayering flattens and widens the structure, which results in having fewer staff overall and a greater number of employees reporting to each individual manager. HRM advocates claim that the flattened structure works well since empowered, multiskilled employees need less supervision than did their bored and dissatisfied 1970s and 1980s counterparts. Their extra responsibilities draw them into the job and since they are making decisions and solving work problems, they feel more committed to the achievement of successful outcomes.

Organisation Development

Organisation Development (OD) involves implementing planned programmes which are designed to enhance organisational effectiveness and employee well-being through the use of the techniques of the behavioural sciences. The improvement of organisational effectiveness is the main aim, and OD attempts to achieve this through implementing a planned series of change-interventions. The *change function* of these interventions is designed primarily to help individual employees to work together more effectively, and attempts to alter such behavioural factors as attitudes, the quality of interpersonal communication, problem-solving and decision-making. Changes such as these tend to improve individual work performance and thereby increase levels of job satisfaction. Typically, the organisation's spans of control and overall structure have to be altered to accommodate the outcomes of the interventions, and the ultimate change is to the culture, which becomes more conducive to the achievement of objectives.

While explanations of the concept of OD normally would be found in a study of managing organisational change, it is included here because it has a respectable track record as a medium through which human well-being and organisational enrichment are considered together. Old-fashioned ideas about separating the planning and doing of work, who possesses power and authority, in fact the whole of the control/compliance workplace paradigm have no place in an enterprise that has embarked upon an OD programme. The values that underpin OD activities may be summarised as follows:

- *Treating employees with respect.* Individuals are regarded as self-starters, responsible, caring and conscientious. They are treated in a way that allows them to retain their dignity and made to feel that their work effort is valued.

- *Mutual trust.* The OD culture is one of openness, mutual trust and respect, mutual support and authenticity.

- *Power.* Power and leadership are more frequently found in expertise than in positions in the hierarchical order, and the formal 'who's who' types of 'pecking order' distinctions are deliberately blurred.

- *Frankness and honesty.* This is also evident in the OD culture. Interpersonal and other problems are openly confronted and solutions found.

- *Ownership of change.* Employees who are to be affected by changes are consulted, their ideas seriously considered and their participation in effecting changes elicits their commitment to successful outcomes.

OD's most valuable 'plus' is that it works. In the 1970s, when it had been in use for some twenty years, doubts about its validity began to emerge after several academics criticised it for being indefinable and naive. Still, there are some pretty important factors around which have never been defined, yet have an important bearing upon human and organisational well-being. No one, for example, has ever produced an acceptable definition of human intelligence, yet we all think we know what it is. As the saying goes, 'I cannot define an elephant, but I know one when I see one'!

Criticism in the 1970s caused OD to fall into unjustifiable disrepute for a few years, but since the mid-1980s it has enjoyed the benefits of a resurgence. The Americans now call it OE, meaning 'organisational effectiveness', while various euphemisms are used to refer to systems the principles and techniques of which are remarkably similar to those of OD. In any case, managers today tend to take an eclectic view of ideas and systems through which organisations may be managed. If we were to scan across the managerial spectrum and stop it in mid-flight as it were, we would find that most managers are operating according to a system which is a hybrid (or is it mongrel!), that has been bolted together using selected components of a wide variety of systems, chosen on the basis of their merits as 'suitable' for running *this or that particular* organisation; they are all different from each other.

Conclusion

It was not until the final quarter of the twentieth century that managers began to realise that there were advantages in extending their perceptions of employee well-being beyond the limited requirements of health and safety legislation. It is now some seventy years since ideas were advanced about how managers might develop job satisfaction, job involvment and motivation within people at work. The human relations approach, which began in the 1930s, has been modified and refined considerably, and much of what was expounded then has, in very recent years, been incorporated into the principles and techniques of human resource management. In one way this attempt at blending the two approaches to management – HRM and the human relations approach – has caused some confusion. While non-HRM theorists and managers regard 'involvement' as an employee's attitude towards, and affinity with, the actual work that he or she carries out, those who defend HRM pair 'involvement' with 'commitment' and say that it is important to elicit these attitudes, since they improve work performance, although they are yet to produce evidence in support of this assertion. On the other hand, the writers of the studies that have been mentioned in this chapter have produced considerable evidence to support the view that it is *job* involvement, rather than commitment to the organisation, that enhances performance. After all, assessments of an individual's performance are related to his or her job.

It is important to bear in mind that while the industrial work paradigm changed markedly in the twentieth century, the purposes and objectives of organisations remain the same, which are to survive and develop; it is the technology, or the means of achieving those purposes and objectives, that has changed. Similarly, while the techniques for motivating, involving and satisfying employees have changed and developed extensively, the organisational motive for this also remains largely unchanged, which is to maximise human performance.

Experienced managers will have witnessed the beneficial effects that job satisfaction and job involvement have on employee well-being, and will have seen improvements in punctuality and reductions in sickness absence. While it is still true that most managers working at the top end of organisations are indifferent to the plight of stressed employees (Currie, 1991), their number is reducing as they gradually realise the financial benefits of treating employees with dignity and respect and of being open with and supportive of them. It is hoped that sooner or later the strategies and policies that are designed to achieve organisational success will be integrated with those designed to foster employee well-being, and that this practice will become widespread.

References

Adams, J.S. (1961) 'Toward an understanding of inequity', in R. Likert (ed.), *New Patterns of Management*. Maidenhead: McGraw-Hill.

Herzberg, F.W., Mausner, B. and Snyderman, B. (1957) *The Motivation to Work*. New York: Wiley.

Maslow, A.H. (1987) 'A theory of growth motivation', in A.H. Maslow, *Motivation and Personality*. New York: Harper & Row.

Mayo, E. (1933) *The Human Problems of an Industrial Civilization*. New York: Macmillan.

Vroom, V.H. (1970) *Management and Motivation*. Harmondsworth: Penguin.

CHAPTER 6

Managing diversity

Introduction

Organisations vary in their approaches to formulating ethical and legitimate strategies and policies on discrimination, and it is possible to distinguish between two main types of approach. First is the equal opportunities approach, in which the term 'equal opportunities' is a blanket expression that attempts to cover all aspects of discrimination. It is a traditional and administrative approach that sets out to ensure compliance with legislation through the promotion of policies that are designed to ensure fairness at work and equal treatment, although, as we shall see, treating all employees equally does not always produce fairness. The equal opportunities approach seeks to ensure that the organisation meets its legal obligations and, on moral and ethical grounds, defends the equal rights of all individuals and groups, including minority groups.

The second, 'managing diversity', is a more recent approach that differs in strategy from the equal opportunities approach. While the managing diversity approach incorporates all of the relevant legislative provisions in the organisation's internal policies, it does not perceive legal compliance to be its only purpose, in that it is not exclusively a response to an external requirement. The managing diversity approach states the business case for providing equal opportunities and attempts to ensure that the organisation and the individuals benefit from the differences in employees' attitudes and the extra variations in skills that have emerged as a result of changes in the make-up of the communities from which the workforce is drawn. Managing diversity is a vibrant and dynamic approach that is more likely to succeed than legislation, codes of practice and pressure groups; while legislation may have the capacity to force changes in people's behaviour, it is unlikely that it will ever succeed in changing attitudes. Changes in workplace behaviour that are legislated through internal policy, however, are not only a means of achieving equality and fairness but are also the medium through which employees may experience a culture of genuine acceptance, which is far more likely to change attitudes.

In the managing diversity approach, strategies and policies on discrimination are integrated with those that drive the organisation forward and promote the achievement of its objectives, emphasising the idea that equal opportunity provisions are designed to embrace all employees, including those from the indigenous population as well as employees who work for customers and suppliers, which is an approach that aligns well with the principles of human resource management. The equal opportunities approach, however, regards actions on the part of the organisation as responses to external requirements with which the organisation must comply, and are thought of as somehow separate from those that drive the business forward.

Discrimination

The first part of this chapter defines discrimination and analyses the various forms that it can take. In the second part we explore the steps that organisations can take to eliminate, or at least moderate, unacceptable attitudes and behaviour that can cause distress to particular individuals and minority groups. The chapter also points out that if managers are to develop a working environment that is concurrently conducive to employee well-being and high productivity, then they need to understand how members of minority groups perceive their work situations. Competition in the global economy is fierce and organisations can ill afford to turn away genuine talent by consciously, or unconsciously, adopting unacceptable discriminatory attitudes towards individuals and minority groups. Finally, we describe how unfair treatment and failure to provide equal opportunities can lead to stress, demotivation and falls in levels of productivity. This is a sensitive subject and is likely to remain so for many years.

The word discrimination may be taken to imply such positive human qualities as discernment, judgement, refinement, taste, choice, discretion or preference, but it may also imply unacceptable attitudes such as bias, bigotry, favouritism, intolerance and prejudice. In the workplace, the negative aspects of the definition are at the centre of interest and organisations are keen to be seen as non-discriminatory providers of equal opportunities.

Societal discrimination

Discrimination, as we know, is a world-wide societal feature, but the reasons behind the prejudices and preconceptions vary from one country to another. In African countries, the perception of black people as second-class citizens began with colonisation, largely by the Europeans, and in some parts survived legally until the 1990s, although it still persists in the minds and actions of many of the descendants of European settlers. In the USA, discrimination still survives informally over many issues, despite strict and far-reaching legislation proscribing it, especially in matters of employment which, unlike in many other countries, includes mandatory equal opportunities policies.

In some countries, such as the USA, Canada, Australia and New Zealand, people of a wide variety of ethnic and cultural origins actually established the country in its modern form, and seem after the passage of time to have always been present. Now, however, they discriminate against the descendants of the ancient indigenous peoples. To the Europeans, a significant presence of people from different ethnic and cultural backgrounds is largely a post-Second World War phenomenon.

All societies contain groups that are the targets of discrimination. The prejudices that cause discrimination are usually unfounded and are expressed in very subtle ways, maybe through body language, or through the adoption of an obvious attitude of superiority, perhaps when just conversing. One very worrying and not so subtle trend that has developed is the targeting of minority groups, in which the prejudice is expressed in the form of physical violence, sometimes resulting in serious injury or even death.

Recent years have seen a dramatic increase in the numbers of people moving into the more advanced, industrialised nations to escape from Third World poverty and/or from oppressive conditions. Not all of the host countries' indigenous populations have welcomed these immigrants with open arms. Many perceive them as a threat to their comfortable lifestyles, including their security and their jobs, while to others, especially very mature people, they invoke the images and preconceptions they learned when they were children. The advanced, industrialised nations have produced legislation that proscribes discrimination and requires the provision of equality of opportunity and fair treatment, not only in the workplace but in all areas of life. Organisations too have legislated internally against the unacceptable treatment of minority groups through their policies and procedures. The detail of the provisions of national legislation varies from one country to another, but broadly they all follow the same basic principles.

Legitimate discrimination

A discriminatory attitude has a role in business. Selection and promotion systems, for example, are overtly discriminatory since we are forced to choose just one from a number of candidates, offer the position to him or her, and not to the others. Similarly, decisions about who is to be selected to receive or not to receive training in some specialism force us to discriminate. Clearly, in such situations we are rewarding some people and not others, sometimes when the difference between them is extremely marginal. In these processes we are trying to predict performance and so we have to select those whom we believe to be best for the job, and we do it by discriminating in favour of some individuals and against others. In this way, some kinds of discrimination are acceptable, indeed are vital, so long as the grounds upon which we do discriminate are exclusively related to the position, promotion, training or whatever the target of selection happens to be. On the other hand, it is unlawful to discriminate against employees by behaving unfairly towards them, or by failing to provide them with an equal opportunity for reasons that are not related to their ability to meet the demands of the position or the training, for example because of their race or sex. It is, therefore, the reason why one is discriminating that determines its legality. Since it is impossible to legislate against discriminatory attitudes, the law relating to this subject can only proscribe behavioural acts and omissions that are unfair because they place someone at an unjustifiable disadvantage, or which *directly* or *indirectly* fail to provide an equal opportunity (see Chapter 8 for definitions of direct and indirect discrimination). Such acts and omissions have their roots in certain individuals' prejudiced perceptions that cause discriminatory attitudes. Although most managers would hotly deny that they possess such attitudes, there is plenty of hard evidence to support the view that they do.

Conscious discrimination

There are organisations and individuals who deliberately discriminate against others on unjustifiable grounds. Conscious discrimination is usually based upon unfounded beliefs and assumptions, first, about individuals because of their appearance, personal style or command of the language, and second, simply because of their sex or ethnic origin. Deliberate discrimination is far more frequently the act of an individual than an organisational manoeuvre. This is because it usually results from personally held beliefs about others that have been learned during the individual's development and socialisation period, and often they are beliefs that have been internalised and held for many years. In most cases when individuals deliberately discriminate, they are failing to follow organisational policy.

It is clear, however, that in some small and medium-sized organisations, and in isolated outposts of some large organisations, pressure to discriminate is applied to managers and professionals who are handling recruitment and selection processes, and on rare occasions it has been known for managers and professionals to be instructed to discriminate. Sometimes this is done with good intent. When, for example, senior managers are concerned about the prospect of being accused of discriminating against women because the male–female balance in a section or department of the organisation is one sided, say in favour of men, to redress the balance they ask for females, rather than males, to be engaged. In some countries, the USA for example, this may be regarded as legitimate because of its obvious underlying purpose, but in the UK and Europe it would be regarded as positive discrimination against men, which is unlawful.

Unconscious discrimination

Everyone, regardless of their sex, race, creed, colour or ethnic origin has preferences and prejudices of one kind or another, not only about people, but about political and religious causes and beliefs, social concepts and situations ... everything and anything that they have ever encountered and dealt with in the environment and culture into which they were socialised. The values and beliefs that people have are acquired through their experience, and they internalise them. Values and beliefs, which are placed in orders of importance and priority, determine people's evaluated perceptions of and attitudes towards things which, in turn, determine their behaviour around them.

Because older and long-serving employees were socialised long before the advent of unlawful discrimination and political correctness, they may have great difficulty in suppressing their preferences and prejudices and in changing their perceptions and attitudes, even when it becomes legally necessary. Because of *when* they were reared, they were taught things which today would be regarded at best as politically incorrect and at worst as illegal. If, for example, they were English and were in their schooldays between 1939 and 1945, parents' and teachers' remarks, and indeed government propaganda, will have given them a perception of German, Italian and Japanese people that would mystify and horrify today's youngsters, who have had an entirely different social schooling. For these reasons, there are situations in which what is intended to be an innocent remark reveals a well established long-held belief which is now regarded as unacceptable.

Values and beliefs that lead ultimately to particular kinds of behaviour are handed down from one generation to the next, often inherited by many successive generations. This inheritance is acquired at an early age, when children are keenly receptive to suggestion and ideas, and values and beliefs that are internalised at that stage in their lives become deeply ingrained in the following years and are therefore difficult to change.

The social effect of behaviour that results from this phenomenon can be amusing, but it can also be deeply embarrassing or painful:

In the 1980s and 1990s, British television was showing the American weekly drama, *LA Law*, which was enjoyed by an old man, his children and grandchildren. In one scene, a female lawyer, addressing her black male colleague, asked him a long and very complex technical question. Before he could reply, the old man turned to his family and said, 'Fancy expecting a black man to know the answer to a question like that.' The grandchildren looked embarrassed and dismayed, 'Grandad!' said one, 'You musn't say things like that.'

Clearly, the old man was still carrying the social baggage that had been handed down for generations from his ancestors, who had been involved in nineteenth century military actions in Africa and India.

The old man's perception of and attitude towards black people was based upon a 'taken for granted' belief that could never be dislodged by legislation and which could easily be inherited by the generations that follow him, which includes people who are working in organisations now. Clearly, it will take a few more generations to eradicate this kind of long-held belief.

Today, small children are given toys at Christmas and on their birthdays. Girls are given nurses outfits, cookery sets, and doll's houses. Boys are given train sets, toy soldiers, and carpentry kits. Are they being prepared for something later in life? Television advertisers show boys and girls concurrently being introduced to computers and the Internet, but at that stage, that is fun. The train sets indicate what *real* work is, and the doll's houses provide the firmest indication of what the girls will be doing in the future. It is this kind of unconscious discrimination that influences the shape of those values and beliefs that will live longest in the minds of future generations. Discrimination has a long tradition.

Equality and fairness

While employees have a legal right to be treated equally and fairly in the context of their contractual rights, it is not always possible or practicable to treat people equally and fairly at the same time, since equality and fairness do not always go hand in hand. There are occasions when, if everyone is treated equally, unfairness is the result; it depends upon one's understanding of equality. For example, to provide physical working conditions that are exactly the same for everyone could be perceived as equal treatment; but if one of the employees is disabled and, as a consequence of his or her disability, is unable to work as comfortably or as effectively as the other workers in the physical conditions provided, the provision will be seen to be unfair, or as a failure to provide an equal opportunity. In Europe, and specifically in the UK under the Disability Discrimination Act 1995, the employer has to be prepared to make reasonable adjustments to the physical conditions so that the disabled employee is not placed at a disadvantage.

Individual differences

The truth is that people are not all equal; people are more or less intelligent, more or less dextrous, more or less experienced and differently experienced from each other. There is a host of situational, physical and psychological differences between individuals that render them unequal to each other. Indeed, it is these very differences that provide the basis for acceptable and legitimate discrimination, in which they make some people more employable or more promotable than others. Rather than treat all employees as equals, it is more honest, more practical, more productive and more mutually satisfying to recognise and accept their differences and treat them fairly, which may mean providing some people with physical working conditions that take their disabilities, as well as their abilities, into account.

Indeed, while organisations that have adopted the managing diversity approach aim to treat people fairly, and provide equal opportunities in accordance with the law, they also have seized the opportunity to take advantage of the different knowledge, skills and attitudes that members of minority groups have brought with them, since their contribution provides added value to the organisation. We have to learn to assess people in terms of what they *can* do, rather than what they *cannot* do. In this way the disabled or minority individual benefits, and the organisation does not miss out on acquiring valuable skills and knowledge.

Minority groups

People are categorised as 'minorities' when they: are women; have a particular skin colour; follow a particular religion; are disabled; belong to a particular age group (e.g. child-bearing age, or over 40); belong to a particular race; have a certain ethnic background; are transsexual or homosexual. Anyone who happens to fall into one or more of these categories can become the victims of other people's prejudices. Some of the above categories are covered by legislation and some are not. In the USA, it is illegal to discriminate on the grounds of age, while in Europe it is not, at least not at the time of writing. In the UK, the government has launched an initiative entitled 'Age Positive', and has undertaken to introduce legislation that proscribes discrimination on the grounds of age before 2006.

Some assumptions about minorities

The assumptions listed in Table 6.1 are quite common among managers. Readers may care to test their own assumptions by covering the right-hand column and responding 'true' or 'false', to the assumptions listed on the left.

Table 6.1 Common assumptions among managers

Assumption	Reality
1. There are important differences between men's and women's work performance.	*False.* Studies of employees' performance in a wide variety of jobs indicates no difference.
2. While men are likely to be highly motivated, have a greater competitive drive, are better learners and very sociable, women are superior at problem-solving, analytical skills and predictive skills.	*False.* Research shows no differences between men and women in any of the skills listed.
3. Women are more willing than men to conform to authority.	*True* (Quinn, Staines and McCullough, 1994).
4. Men are more aggressive than women and have stronger expectations of success.	*True.* Reference as at 3 above.
5. There are no differences between men's and women's productivity rates.	*True.* Reference as at 3 above.
6. Men experience higher levels of job satisfaction than do women.	*False.* Reference as at 3 above.
7. Women's absence rates are higher than those for men.	Current research (Garrison and Muchinsky, 1994) indicates that this is *true.*
8. Married employees have fewer absences, lower leaving rates and tend to be more job satisfied than their unmarried work colleagues.	Research shows that there are strong indications that this is *true.*
9. Conscientious and satisfied employees are more likely to be married.	*True.* Reference as at 8 above.

10. Women as leaders are more likely to be democratic than men as leaders.	*True*. Reference as at 3 above.
11. Employees' productivity decreases with length of service.	*False*. Research carried out by ICF Inc. (1995) for the American Association of Retired Persons.
12. Long-serving employees have a low absence rate.	*True*. Reference as at 11 above.
13. Long-serving employees are likely to be job satisfied.	*True* (Kacmar and Ferris, 1990).
14. Long-serving employees are less likely to leave.	*True*. Based on fears of change, failure, loss of rights, they also favour routine.
15. Women are less susceptible to occupational stress than are men.	*False*. Research indicates the reverse (Cooper et al., 1997).
16. People over 50 are less productive than younger people.	*False*. Reference as at 11 above.
17. People between 40 and 65 are more experienced than those between 20 and 40.	*False*. Experience is not a function of time. Many under 30s are more experienced than other older workers.
18. People over 50 are less likely to leave than those under 50.	*True*. They do not wish to lose pension values, long service holiday entitlements, etc.
19. Resistance to change increases with age.	*True*, but research shows that the trend is reversing.
20. Workers aged 55 and over are the fastest growing sector of the workforce.	*True*. Reference as at 11 above.

Women as a minority group

Women are discriminated against if they are black, Asian, homosexual and all or any of the categories that are the targets of prejudice, but mostly they are discriminated against simply because they are women. Many men, and even some women, harbour the belief that at heart women are not career people, they have a different agenda from men, and their highest priorities are with their homes and families. In most organisations, therefore, the greatest number of women are found in the lower sections of the workforce doing part-time work. It could be argued, of course, that this is where the greatest number of *all employees* are found, full- and part-time, but when we look *vertically* through the hierarchical order we find that the further up we go, the balance between males and females shifts in favour of males, especially white males. In fact we find more white males than the total number of all other employee categories, including ethnic differences, whereas in the absence of discrimination we should find a percentage that reflects or is reasonably close to the men–women balance at or near the bottom of the hierarchical order.

In the area of employment, we should not be too confident about referring to women as a minority group, since in many countries working women either outnumber working men, or the balance is around equal. Some writers argue that traditional organisations in Europe encounter problems in accommodating minority groups because they are accustomed to employing and catering for the needs of people whom they regard as 'normal', in other words white, able-bodied males, and that the organisation's structures and processes have been built around this perceived normality. But the argument is not totally sound. Earlier in this chapter it was pointed out that the growth of minority groups in UK and European organisations is a post Second World War phenomenon. But this applies more to minority groups of different ethnic origins rather than to women, and the structures and processes of organisations are unaffected by employees' ethnic origins. The employment of disabled people is another issue altogether, and it is one that does affect an organisation, not only in terms of structures and processes but the physical work environment too.

Women, on the other hand, have been working in industry in the UK and Europe almost since the beginning of the Industrial Revolution. For example, the shop floors of cotton and wool mills were almost entirely occupied by women and when, thanks to the business success of Remington and Sons in the USA in 1867, the typewriter made its debut, women were employed in offices too. The employment of women in a variety of workplace roles received a further boost during the Second World War, when men were conscripted for military service. The positions that were occupied by women, however, have almost always been at or near the bottom rungs of the ladder.

Sadly, even with such a wealth of experience of employing women, many organisations, even today, appear to have difficulty in treating women with fairness and equality. Today women more than men occupy part-time positions, which in most organisations exist at or near the bottom of the hierarchical order. It is, therefore, when we look at the kinds of work to which women are and are not admitted that the equal opportunities question arises. Usually for reasons of convenience more women apply for part-time positions because they adopt most of the responsibility at home, ensuring, for example, that the children get to and from school safely and that the housework and shopping are done. But there are further reasons why some employers discriminate against women. First, they are reluctant to employ young women because they fear that they may wish to take time out or leave altogether to have children, and if they have been given senior positions this could be very inconvenient. Secondly, some men believe that women are not usually emotionally stable enough to occupy positions of responsibility, which of course is just pure, unsubstantiated prejudice; and thirdly, some men still try to shelter behind the old fashioned inherent prejudice about the whole idea of women working. Those who do not try to hide their prejudice will say in private that 'a woman's place is in the home'.

In Europe, new legislation has enhanced women's maternity rights, and this is likely to exacerbate the problems of discrimination, especially at the initial selection stage. Fathers too now have a legal right to take time off when their children are born, but whether or not they do so is their choice; also, the father's entitlement is for less time, and whether or not they are paid during their absence is left to the discretion of the employer which implies that fathers will only take the time off in those households that can afford it.

Racial and other minorities

Race is said to include a person's colour, ethnic origin and nationality. The origins of prejudice on such grounds are discussed above, but individuals and groups of particular religions are also the targets of discrimination. Society labels minority groups and attributes negative and unfounded characteristics to them. These attributions have existed for many generations and have developed into prejudices which will prevail for generations to come. It is not surprising that such prejudices are transferred into the workplace. In countries where it is not unlawful to discriminate on religious grounds, many organisations have developed policies that legislate against such discrimination.

Equality

Equality means treating *all employees* in the same way, and offering equality of opportunity over such matters as, *inter alia*, selection, training and promotion. It also means equal treatment in relation to

---

pay and other terms and conditions of employment. We all know, of course, that in many countries there is legislation, the provisions of which demand that organisations provide equality in these ways, but when the relevant decision-makers are prejudiced in their attitudes towards minority groups, it is not difficult for them to provide reasons why they have screened a person out of a selection list or bypassed someone who could have been promoted. We deal with the legal aspects of these matters in Chapter 8, but the point that is being made here is that exercising prejudice as described above is not in the best interests of the organisation. It is the organisation's policies that should indicate managers' decision-making routes when they are processing applications that lead them to making choices between people. If all of the decision-making criteria were generated by individual managers, the result would be chaos. Problems arise when the organisation employs managers who ignore policy and allow their personal prejudices to influence their decision-making 'criteria'. The likelihood that such a manager will appoint someone who is not the best person for the job is very high indeed, which means that the organisation will suffer as a result. It also means that more worthy applicants who have been bypassed, or deselected for reasons other than their ability to do the job, will suffer too. They will be demotivated and may even leave if they feel that they can get a fairer deal elsewhere. The fairest course of action, and the one that is in the best interests of the organisation, is to set the criteria so that they relate directly to the object of selection, which might be a job, promotion, transfer or training. If such criteria fail to produce someone suitable, we have to look elsewhere.

Approaches to the provision of equal opportunities vary. In the UK and most European countries, the perceived need for the provision of equality has its roots in the concept of fairness and the equal treatment of people regardless of their sex, marital status, colour or ethnic origins. In the US, however, equality is regarded as a civil right and conformity to the related legislation is monitored through statistical information provided by employing organisations. This information should show that the make-up of the workforce is a reasonable reflection of the make-up of the population in the recruitment catchment area of the organisation. Where the information shows a discrepancy between the workforce and population make-up, the organisation may attempt to correct the balance through 'positive' discrimination. Sometimes referred to as 'reverse' discrimination, the underlying idea is, when recruiting, for example, to discriminate in favour of the minority groups that are needed by the organisation to achieve the appropriate balance.

In Europe, positive discrimination is illegal, but this should not prevent organisations from taking positive action to correct imbalances between the positions occupied by male whites and minorities. It could be, for example, that while there is an acceptable balance across the whole workforce, the balance between occupants of lower, middle and higher level jobs is discrepant. The organisation may question this. Why, in some organisations, do minorities routinely deselect themselves when applications for promotion are called for? Do they feel that it would be pointless for them to apply; that because of their sex or ethnic background, they would not be welcome in the middle and upper echelons? And when minorities do apply, but fail to meet the required criteria, or fail to pass particular tests, the organisation may take steps to discover why this is so. Many of these problems can be solved through training and/or counselling, particularly those that are experienced by recent immigrants, which may be due to a language problem or a failure to understand a particular aspect of a culture that is new to them:

> In an engineering factory, an ethnic minority group of nine machine operators complained that the system for selecting chargehands and supervisors discriminated specifically against them. In the past, they had applied for such positions, but had

been turned down. Another batch of applications had been called for and it was noticed that this time, none of the machine operators applied. The personnel chief wanted to know why. First, he analysed the selection process, which lasted a day, and included several occupational tests. When he examined the selection records, he found that they had all failed because they could not handle the tests, and in particular, the test of leadership ability. He called in a consultant occupational psychologist who, after analysing the tests, told him that they were unfair and did indeed discriminate against the ethnic minority candidates. It turned out that the candidates in question did not lack leadership ability at all; the short-coming was in their test-taking ability. Subsequently they were trained and counselled in test-taking, and now, three of them are chargehands and two are supervisors.

Disability

When selectors are considering disabled people for employment they tend to appraise them in terms of what they cannot do, rather than in what they can do. Also, they demonstrate compassion for the candidate and express their sorrow at not being able to offer them the job, when all the time, if they really thought about it, they could offer them the job, and if they are the best person for it, *should* offer them the job, not only so far as the law is concerned, but for the benefit of the organisation too. Disabled people have been turned down for jobs on the most spurious grounds. In one instance, the applicant, a victim of the thalidomide debacle, had been born with a malformed body, but had not allowed this to deter him from becoming a qualified and extremely proficient computer operator. He was turned down on the grounds that when he sat in the chair facing the worktop, he was too short to reach the computer keyboard. Undoubtedly the reader has already solved this 'problem' by either raising the chair or lowering the machine. Even if it had meant completely redesigning the whole work station, the individual should not have been deprived of the job, nor the organisation of the services of a first rate operator. Organisations simply cannot afford to turn away talent.

Political correctness

This is a subject that has produced many problems and considerable confusion in organisations. To ensure politically correct behaviour one needs to understand the underlying reason for its existence. Behaviour based on a lack of such understanding will, sooner or later, result in political incorrectness, which rightly or wrongly may be perceived to be the product of a discriminatory attitude. The purpose of political correctness is to show an attitude of equality through one's speech, writing, the general treatment of people and in the handling of human relationships. To many people, politically correct behaviour does not come naturally. The need for it is an indication of massive changes taking place in social structures, culture, literature (including grammar), perceived status and the conduct of relationships. In all formal and in some informal situations, political correctness has become the socially acceptable form of behaviour and indeed is the norm in many circles, although its associated terminology has come in for considerable criticism in the past decade or so, since one of its major influences has been to modify language.

It has been said that in some areas politically correct terminology has gone over the top, in that not only does it fail to recognise gender where it should, but it replaces reference to the sex of an individual with expressions, such as 'chair' and 'person'. Why, they ask, do we not refer to or address the person who actually is in the chair as chairman or chairwoman? And why has *people*, the plural of person, been replaced with *persons*, which is regarded as non-sexist? Is there something sexist about the word people?

There are positions which traditionally have been held by men for many years, and others that have been held exclusively by women, but to be politically correct when in the general sense we refer to people in these positions, we have to use either the plural, or state both genders in order to show that the incumbent could be a person of either gender. The offices of Lord Chancellor and Lord Mayor were obviously titled on the assumption that the holders of such offices would be men. In fact the title is assigned to the office rather than to the sex of the individual who happens to be the incumbent, and so, unlike 'the chairman', it remains in force.

Most frequently, speaking involves addressing people directly as individuals or in groups, while writing most often takes a 'first' or 'third' person form. Either way the need for political correctness has caused us to alter our use of particular terms and phraseology. In the use of spoken and written communication in many areas of life, and particularly in education and employing organisations, political correctness has taken precedence over what used to regarded as the 'correct' use of language by observation of grammatic and phraseological requirements. Now, and one suspects for many years to come, people in conversation or when writing find themselves struggling to achieve politically correct statements, and on occasions they fail to communicate with total integrity of meaning. To them the language has to be learned all over again. The truth is that change, most often social and technological change, has always influenced vocabulary and terminology, and we too have to change accordingly.

Equal opportunities policy

In most countries having an equal opportunities policy is not a legal requirement (the USA being one of the few exceptions). Compliance with equal opportunities legislation, however, is a requirement and the formulation and implementation of a policy will increase the likelihood that compliance will be efficient and effective. There are variations in the provisions of legislation, for example age discrimination is illegal in the USA, while in the UK it is merely frowned upon. Organisations, however, should not assume that they are limited to what is required in law. So long as they comply with what the law does require, they are free to draft policy that demonstrates the intention to treat all employees fairly and equally regardless of, for example, sex, marital status, race, creed, colour, religion, ethnic origin, disability and whatever other distinguishing feature may cause people to be categorised as members of a minority group. Some of these categories are covered by law and some are not – it varies from one country to another.

On the question of age, for example, a recent development is the employment of people on the grounds of their capability to do the job, but also on the grounds that their maturity and experience, which usually means over 50 years of age, will enable them to relate to customers with a greater degree of understanding. Enterprises that have taken the lead in this respect include supermarkets trading in food, DIY supplies and household furnishings. Such companies have realised that their mature customers are much more likely to relate easily to people of their own level of seniority, rather than '... be served by some inexperienced young "whippersnapper"', as one survey respondent said.

Where legislation proscribes age discrimination, it could be argued that to actively seek out mature people places younger candidates at an unfair disadvantage; it may even smack a little of 'reverse' or positive discrimination, but in countries where the law ignores the plight of mature people who happen to be unemployed, the practice is perfectly legitimate. There is a deep well of skilled and experienced people who are physically and mentally fit, yet who find themselves in an age trap in which prospective employers regard them as too old for the job, while they regard themselves as too young to retire. The skills and experience which are largely being ignored by industry are truly invaluable. Such people usually bring with them a high level of motivation and a set of values that seem to be hard to come by in industry at present. One early middle-aged employer was heard to pass a sarcastic comment about 'only being able to keep these ancient gems for ten years at the most', but when he was asked how long he kept his younger employees, he went silent.

Monitoring policy

Most managers are at least broadly aware of what is acceptable and what is not, and how the provisions of legislation on sex, disablement and race discrimination influence their behaviour, especially in terms of communication style, decisions and actions. Normally, therefore, they do not consciously discriminate, but one problem is that most discrimination and political incorrectness that takes place occurs in offices and at shopfloor levels, usually between and among shopfloor and office workers in the manager's absence. Even the managers who are aware of this do not really know how to prevent it and can only deal with it effectively when complaints are made.

One approach is to take positive steps to monitor the effectiveness of the organisation's equal opportunities policy. This may be done by conducting attitude surveys through the use of interviews and anonymous questionnaires, scrutinising selection, training and promotion decisions and applications, and analysing staff turnover figures at departmental and sectional levels. The volume and nature of complaints of discrimination and deteriorating race relations is also important, but it is better culturally and in terms of productivity if the policy is monitored *before* such complaints arise. The results of these analyses will, by their nature, imply the kind of action necessary to correct any unacceptable situations.

The purposes of the activities described above will be observed by the staff who will realise that the organisation is committed to equal opportunities and good race relations. This may be further reinforced by a specific statement from the top managers, which might say:

> While this company realises that there is discrimination elsewhere, we wish to make it clear that no employee, customer, supplier or any other person or organisation associated with us now or in the future, will be treated less favourably than others on grounds of their sex, marital status, race, creed, disability or sexual orientation. No minority group or individual member of a minority group will be placed at a disadvantage by virtue of any conditions or requirements that are not believed to be necessary for the completion of a particular job or contract.

It is strongly recommended that the organisation develops and publicises an equal opportunities policy, even though this is not a legal requirement. Ideally a full policy statement will be included in the employee handbook. (For an example of a full policy statement on equal treatment see Chapter 8.)

Major discriminatory factors

Candidates for employment feel that they are being unfairly treated when in their perception:

- their initial applications are rejected even though it is clear that they are eminently qualified to meet the demands of the job;

- the recruitment advertisement discriminates against them by virtue of its content, e.g. it asks for a physical or intellectual quality that is not essential for the job;

- the structure or nature of the selection process varies from one candidate to another;

- selection tests discriminate against them.

Established employees feel that they are being unfairly treated when in their perception:

- the value of their work performance is at least equal to that of their colleagues, while the related rewards are not;

- they are eligible for promotion, training or special projects, but are overlooked when such selection decisions are being made;

- they are excluded from informal events, or ignored when they do attend;

- they are ridiculed by other employees, including managers, because they have some distinguishing personal feature such as a disfigurement or disablement, they are a woman, or a member of a minority group;

- they are selected for redundancy when their case for staying is equal to or stronger than a fellow employee who has not been selected.

The above lists are not exhaustive; they are included to give the reader a general indication of the nature of factors that are regarded as discriminatory. Most of the items on the list are illegal, yet they are found quite frequently, with the notable exception of illegal recruitment advertisements, the number of which has reduced dramatically in recent years, which is due to the extra care taken by advertisers and the keen awareness and vigilance of advertising agents and the media, who are just as amenable to the law as the advertisers themselves.

Impact on well-being

When, for any of the reasons listed above, people feel that they have been unfairly treated, they experience the sting of injustice. They feel hurt … slighted … and in many cases frustrated, because they feel that there is little or nothing that they can do about it. The feeling that others consider you to be somehow inferior preoccupies the mind; it dominates one's thoughts. Individuals, of course, are more or less sensitive, and therefore the degree to which they are affected by unfair treatment varies. Friends advise them to 'rise above it', but one would have to be exceptionally tolerant or tough-minded to be unaffected by some of the treatment that is handed out, even today.

Perceived unfairness is a significant demotivator. Victims of discrimination become alienated by the way they are treated, and as a result the value of their work suffers. They become less amenable to accepting performance targets, and their absence rates rise. After all, they think, if that really is what they think of me, why should I bother? A strong-minded individual will eventually leave and take his or her talents elsewhere. While the more sensitive individuals are less likely to leave, they are more likely to experience the effects of stress.

The feelings that are inculcated by discrimination are long-lasting and powerful determinants of behaviour. Where, for example, individuals feel that their fate is to remain at the bottom of the organisational ladder, they will make assumptions about the kind of behaviour that is expected of someone in that position. In other words, they will abandon their ambition to make progress. If they perceive, from the discriminatory behaviour of the organisation, that others think that their talents should lie dormant, then they will. The problem with this is that feelings of under-utilisation, and that one's true potential is being ignored, can induce stress. It is true that *over*work also induces stress, but most people do like to be given a positive challenge, and they like to feel mentally stretched by the nature of the work they are given, and they also like to feel that their work is perceived by the organisation as valuable.

Conclusion

Human failings will always prevent the achievement of perfect equality and fairness in the treatment of people. Experience has shown that legislation, codes of practice and, to a lesser degree, the activities of pressure groups have led to some progress, but historical evidence shows that there is still a long way to go. Largely people have learned from their mistakes. It is managers' decisions and actions that can breach the letter and the spirit of the law, but there are severe problems in this respect.

The ultimate solution is a long way off and will not be achieved through legislation alone. It will take a large-scale educational and cultural change at societal level to produce genuine attitudes of equality and fairness. If the organisation's ability to retain its core staff, and if its reputation as a fair employer are to survive, the attitudes of its managers must demonstrate genuine acceptance of diversity and a firm belief in equal status and fairness.

The range of stressors to which women are vulnerable is greater than that of men. Bullying male managers see them as an easy target, and they and other male workers discriminate against them when they sexually harass them. Most men fail to understand that this kind of behaviour can inflict deep and long-lasting psychological scars upon women and can cause feelings of fear and insecurity.

References

Arnold, J., Robertson, I.T. and Cooper, C.L. (1997) *Work Psychology*. London: Pitman.

Garrison, K.R. and Muchinsky, P.M. (1994) 'Attitudinal and biographical predictors of incidental absenteeism', *Journal of Applied Psychology*, June, pp. 385–89.

ICF Inc. (1995) *Valuing Older Workers: A Study of Costs and Productivity*, a report prepared for the American Association of Retired Persons.

Kacmar, K.M. and Ferris, G.R. (1990) 'Theoretical and methodological considerations in the age–job satisfaction relationship', *Journal of Applied Psychology*, April, pp. 201–7.

Kelly, R.M. (1991) *The Gendered Economy: Women, Careers and Success*. London: Sage.

Quinn, R.P., Staines, G.L. and McCullough M.R. (1994) *Job Satisfaction: Is there a Trend?*, Document 2900-00195. Washington DC: US Government Printing Office.

CHAPTER 7

Managing individual differences

Introduction

In Chapter 6 we dealt with managing differences between people in terms of their sex, race, creed, colour, age and so forth, in fact anything in their cultural background that sets them apart from the indigenous population, and we were examining ways in which managers could ensure the provision of equal opportunities. Here, we explore the differences between and among all individuals, regardless of their sex, race or other features.

Personal differences between employees have a profound effect upon the manager's ability to manage, especially when the groups are large, as they are inclined to be when the organisation has adopted human resource management principles. It is well known, of course, that all individuals are different from each other in terms of their genetic inheritance, but in this chapter we are more concerned with the psychological differences that people acquire through their encounters with the environment, and from the development of their personalities as they progress through childhood and into adulthood.

Socialisation

It is also worth exploring the ways in which people are alike, similarities that develop within people as they are socialised into the communities and cultures into which they are born, which is a process that continues throughout life. Through being rewarded and punished, usually at first by parents and teachers, we learn the difference between behaviour that is socially acceptable and behaviour that is not. We learn the rituals and norms of our society, and since most of us wish to be accepted, we adhere to them. The outcome of this is that people who have been born into the same society all speak the same language, dress in a similar fashion, and adopt similar patterns of behaviour. In other words, they all follow the same societal norms and rituals. There are, of course, those who choose to deviate from the behavioural norms of society by committing acts of violence and dishonesty, for which in most cases they are eventually punished, and attempts are usually made to correct their behaviour. This chapter, however, deals only with normal people in normal situations.

Why we are all different

While on the one hand our behaviour is similar to each other's when we do things that we believe would meet with society's approval, the personal style with which we actually carry out that behaviour is influenced by our personalities. Our personalities begin to develop while we are being socialised, but we all interpret the environment in different ways, so that the likelihood that two people will develop exactly similar personalities is about equal to the likelihood that their fingerprint patterns will be the same. To adhere to the norms of society, therefore, we do similar things, but the ways in which we do them are unique to each individual.

We are all reared in different home environments by different people with their own unique patterns of values, beliefs, perceptions, attitudes and behavioural inclinations. According to the above description of socialisation, we are taught many similar things, but our perceptions and interpretations of them vary. For example, people in the society into which we were born may hold democratic values, but the families within that society vary denominationally in their political and religious beliefs; they belong to different socio-economic strata, play different sports and send their children to different schools. To some of them, education and living standards are high values, whereas to others they are unimportant. As children we tend to adopt the values and beliefs of our parents, but we change them later when we go to school and learn about the other pupils' general upbringing and family lives and their values and beliefs. As we mature and develop further, we change them yet again when we start work and become further influenced by what we see and hear.

Some of the values and beliefs that we adopted at an early stage stick with us, some for the rest of our lives. Others are more malleable, more amenable to change. Eventually, we adopt a particular lifestyle and standard of living, which to a great extent, reflect and are supported by our values and beliefs. Ultimately, each one of us becomes a wholly unique and distinctive individual.

In the general sense, therefore, it can be said that our personal interpretations of our environmental experiences gave us our values, beliefs, perceptions, attitudes and motivations, which of course determine our behaviour. A manager running a department which is staffed by, say, twenty people, is leading, motivating and influencing the behaviour of twenty entirely unique individuals, and the greater the number of people, the greater the mixture of values, beliefs, intelligence levels, perceptions, attitudes and motivations.

Perception

Even as we pass people in the street, a fleeting assessment of them floats through our minds; these first impressions account significantly for our subsequent perceptions of people. Perception is a mental *process*. It is the process that gives us the ability to make sense of the world around us through the variety of sensations that we experience, such as colours, shapes, sizes, noises, tastes and textures. Perception enables us to interpret and organise them in a manageable way. In fact the organs of sensory perception – eyes, nose, ears, mouth and skin – are our personal media, carriers of messages made up of sensations, whereas perception itself is something that takes place in the brain. Sensation alone is insuffient for perception to take place. The sensations that we experience must also have meaning before it can be said that we have perceived something; *perception = sensation + meaning.*

Selective perception

The things that we are capable of perceiving are not presented to us in a piecemeal or isolated, one-at-a-time way. There are literally millions of environmental stimuli around us all the time, and mostly they occur in patterns. As we develop from childhood, we become accustomed to them; we take them for granted, and in perceptual terms, we select from them. What we select is determined by what we *need*, *expect* and *wish* to perceive. Also, our 'built-in' value systems cause us to assess what we perceive and from this we develop preferences and prejudices. There are situations and objects that a group of people would see as similar. A group standing looking at a piece of furniture, for example, would all agree that it is a table. What they might disagree about, however, is whether or not it is a beautiful table. In the area of selective perception, therefore, we are also dealing with our values systems.

Perception in the workplace

Of all of the ways in which we are different from each other, the way we perceive people, ideas, concepts and situations is one of the most important. Our beliefs and values, goals and motives, personality characteristics and past experiences combine to determine how we perceive things. In the workplace we have perceptions of the people around us at work – working colleagues, the boss, subordinates, customers and suppliers. We have feelings and beliefs about the nature of the work we do, about the organisation we work for, its policies and goals, and indeed we have also developed perceptions of the whole idea of work, and of working for a living, and whether or not that is a good thing. An understanding of the process we call *interpersonal perception* is useful in our attempts to understand people's workplace behaviour.

Ineffective communication, for example, is often attributed to weaknesses on the part of the sender and/or the recipient. Critics of such weaknesses seldom identify insufficient understanding of interpersonal perception as the problem. Usually they attribute poor communication to lack of clarity in the message or a general lack of understanding of the mechanistic principles of communication. But no matter how well 'tuned in' people try to be when they are sending or receiving messages, there is no escape from the fact that the recipient's perception of the importance or credibility of the message is strongly influenced by his or her perception of the sender.

Perceptions of the work of others

So far, we have seen that everyone lives in his or her own perceptual world. We all have our own orders of priority and unique value systems. In the workplace, we often fail to have sufficient regard for other people's priorities and value systems. The company accountant, for example, may appear irritated, or even downright furious, when the production manager has failed to produce his monthly figures on time. To the accountant, getting the figures in on time from the various managers tops the list of priorities towards the end of the month, whereas the priorities of the production manager are quite different. Similar altercations occur, for example, in hospitals, when a business manager's priorities are different from those of the senior consultant, whose principal concerns are with his or her patients.

The influence of perception on motivation

It has been said that a manager's job is to motivate people, but technically there is no such thing as an *un*motivated person. Individuals are always motivated to do something. They are, therefore, already motivated when they come into the workplace. The question is, however, motivated to do what? Go across the office and chat to Charlie? Get on to the Internet for a while? A manager's job is to motivate people to do what he or she wishes them to do – in other words, it is to *change* their motivations. A significant proportion of the disciplinary problems that managers have with individuals are due to perceptual differences between what the organisation and the individual see as desirable and acceptable behaviour.

Perceptions of work situations

Since our thought processes are different from those of other people, our perceptions of situations are also different. Human beings are very adaptable, and when we find ourselves in a particular situation we try to adapt to it. Some psychologists believe that we simply *respond* to situations; indeed, *behaviourism* is a world-wide school of psychological thought which is based entirely upon the idea that our response to environmental stimuli accounts for all of our behaviour. This kind of psychologist is likely to recommend that we motivate our staff by setting up the kinds of work situations to which they will respond with the behaviour we desire. Behaviourism was first propounded in 1913 and the terms used in its technical vocabulary have pervaded the literature of psychology ever since. There have been many developments in the field of occupational psychology since 1913, and today psychologists tend to be eclectic in their approaches to solving problems in the workplace.

In fact, everyone reacts differently to the same situation. To some extent, the situations in which people find themselves do influence how they will respond, but the response of individuals is also determined by his or her unique interpretation of a situation. For these reasons, different people approach the same problematic situations in different ways. People *interact* with situations, rather than merely respond to them, and it should also be remembered that the person in the situation is also a part of it. If, therefore, you take an individual out of a situation and replace him or her with someone else, you have changed the situation. For example, if one person experiences the effects of stress from being in a particular job situation, it may be that the same job situation may have a different effect on someone else. A similar principle may be applied where an employee is not motivated to perform at the required standard, but would be motivated in a different job situation.

It is worth noting that an individual's perception of the job has by far the strongest influence over the degree to which that individual is motivated to work. Managers can only do so much. The job itself should be designed like a product that is screaming out to be used. By the time people are old enough to go to work, they are experienced enough to have learned that their behaviour has outcomes. Some outcomes are pleasurable and others are painful, and people usually are motivated to repeat the kinds of behaviour that produce the pleasurable outcomes. To an extent, most managers have the authority to offer marginal rewards to employees for carrying out specially delegated work, but it is up to the manager to identify the kind of reward that would appeal to particular employees.

From what is said above, it is clear that all members of staff will see the same thing in his or her own particular way. Even two people who are doing exactly similar work will have different perceptions of their jobs, and will each apportion a different level of importance to it. This will influence the level at which they are motivated to do the job, and more importantly, the nature of the incentives that are likely to increase their motivation. The truth is that most people are not doing exactly what they would like to be doing for a living and most are carrying out work that has been planned by others.

Coping vs expression

Think about your own job for a moment. How much of the content of your job was planned by someone else? For example, if your work involves you in filling out forms, who designed the forms? If you operate a machine, who determines the settings? If you use systems, who designed them? Is your job ideally the job you would be doing if you had the choice? If not, what are your needs and expectations from a job? Do you want to spend every day following someone else's blueprints? Or would you prefer something in which your own original inputs predominate? All jobs are divisible in this way. When you are following someone else's task design, you are said to be *coping*, and when you are imposing your own personal style on your work, you are said to be *expressing* yourself. Some people prefer most of their job to be coping, while others prefer largely to express themselves. The preferred *coping-expression balance* is determined by individually different psychological needs. The way in which jobs are designed produces a coping-expression balance that could be anything from say, 10 per cent to 95 per cent coping, and vice versa. Also, by their very nature, some jobs can only be carried out by people with a high preference for coping or with a high preference for expressing themselves.

Artistic professions, for example, tend to lend themselves to a high degree of expression and a moderate degree of coping. Actors *cope* with the rules of stagecraft, but they express themselves through their own personal interpretations of the roles they play. Painters cope because they all use roughly the same kinds of techniques and materials, but we can tell a Rembrandt from a Goya because the artists have stamped their personalities on their work.

Similar principles apply to many commercial and industrial occupations. Managers have to cope with the limitations imposed upon them by internal policies, budgets and other controls, but they may express themselves through the way they communicate, through their leadership styles and generally through the way in which they run the department. Workers who actually produce the products and services have to cope with work methods and procedures, but they may express themselves through their team membership behaviour and through the quality of their work.

On the other hand, the job of an employee in the inspection department of an automobile plant was to check that the door locks worked efficiently and that when the doors were closed they were flush with the apertures into which they fitted. The system for doing this was one in which two employees, one on each side of the assembly line, stood facing each other. The cars moved slowly between them which gave each one access to one of the side of the car, and as the cars passed by the men opened and closed the doors, checking the locks and door flushing as they did so. And that was it: their job was to open and close car doors all day, every day. One hundred per cent coping? Not on your life!

The plant regularly accepted parties of visitors from schools, clubs and other organisations, and hardly a day went by without at least one visit. One of the men on the car door job stood there, usually bored out of his mind, but dying for the next party of visitors to come around. When it did, he went into a little act. As the guide was explaining the job to the visitors, his act began. He showed that he could do the job blindfolded, he could do it with his back to the car – he could even tell whether or not the lock worked just by listening, which involved one of the visitors opening and closing the door. He showed the visitors several more little tricks with the doors and locks, and this, of course, was where he got his psychological kicks. He thoroughly enjoyed his job. Technically, it was almost 100 per cent coping, and it is true that his 'little act' was not an integral part of his job, but without it he would not be able to add an 'expression' component to his daily routine.

The importance of coping and expression

All individuals have their own ideas about how much coping and how much expression they need in their jobs. The preference for a particular balance is a relative thing. While on occasions some people may say that they wish they had a job that 'challenges' them, or one through which they can express themselves more, they seldom do anything about it. Those who are unhappy with what they do for a living tend to put up with it anyway – they need the income and other benefits and often are too afraid to risk moving into a new position. On the other hand, some people feel ill-equipped to meet the challenges of their jobs. They are in positions that stretch them too far, and suffer from the effects of stress as a result. They long for jobs with less responsibility, jobs that do not require too much personalised input.

In Chapter 5, we saw the differences between 'content' and 'process' theories of motivation. In Maslow's terms, we know that one person's 'lower order and higher order needs' will be different from those of another person, who may be doing exactly the same kind of job (Maslow, 1987). From Vroom's framework, we saw that individual's 'expectancies' will also vary from one to another (Vroom,1964). This is simply because different people see the same things in different ways.

Attitudes

An understanding of attitudes is extremely important to the manager's understanding of workplace behaviour. Employees' attitudes will determine how they will behave, and managers need therefore to understand how they are formed and the various techniques that are available for measuring and, where necessary, changing them. An attitude is a mental predisposition to behave consistently towards a person, object, concept or situation. One's attitudes are the cumulative product of the learning one has assimilated through the experiences of socialisation and personality development.

The characteristics that determine our perceptions also determine our attitudes towards people, objects, concepts and situations. Attitudes, therefore, are determined by our values and perceptions, which give us feelings and beliefs about things which, in turn, influence our behaviour towards and around them. The target of our attitude – the person, object, concept or situation – we call the 'attitude object'. Since attitudes influence behaviour, it is important for managers to understand the attitudes that are held by their staff. We saw in the previous chapter that there are negative attitudes that can result in undesirable behaviour towards, say, women or members of minority groups.

Measuring attitudes

We should never leap to conclusions about employees' attitudes when we observe particular characteristics of their behaviour. Attitudes vary from one individual to the next and their behaviour when they are in groups, perhaps with their work colleagues, is quite different from their behaviour when they are alone. Observing behaviour can signify something about an individual's attitudes and if the attitude that is indicated could be the basis for undesirable behaviour, perhaps towards others, then the manager may feel disposed to organise a formal and more objective attitude survey. Since we are dealing with human beings, the results of surveys are never totally accurate and reliable. However, on the grounds that information obtained through a survey is better then guesswork and certainly better than no information, it is a good idea to monitor employees' attitudes through the use of formal surveying techniques.

The semantic differential scale

There are several techniques for measuring attitudes and one sometimes finds the semantic differential scale, which is often used for market surveys. The semantic differential, despite its name, is quite a simple scale; Figure 7.1 is an example.

People are asked to respond by circling the number over the phrase that most accurately reflects their feelings about the statement above the grid. The implication here is that the difference between the meanings in the phrases reflects the numerical difference between the numbers, which in this case is 1.

Central heating is bad for one's health

− 3	− 2	− 1	0	+ 1	+ 2	+ 3
Strongly disagree	Disagree	Mildly disagree	Don't know	Mildly agree	Agree	Strongly agree

Figure 7.1 A semantic differential scale.

The Thurstone scale

One of the most frequently used techniques is the Thurstone scale. Thurstone (1933) thought that the semantic difference between a number of phrases was unlikely to be precisely the same as the numerical difference between the related weightings. In order to produce a more accurate reflection of attitudes, a set of phrases was needed that could be modified until they were as accurate as possible. The process through which he achieved this was very complex and time-consuming. For objectivity as well as accuracy, he recruited around 50 'judges' to assess each of 11 statements and the semantic difference between them. He used 11 statements, which the judges graded progressively from negative to positive. Each judge tried to achieve an even semantic distance between the statements by modifying them. Where the semantic difference between the statements was not thought to be exactly equal to the difference between the related numbers, he changed the numbers, again with the assistance of the judges (see Figure 7.2).

When the questionnaire is distributed, the column containing the numerical values is omitted. The values appear only on the master copy which is retained by the surveyor. Respondents are asked to tick every statement with which they agree. The survey form should be designed to preserve the anonymity of the respondent.

To measure the attitude demonstrated, an average is calculated simply by totalling the numerical values of each ticked statement and dividing by the number of ticks. For example, if a respondent had ticked statements 4, 5 and 6, the numerical value of the respondent's attitude would be 7.3, which would have been calculated thus:

$$\frac{8.2 + 7.4 + 6.3}{3} = 7.3$$

Value	Statement	Tick
11	1. The HR department provides an excellent service	
10.8	2. All in all, HR provides a very good service	
9.9	3. Mostly, the HR department provides a good service	
8.2	4. Most of the time HR service is good	✓
7.4	5. The HR service is fairly good	✓
6.3	6. HR here is probably as good as any other	✓
5.1	7. The HR people seem to be in need of a little training	
4.6	8. The HR department has room for improvement	
3.2	9. The HR department' service is pretty poor	
1.7	10. The HR department is disorganised and ineffective	
1	11. The HR department is hopelessly inefficient and ineffective	
	Total score	

Figure 7.2 Example of a Thurstone scale.

To measure the average attitude of a group of people a similar formula is used. All of their individual averages are totalled and divided by the number of people in the group. Attitudes may range from 'low negative' through medium to 'high positive', thus:

1.0 to 3.75 = low negative
3.75 to 5.5 = high negative
5.5 to 8.25 = low positive
8.25 to 11.0 = high positive

Response bias

Sometimes the subject of an attitude survey is a delicate and sensitive matter. Surveying attitudes towards, say, women at work or immigrant workers can be misleading to the surveyor. There is legislation and social change that does not always allow genuine attitudes to surface. People are aware of the expressed, and tacit, rules of political correctness and their responses to statements on a questionnaire are not always an accurate reflection of their true beliefs. Even when the surveys are anonymous, individual respondents still raise a barrier between their true beliefs and the kind of answer that they think would be appropriate. It is only when we compare employees' actual workplace behaviour towards members of minority groups with their responses on the questionnaire that we can observe a discrepancy. Another form of response bias occurs when the respondent abandons any intention to respond truthfully. Instead, they provide an answer that they think the surveyor wishes to see. Sometimes this is done with the best of intentions, for example by respondents who wish to 'help science' or to help the surveyor to achieve a 'good result'.

The intrusion of response bias into a questionnaire is unavoidable, but it is possible for a well trained and experienced practitioner to detect it. When the issue is important to the organisation, it is advisable to commission a consultant who is an expert in this field to carry out the survey. An important additional advantage of using a consultant is that his or her analysis of the results will not be affected by prior knowledge of the respondents.

Changing attitudes

It is said that if we know where we are going, then we are more likely to get there, but it is equally important to know where we are starting from. Measuring attitudes in the workplace gives us that starting point when we wish to change attitudes. Using the Thurstone scale tells us not only whether attitudes are positive or negative, but the degree to which they are one or the other. But changing attitudes can be a complex business.

When we are making changes, we have to be clear about precisely what it is that we wish to change. If, for example, measurements indicate that the workforce's attitude towards the organisation's equal opportunities policy is negative, then we have two choices. First, we can leave the policy as it is and try to change people's attitudes towards it, or secondly, we can change the equal opportunities policy by turning it into one towards which the workforce attitude would be positive. By taking the first choice, we will have tried to change the people's attitudes, but by taking the second choice, we will have changed the equal opportunities policy, while the workforce attitude remains unchanged, since the attitude towards the old policy will be the same as it was beforehand; we will not have changed the attitude, but we will have changed the attitude object.

It may be that there are very good reasons why the employees have a negative attitude towards the equal opportunities policy, and after re-examining it managers may identify areas for improvement, in which case it would be right to change it. On the other hand, there are strategies, policies, procedures, benefits and services that are designed by the organisation which it would be unwise to change, even though employees may have a negative attitude towards them. If, as an example, we consider an organisation's HR strategy in which, in the light of fierce global competition, it has been decided that a lean and flattened structure with a smaller but multiskilled workforce would enable the organisation to compete more effectively and stay alive, then clearly the strategy has to stay. But it is also clear that the reorganisation that would be necessary to achieve this would involve a redundancy programme, and obviously the employees' attitude towards that would be negative. In such a case, the organisation would need to retain the strategy and attempt to change the employees' attitude towards it. Otherwise, the organisation may not survive, and everyone would lose their jobs. While it can be difficult to change people's attitudes, it is possible to do so through the use of persuasive information and group exercises.

In many industries and professions the need to change people's attitudes is an essential ingredient to success. Advertisers do it when they are wooing prospective purchasers; politicians do it when they are canvassing for votes, or addressing a particular parliamentary Bill; animal rights activists, environmentalists and anti-abortion groups do it when they are stating the underlying purposes of their cases.

Persuasive information

All of these groups and individuals are trying to change people's attitudes through the use of persuasive information. In industry we try to reduce accident rates by changing employees' attitudes towards health and safety at work. We post notices in strategic positions in the workplace, warning of the possible consequences of carelessness, daydreaming on the job, failing to report faults and other dangers, such as oil patches on the floor, and so forth.

As we know, attitudes are influenced by people's experiences and their perceptions, feelings and beliefs about things, and of course attitudes determine behaviour. People's attitudes towards things will change if they receive sufficient information, information that is impressive and sound in the arguments it uses to foster a change.

Training for change

We may change attitudes when we expose people to training, coaching and counselling, especially when the training is directly related to the attitude object. A one- or two-day training course on health and safety issues can have a significant effect upon people's attitudes. Such a course would have to be directed by an expert who is not only well versed in health and safety, but is also skilled in transferring his or her knowledge, skills and attitudes to the trainees. The course director would also have to have credibility in the eyes of the trainees, since without that nothing will change. Coaching and counselling techniques would be useful when it has been observed that a particular individual's behaviour is threatening the health and safety of employees, including him or herself.

Group exercises

These need to be carefully handled and specially designed to suit the purpose. For an example, we can return to the organisation's strategy for change, involving a lean, flat organisation with a slimmer but multiskilled workforce. One approach to changing attitudes towards the strategy would be to involve employees in it from the outset, in a way that would provide them with a sense of ownership of the project. This can be achieved by presenting the problem to groups of employees and asking them to work towards a solution. Most employees would agree to become involved in such an exercise, although the most extreme and vociferous opponents may not.

Managerial attitudes

The most important attitude that managers have is their attitude towards their staff. Such attitudes vary from one manager to another, since the managers themselves are unique individuals, each with his or her own individually different perception of the ideal 'manager–employee' relationship. According to Douglas McGregor (1960) some managers, whom he referred to as 'Theory X' managers, regard employees as indolent, workshy and in constant need of prodding and supervision, while others, whom he referred to as 'Theory Y' managers, see employees as self-starters to whom work comes easily and is as natural as rest or play. Whichever of these two attitudes a manager possesses will determine how he or she treats the employees. It is clear, however, that the manager's attitude towards his or her own job, in terms of the responsibilities it entails, will also influence his or her treatment of employees. Blake and Mouton (1964) developed the well-known managerial grid which they designed to situate managers' attitudes on a dimension ranging from those who are primarily interested in achieving high productivity, to those who are primarily interested in caring for their staff (see Figure 7.3).

Research using the grid usually pitches most managers at or near the 5:5 – 'middle of the road' mark, and it is said that they should be striving diagonally upwards towards the 9:9 'team management' mark. Accompanying the grid is a questionnaire containing 36 statements to which the manager is asked to respond on a five-point semantic differential scale, ranging from 'strongly disagree' through to 'strongly

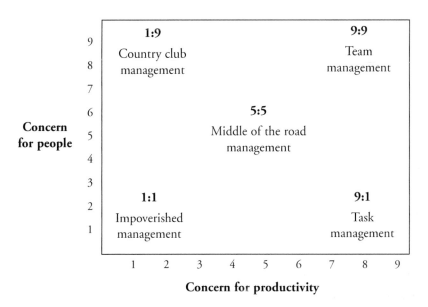

Figure 7.3 The managerial grid (Blake and Mouton, 1964).

agree', and his or her position on the grid is determined by the nature of the responses.

The attitudes of old-fashioned managers cause them to see themselves as members of a kind of privileged and elite squad at the top end of the organisation, remote from the staff and entirely disinterested in the nature of the work and how employees are treated. Middle managers are supposed to be the media through which the strategies and policies that have been drawn up at the top of the organisation are implemented internally, yet few old-style senior managers are aware of how their middle managers treat their staff. It is true, and gratifying, that such managers are a dying breed, and it is doubtful if they would ever have learned that 'management' is not something you *are*, it is something you *do*. While it is true that management is important, it is a process, one of the many that keep the organisation's wheels turning. Modern managers try to get to know their staff as well as they can, certainly to the point where they can predict their behaviour in workplace situations with a reasonable degree of accuracy. They understand that they are leading the people who are directly involved in producing the product or service upon which the organisation depends for its survival and further development.

In well managed organisations, there is a sound business purpose underlying the style with which employees are led. In a supermarket, for example, the managers are acutely aware that the shop workers who replenish the shelves, serve behind the counters and operate the checkout stations are customer-facing employees. They are there to ensure that the customers are treated with respect and courtesy and that the customers get what they want. Even though such staff are a way downstream from the senior managers, they are the employees who guide customers to the products they are looking for, and who are not incidentally responsible for collecting every penny that the organisation takes.

In this situation, the place is organised and managed so that the customer-facing employees are themselves well served with everything they need to do their jobs efficiently and effectively. These are the staff who impress the customer with the services they provide, which in turn fosters customer loyalty. In fact, they are the most important staff in the entire organisation and many managers see their own role as one of attending to their staff's workplace needs. In this situation, managers who bully their staff into doing what is required, or adopt an 'ivory tower' attitude of superior indifference to them (which far too many do), will inculcate the wrong kind of staff attitude altogether. It is an attitude that customers are also quick to observe, and as a result may decide never to shop there again. In addition to the humane side of treating staff as individuals, and with respect and dignity, there is a sound business case for it too, since staff will treat the customers in the way that they themselves are treated.

The manager's attitude towards employees will be communicated through his or her managerial style, manner of communicating and actual treatment. Where the manager's attitude is positive and encouraging, employees feel that they and their work are important, and they will be motivated to perform accordingly. Employees who work with such managers are less likely to experience the effects of stress and more likely to feel appreciated and understood. Relationships such as this will become part of the culture of the workplace and this will be communicated to the customers who will enjoy dealing with the organisation.

Implications for well-being

There is a wealth of evidence to support the view that employees will respond positively to organisations that show an interest in their well-being. When attitude surveys are carried out on stress, the pension scheme, the staff restaurant and in fact on any benefit or provision that affects the well-being of the employee, just the very fact that it is being done is an indication that the organisation cares about its staff. Many managers harbour fears of 'going too far' when it comes to caring for employees, but they should reconsider. After all, can one 'go too far' when one is actively showing an interest in the most important resource in the organisation? Go too far along a non-caring line and the organisation will suffer as a result, through reduced performance and lost productivity.

This is not to say that we should mollycoddle employees by rushing to attend to their every need or wish. We should, however, without being over-indulgent, develop relationships of mutual trust and respect. In this way, employees will feel genuinely valued and feel that their work is appreciated and worthwhile. After all, employees are not stupid – they understand that the needs of the business must come first. Involving people in this way encourages them to take up training opportunities to improve their performance and generally to become involved in what is going on in the place.

While some managers possess a healthy degree of natural ability in building up this kind of goodwill, others seriously lack sensitivity. It should borne in mind that goodwill, mutual respect and trust between managers and employees may take a long time to establish, but can be destroyed irrevocably in a matter of seconds. When, for example, senior managers in a UK organisation concurrently announced an 11 per cent salary increase for themselves, and a 3 per cent increase for the staff, they were telling the employees, via the announcement, that they had scant regard for them, or for the value of their work. Also in the UK, just before Christmas 2000, at the very height of what is regarded as the 'season of goodwill', a car plant announced that a massive redundancy programme would be 'actioned next year' because the plant was to close down; certainly this was an announcement that could have waited a month. Obviously, the employees, not knowing who were to be transferred to other plants and who were to leave, had an unnecessarily miserable and anxious Christmas.

Conclusion

All individuals live at the centre of their own perceptual world. When others recognise them as individuals, it enhances their self-esteem and makes them feel special. If a relationship of mutual respect and trust is to develop, managers need to be able to relate to employees as individuals.

All normal individuals have been born into a particular society with its own cultural norms, values and beliefs, and people learn to conform and behave in ways that they think will meet with the approval of their peers and elders. The families within which people are raised have their own sets of values, beliefs and allegiances to political ideas and religious denominations, and these are handed down to the children.

The differences between individuals have a profound effect upon the manager's ability to manage, and individual differences are now more complex than they have ever been. The workplace is a microcosm of the society in which it is set, which today is made up of a mixture of people from many different parts of the world. Many new immigrants have been socialised into cultures with which members of the indigenous population are unfamiliar, which leads to a lack of understanding of the social norms, attitudes and behaviour of new employees from overseas. Most immigrants come to a Western style of developed country in search of a new life, or to escape from an uncomfortable or threatening regime. They have to learn new norms, adopt new values and beliefs, and so forth. In other words, they have to go through the socialisation process again, at the same time as setting up home, acquiring an understanding of the culture of their new workplace and generally handling all aspects of starting a new life, which sometimes also means learning a new language. The last thing they need is to encounter people at work who have a prejudiced attitude.

In the twenty-first century, there is an increasing need for managers to get to know their staff on an individual level, so that they can communicate with them more comfortably and establish a meaningful relationship of mutual respect and trust.

References

Blake, R.R. and Mouton, J.S. (1964) *The Managerial Grid*. Houston, TX: Gulf.

McGregor, D. (1960) *The Human Side of Enterprise*. New York: McGraw-Hill.

Maslow, A.H. (1987) 'A theory of growth motivation', in A.H. Maslow, *Motivation and Personality*. New York: Harper & Row.

Thurstone, L.L. and Chave, E.J. (1933) *The Measurement of Attitudes*. Chicago: University of Chicago Press.

Vroom, V.H. (1970) *Management and Motivation*. Harmondsworth: Penguin.

CHAPTER 8

Legal aspects of employee well-being

Introduction

This chapter explains the legal concepts and legislative measures that are concerned with the well-being of individuals in the workplace. While there are variations in legislative measures between one country and another, in general the types, patterns and provisions of such legislation have been drafted with very similar objectives in mind. Here, examples of differences in specific legislative provisions in particular countries are given when making comparisons. Otherwise, the chapter addresses the law in general and discusses the overall objectives, although managers are advised to apprise themselves of the law in their own states, and may find it interesting to observe the similarities and differences in other states.

On the same note, it is surprising how many managers assume that particular issues are covered by legislation in their own states, when in fact they are not. Two examples of this are discrimination on the grounds of age or religion, which are not by any means widely proscribed. The USA and New Zealand are examples of where discrimination on grounds of age is illegal, but the UK and Europe are yet to include this. In the UK, 'Age Positive' is a government initiative designed to challenge and eliminate age discrimination in the workplace. The initiative is supported by the professional institutions, including the Chartered Institute of Personnel and Development (CIPD), whose members are employed in the HR field. The UK government, having signed the European Directive on Equal Treatment in October 2000, has committed itself to introducing age legislation by 2006, although many large European organisations have already developed and implemented relevant policies.

The chapter also discusses the issue of litigation in which employees take legal action against their employers because their well-being has been adversely affected by the way they have been treated in the organisation. Examples are included to illustrate how the circumstances that lead to such litigation can affect the well-being of the individual, and the health of the organisation in terms of cost, efficiency, effectiveness and reputation as an employer.

The circumstances and situations that potentially may affect employees' well-being are wide and varied. Here, we deal generally with the law that covers well-being, which includes health and safety at work legislation, and specifically with the law on equal opportunities and discrimination.

Finally, we explore internal legislation in which we examine the policies and procedures that are formulated by organisations to ensure that, on the one hand, the organisation has a formal means of regulating and controlling behaviour, while on the other, the individual employees have access to a system of justice, without necessarily having to seek redress externally.

Legal aspects

In law, the organisation has a legal responsibility for the well-being of their employees while they are carrying out the business of the organisation; this includes their mental as well as their physical well-being. For practical reasons, organisations delegate this responsibility to their managers. There is a considerable amount of legislation to cover these aspects of management, and there have been cases, the specific implications of which have led to judgements that have created precedents which can be referred to in future cases. Also, organisations should be aware that while inappropriate actions and/or omissions may expose them to the possibility of litigation on the part of employees or ex-employees, the same actions and/or omissions may also make them vulnerable to prosecution by authorities that have been deputed by government to enforce legislative provisions.

Sex and marital status

Unlawful discrimination on the grounds of sex or marital status is defined under two main headings: *direct* and *indirect*.

Direct sex discrimination

This occurs when a person is treated, on the grounds of their sex, less favourably than a person of the opposite sex is, or would be, in similar circumstances. This may involve treating a woman less favourably because she is a woman. An example of this might be related to recruitment in which a woman has applied for the kind of job that is traditionally male dominated, such as plumbing or welding; her application is not treated seriously and she is turned down because she is a woman, whereas the selection decision should be made on the basis of an applicant's qualifications for and capability to do the job, and should not be related to their sex.

Indirect sex discrimination

This occurs when a requirement is attributed equally to men and women, but the requirement is loaded in favour of one sex or the other, so that either most men or most women would be placed at a disadvantage because they find it harder to meet because of their sex. For example, the UK Civil Service was adjudged to have indirectly discriminated against women when they imposed an age bar of 28 on promotion to executive officer grade. The judgement was given on the grounds that at this age most women would not be likely to be ready for promotion, since they would be raising a family.

Direct discrimination

On the grounds of marriage this occurs when a person, because for example of his or her married status, is treated less favourably than an unmarried person, or would be treated in a similar situation. An example of this might be where an employer shelves a person's promotion on the grounds that his or her marriage and home obligations could take precedence over those related to the higher position, such as staying back late to complete a task.

Indirect discrimination – marital status

The criteria for this are similar to those for indirect sex discrimination so that, for example, the requirement is loaded against married people, thus placing them at a disadvantage. In a matter of promotion, for example, in which requirements for the higher position are to work longer hours and/or spend time away from home, single rather than married people would be much more likely to be able to meet this requirement. This kind of 'loading' is unlawful where it can be shown that the requirements, such as those mentioned above, are not essential for the job to be carried out efficiently and effectively.

Indirect discrimination on the grounds of marital status can be very difficult to detect. It is not so overtly perceptible as other forms of discrimination and evidence of it is usually particularly hard to find and present.

Related legislation

The objectives of UK legislation that is concerned with employee well-being are similar to those in most Western industrialised nations, and here the initial legislation on sex discrimination was the Equal Pay Act, which although enacted in 1970, did not come into full effect until 1975. This Act was subsequently amended by several sets of statutory regulations and instruments in 1983 and 1984. Broadly, the purpose of this Act is to require that a woman's pay should be equal to that of a man. The Sex Discrimination Act 1975 came into effect at the same time as the Equal Pay Act, and the purpose here was to provide for equality for both sexes and also to outlaw discrimination on the grounds of an individual's marital status. These Acts have been followed by:

- the Equal Pay (Amendment) Regulations 1973;

- the Employment Protection Act 1975;

- the Employment Protection (Consolidation) Act 1978;

- the Employment Act 1989;

- the Social Security Act 1989;

- the Trade Union and Employment Rights Act 1993.

Further legislation has since been enacted as a result of European directives, such as the Human Rights Act 1999. It is assumed by many that legislation of this type is aimed at women, who were regarded, with considerable justification, as major targets for discrimination. In fact, while the original objective of the legislation is to outlaw discrimination against women, much of it proscribes discrimination against any person, regardless of their sex. There have been successful discrimination actions brought by men, but the number of these, compared with similar actions brought by women, are few.

The Equal Pay Act 1970 and the Equal Pay (Amendment) Regulations 1983 delineate circumstances in which equality is demanded:

1. *like work*, where a man and a woman are doing work of the same nature;

2. *equivalent work*, in which pay must be equal when jobs that are being carried out by men and women are equally rated, for example, under a job evaluation scheme.

3. *work of equal value*, in which a woman can show that the value of her work is equal to that being performed by a man. The most well-known European example of this was when a woman working in Camel Laird's shipyard on Merseyside in the UK claimed that her work as a cook was equal in value to that of a craftsman, such as a painter or joiner. For work of equal value to be established, the claimant has to show that the demands of the job in terms of skills, effort and decision-making make it equal in value to the organisation as those of a higher paid job. To claim under this regulation, the work need not be similar, and there does not have to be a job evaluation scheme.

In relation to the third circumstance, work of equal value, the claimant must be (a) employed by the same employer; (b) employed by the same employer in an installation that is covered by the same terms and conditions; and (c) be able to show that the alleged 'equal value' job is occupied by a person of a different sex. An employer, however, may successfully defend the decision to pay less to one person than to another and may counter the claim by showing that the pay should remain different on the grounds of a 'genuinely material factor' (GMF). The higher paid person is receiving more, not on the grounds of being male, but because he has earned incremental increases through long service, and/or that he is more highly skilled and qualified and, therefore, more productive than the lower paid person.

Sex discrimination

While the Sex Discrimination Act 1975 provides for the equal treatment of men and women in many areas of life, for example applying for a home loan or bank overdraft, we are principally concerned with the way in which it regulates the provision of equal treatment in employing organisations. The main areas in which failures to provide equal opportunities to men and women are most frequently found are:

- recruitment and selection;

- promotion;

- training opportunities.

Recruitment and selection

This area of the legislation covers discrimination on the basis of sex or marital status in relation to employees and potential employees. It is sometimes convenient, for purposes of explanation, to regard recruitment and selection as two separate processes, in which recruitment begins when a vacancy appears in the organisation and ends when all of the applications have been received, while selection begins with screening the applications and compiling a list of those who have been selected to be interviewed for the position and ends when the vacancy has been filled.

The potential for discrimination arises when a job requisition is being written. This document is based upon an analysis of the demands of the vacant position and lists the knowledge, skills, qualifications, experience and any other personal qualities that are needed to meet the demands of the job. The same job analysis provides the information upon which a job description and person specification are produced, the main features of which appear in the recruitment advertisement.

Early in this chapter we defined *indirect* discrimination, and from the definition it can be seen that those who write the documents referred to above may, accidentally or deliberately, include requirements that do not apply equally to potential applicants of both sexes, and/or equally to people regardless of marital status, when in fact the requirements are not essential to the job. A recruitment advertisement that contains such requirements indirectly discriminates against one sex or the other, or one status or the other, and therefore would be regarded as illegal.

On the question of *direct* discrimination, this could happen if, for example, an advertisement asks for a 'Girl Friday' when the job could equally be done by a man. Today, however, this kind of 'howler' is extremely rare, since advertisers, agents and the media are keenly aware of the rules governing such announcements. Direct discrimination is much more likely to occur when candidates are being interviewed or undergoing a selection test. Examples of this would be where the structure of the interview and the types of questions asked were different for a female candidate from those for male candidates, or if interpretations of test results are influenced by the fact that she is a woman. Either way, both of these examples would be regarded as direct discrimination.

Promotion

Examples of direct and indirect discrimination in respect of promotion opportunities would be very similar to those given for recruitment and selection, since the process is similar for both; that is to say, interviewers are looking for the best person for the job and trying to predict in-job performance. There is one exception to this, however, which is where the culture of the organisation is such that few women are applying for senior positions on the grounds that they feel they would be wasting their time. Women have not been told directly that they are not regarded as 'management material', but it is clear from managerial attitudes that this is the case. The UK Civil Service case, described above, is a good example of indirectly discriminating on grounds of sex.

Training opportunities

The most frequently found form of direct discrimination where training is the issue occurs where women are treated less favourably because they are not considered for management training courses, or for courses that are designed to develop people in certain forms of specialism. Direct discrimination also occurs when the organisation has failed to think things through properly when establishing criteria for training. For example, there are organisations in which bypassing women for training occurs regularly, and has become a 'taken-for-granted' habit. The culture is such that selecting women for training simply does not enter people's heads. Often it takes a formal complaint to a tribunal to shake things up and force the organisation into correct practice.

Benefits and services

Where organisations provide benefits, such as a pension scheme, a house purchase scheme with a 'below market' rate of interest, a private health scheme, or services such as an employee assistance programme or even carparking facilities, access should be made equally available to men and women.

Dismissal

When organisations are selecting people for redundancy, it is illegal to load the redundancy programme in favour of one sex or the other. Women experience unfair treatment when such selections are being made. When the organisation's objective is to reduce the number of staff women find themselves further up the list than men. It is thought that this is the result of that 'taken-for-granted' attitude again, in which it is assumed that the need of men, the bread winners, to remain in employment is greater than that of women.

Racial discrimination

In the UK, under the Race Relations Act 1976, it is illegal to discriminate against people on the grounds of their race, although it is perfectly possible to discriminate against someone on the grounds of their sex who also happens to be a member of a minority group. An example of this would be if an Asian woman was not considered for management training (see paragraph on training opportunities above). If this were to happen, it would be discrimination on grounds of the sex of the person if the others selected for training were men, but on racial grounds if the others selected for training were made up of roughly equal numbers of white men and women.

Definitions of *direct* and *indirect* discrimination on racial grounds are very similar to those that have been defined for sex discrimination.

In this context, the word 'race' means colour, race or nationality, ethnic origin or national origin. The legislative demands in respect of racial discrimination are very similar to those for sex discrimination, and normally it is found that the less favourable or unfair treatment has occurred in respect of the same kinds of issue: recruitment, selection, promotion, training opportunities, benefits and services, and dismissal.

An example of direct discrimination on the grounds of race, therefore, would be to select an indigenous, white person for a job or for promotion when it is clear that, say, a West Indian applicant possessed superior qualities that were directly related to the job. Indirect racial discrimination occurs when, for example, a condition or qualification that is not an essential qualification for the job is demanded. Asking for a good standard of writing and speaking in English for a job digging holes on a building site, for example, is an obvious example of indirect racial discrimination, since the ability to do the job would be unaffected by one's command of English, and applicants who were minority group members, who had not been in the country for long, would be placed at an unfair disadvantage.

Disability discrimination

In the UK, the initial legislative attempts to provide disabled people with protection from discrimination were the Disabled Persons (Employment) Acts 1944 and 1958. The protection provided by these Acts was generally regarded as inadequate, and those representing disabled people actively campaigned for improved legislation. The main objectives of the 1944 and 1958 Acts were to assess, rehabilitate and train or retrain disabled people, and to develop a register of disabled people. Also under these Acts, certain jobs were reserved for disabled people only, and the Acts further provided that employers with more than 20 employees were required to sustain a quota of people with disabilities comprising 3 per cent of the workforce. Employers did not make special efforts to meet their obligations under these Acts, and most employers either disregarded them or were unaware of them as a legal requirement. Certainly, the number of prosecutions related to these Acts hardly crept into double figures.

The Disability Discrimination Act 1995, which came into force towards the end of 1996, provides the most comprehensive protection that disabled people have ever had in the UK. This Act established two independent statutory councils, the National Disability Council (for England, Wales and Scotland) and the Northern Ireland Disability Council. The purpose of these councils is to advise government about disability matters and the implementation of the Act. They also draft the relevant Code of Practice.

Disability is defined as: *a physical or mental impairment which has a substantial and long-term adverse effect on a person's ability to carry out normal day-to-day activities, and includes progressive conditions such as cancer and AIDS. People who have a disability and people who have had a disability but no longer have one are covered by the Act.*

The 1995 Act contains two main provisions, which apply to employers with more than 15 employees:

1. That it is unlawful to discriminate against potential or current employees with a disability because of their disability, unless the discriminatory action can be justified.

2. That employers must make reasonable changes to the workplace and to the employment arrangements so that a disabled person is not substantially disadvantaged. 'Reasonable change' includes making changes to premises, equipment, providing additional training, and making changes to working hours and the nature of supervision. Reasonable changes may also include the processes of recruitment and selection, the design of documents (large print, etc.), and a willingness to accept an application on tape or other suitable medium, depending upon the nature of the candidate's

disability. The intention here is to make it possible for a disabled candidate to make an application. Often, disabled people have a fax and/or a specially designed computer at home, and there is no reason why a prospective employer should not accept a faxed *curriculum vitae* or an e-mailed letter of application.

It is worth mentioning at this stage that for people with certain types of disability, telecommuting is a particularly attractive work mode.

The European situation

One of the main problems facing the European Union (EU) is to achieve a greater degree of uniformity in terms of the philosophies underlying particular strategies and policies. The principle of equality for both sexes has been on the agenda since the Treaty of Rome in 1957, but as the EU (as it is now) has developed over the years, member states have independently developed their own social policies and legislative measures. Despite what is said above about industrialised countries' legislation having similar objectives, one of the results of their taking independent legislative action is that certain legal definitions, such as that of 'disability', and concepts, such as that of 'equal opportunities', vary from one EU country to the next. And through all of that development little was said about discrimination against the disabled until very recently.

The formulation of the European Employment Strategy, which arose from the Amsterdam Treaty 1997, includes 'equal opportunities' as one of its four main responses to high levels of unemployment among ethnic minorities and women, including several other groups. Under the banner of *equal opportunities*, the perceived problems were (a) the development of conditions in which men and women have equal opportunities in their family and working lives … and (b) high female employment. In fact, in the UK there already is 'high female employment', which has been around 44 per cent of the total workforce since 1995. This appears to be good news in terms of the thrust towards achieving equal opportunities, but the figure is due in part to a slight decrease in the employment of men, and an increase in the number of part-time jobs, the majority of which are occupied by women. Nevertheless, it is safe to say that in some part it is due to the success of the equal opportunities campaign.

Exhibit 8.1

The fact that 44 per cent of the workforce is female may be a laudable achievement in terms of equality of opportunity, but the fact that it is partly due to the predominance of women in lower-order part-time jobs is in itself a comment on the continuing attitude of 'secondariness' for women, which also includes a significant proportion of female attitudes. It is thought that this male–female balance has come about because women regard part-time work as more convenient for them, since it allows them to carry out their home responsibilities of raising the children, shopping, cooking, cleaning and so forth, which can hardly be regarded an 'equality in their family…lives', in the way that the Europeans think it should. It is interesting that in the majority of cases, the idea of the woman taking *part-time* employment, as opposed to full-time, was her own.

European and American approaches

The grounds upon which legislation is drafted vary from one country to another. In the UK, the original legislation (1974) sought to enforce the provision of equal opportunities for all members of society regardless of their sex or race. Increasingly, however, this kind of UK legislation is the result of European directives that have to be enacted in the 15 member countries of the European Union, where the bases are 'equal treatment', 'fairness at work' and 'family friendliness'. Much of the legislation is directed at non-work areas, as well as the area of employment.

In the USA, equality is a civil right, and was first drafted in respect of racial equality:

> I have a dream that one day this nation will rise up, live out the true meaning of its creed; we hold these truths to be self evident, that all men are created equal.

Martin Luther King: Washington, 27 August 1963.

This quote provides a demonstration of the true depths of feeling that people have about equality, and the lengths to which they will go in order to achieve it. Martin Luther King saw the leadership of this powerful civil rights campaign as his vocation, and he did have a significant impact on the shape of US civil rights legislation. Ironically, in 1963, it was perfectly legitimate for him to say, '... all *men* are created equal'!

Subsequently, emphasis was also placed upon equality for women. Organisations are required to meet targets and submit statistics showing the workforce profile in respect of the ethnic make-up and the male–female balance. If the statistics are off target, organisations may redress the balance by deliberately recruiting females, rather than males, and it is perfectly legitimate for them to do this because the underlying purpose of the manouevre is a legal requirement. In the UK and Europe, this would be regarded as positive or 'reverse' discrimination, which is unlawful.

Exemptions

As we have seen, not all discriminatory actions and decisions are unlawful. There are situations in which it would be lawful to discriminate against a particular individual because of his or her sex, age, race, ethnic origin or religion and so forth. In a recruitment and selection process in the UK, for example, the sex of the person might be an essential qualification for the job, which is referred to as a 'genuine occupational qualification' (GOQ). The objectives here are to maintain common decency, such as when recruiting for a toilet attendant who, by the very nature of the job, has to be of one particular sex or another.

GOQs also apply to race. For example, racial discrimination was regarded as lawful when an Englishman complained to a tribunal about a Chinese restaurant proprietor who had advertised for a waiter, stating that applicants should be of Chinese origin and appearance. The tribunal found for the restaurant owner on the grounds that when customers dine at a Chinese restaurant, it is reasonable for them to expect to be served by Chinese waiters, or at least waiters who appear to be Chinese. It was adjudged that if they were served by waiters who were not Chinese, or did not appear to be Chinese, the restaurant would lose its authenticity as a Chinese place with a Chinese atmosphere. Similarly, if the proprietor of a journal that was read by people of a particular religion were to advertise for an editor, it would be reasonable to aim the advertisement specifically at candidates who were of the same religion.

Litigation

This has been widespread in the USA, Canada and Australia for many years, and while employees in other countries have been slow to seek legal advice, the number of cases is growing rapidly in most of the industrialised world. Increasingly, employees who feel that they have been adversely affected, most often experiencing the effects of stress caused by unfair treatment at work, are now turning to the law in search of compensation. It should be pointed out that most of the actions taken against employers – or ex-employers – are settled out of court, and litigants are usually asked to sign an agreement that prohibits them from disclosing important details, such as the amount of compensation paid, to parties who were not involved in the proceedings. For these reasons, it is difficult to identify how many cases are under preparation at any one time, but from those that do reach the courts, it is clear that the number of such actions is burgeoning.

The employee's choice

In the UK, there are employment tribunals which typically hear complaints of unfair dismissal, unfair selection for redundancy, failure to provide an equal opportunity on the grounds of sex or race and other similar complaints. Access to an employment tribunal is free of charge and the proceedings are less formal than those of the courts. The complaint is heard by a panel of three, including a chairman or chairwoman who is a solicitor, and two other members who are usually experienced in management and staff representation respectively. Where the grounds for the complaint have led to the complainant leaving the organisation, his or her complaint to an employment tribunal must be made within three months of the leaving date. The average time taken, from the initial complaint being made to the date of the tribunal, is about six months. Employment tribunals are limited in respect of the kinds of complaint they may hear and the amounts of compensatory awards they are allowed to make.

As an alternative, employees may take action through the civil courts, but when they do, they normally need to engage the services of a solicitor who may, depending on the severity, complexity, or the specialised nature of the action, brief counsel, all of which are cost factors for which the litigant is responsible.

If, however, judgement is found in the litigant's favour, costs will normally be paid by the defendants. The idea of a law practice, such as a firm of solicitors, offering client services on a 'no win – no fee' basis is a relatively recent innovation in the UK, and undoubtedly is one of the factors that has encouraged people to take a legal action which they may not have risked if the charges were to be applied irrespective of the outcome.

Taking legal action through the courts may involve years of preparation and further time waiting for acceptance on to a court's list of hearings. Normally, such actions are those which either cannot be heard by an employment tribunal, or in which the nature of the action is such that it would be preferable for it to be taken to a higher court. Cases heard in the UK involve lawyers representing just one individual, but in the USA lawyers may take up a case on behalf of groups, all group members having similar complaints.

Whether a case is heard by a tribunal or a court, and regardless of who wins or loses, news of the outcome will be covered by the media which can be damaging to the organisation in terms of its reputation as an employer. Employees are usually well represented as litigants, and organisations should be prepared to defend themselves vigorously against such actions. While no two cases are exactly alike, there are some basic facts of which organisations should be aware.

The ex-employee's case

When employees take legal action against the organisation they or the organisation usually will have terminated the employment contract. What the courts actually see, therefore, are ex-employees and ex-employers, and obviously the severence will have had an adverse effect on the employment relationship.

An ex-employee who alleges that stress was caused by the way he or she was treated in the workplace would have to show, first, that he or she is suffering from the effects of stress, secondly, the nature of the link between the stress-induced physical or mental condition and the workplace stressor that caused it, and thirdly, that the employer knew about the employee's plight and did not try to do anything about it.

In a case involving stress, the litigant seeks compensation for loss of earnings, which could also include loss of possible future earnings, depending on the severity of the medical condition of the individual and hence their future employability. The litigant also seeks compensation for other losses, such as medical costs and psychological or other injury caused. Evidence of the individual's medical condition will be produced, alongside further evidence indicating that the individual's medical condition was caused in the workplace. From the litigant's point of view, these two factors – his or her medical condition and the causal link with the workplace – are the main foundation stones of the case.

In such a case, the employee would sue the organisation for breaching its 'duty of care', in which perhaps the employee had been overloaded with work to the extent that he or she found it humanly impossible to meet the workload targets that the employer had set. As a result, the employee has suffered from the effects of stress and seeks compensation. Usually, cases of this nature would go through the courts and, depending on the outcome, the organisation may find itself with a bill for costs running into hundreds of thousands of pounds.

The ex-employer's case

Those defending such actions, therefore, find themselves chiefly preoccupied with disproving the causal link. The ex-employer, while recognising that the ex-employee is suffering from the effects of stress, attempts to show that the litigant's medical condition is due to factors in other theatres of the individual's life, such as problems with finance, or at home or elsewhere. A further consideration is the nature of the medical problem. Stress, for example, has a reputation for causing high blood pressure and/or severe heart problems, but medical research shows that either or both of these complaints could be inherent family characteristics. If, therefore, the defence could show that there was a history of high blood pressure and/or heart problems in the litigant's family, the litigant's case would be severely weakened.

The organisation's case would be considerably enhanced if it could be shown that the organisation freely provided the services of a well publicised occupational support scheme or employee assistance programme, of which the ex-employee failed to take advantage. Also, there are many internal systems, such as a grievance procedure, through which an ex-employee could have complained about his or her work situation. The court will look closely at the outcome of any steps taken by the individual in the workplace to draw his or her situation to the attention of the managers.

When cases such as these are heard, judgment is made on the 'balance of probabilities' rather than the provision of 'proof beyond reasonable doubt', and there are legal factors that may favour or injure the defence case. For example, organisations are required by law to provide a healthy and safe working environment. The legislation on health and safety at work is extensive and fairly complex, but if a litigant's lawyer can show that the organisation failed to meet its legal obligations in a way that has had an adverse effect upon the well-being of the ex-employee, this will weigh heavily against the defence. In most countries, the concept of health at work includes the employee's mental as well as his or her physical health. In Europe, for example, litigants can damage the defence if they can show that regular 'risk assessment' – which is a legal requirement – was not carried out and recorded.

Overall, however, prevention is better that a law suit, and organisations will prefer to develop and implement policies and strategies that are designed to reduce the likelihood that employees would feel that they had just cause to end the employment contract because of the way in which they had been treated, and subsequently turn to the law in pursuit of compensation.

The internal justice system

All organisations have an internal justice system (IJS), which on the one hand enables the organisation to take action against individuals who misbehave and on the other enables the individual to seek a solution to perceived unfairness or ill-treatment. In this way, both sides of the employee relationship have access to a system through which redress may be sought. In most organisations, the formal processes of the IJS are managed through a *disciplinary procedure* and a *grievance procedure*. It is through these components that the organisation seeks to ensure that workers and management are satisfied with the psychological contract that exists between the individuals and the organisation. The use of these components tend to be psychologically negative, since the disciplinary rules, for example, define unacceptable items of behaviour, ranging from minor indiscretions to comparatively serious offences which are referred to as 'gross misconduct', while through the grievance procedure, employees seek redress or solutions to negative situations. Circumstances in which one party or the other is not satisfied by the outcome of the process may lead to recourse to external institutions, such as employment tribunals or the courts.

In addition to formal disciplinary and grievance procedures, there are factors within the organisation that tend informally to regulate behaviour and may, therefore, be regarded as part of, or at least influential upon, the IJS. Such factors include:

- the organisational culture, which is largely shaped by the style of leadership and formal and informal communication, and the atmosphere within the workplace, in which desired behaviour is rewarded and reinforced;

- widespread knowledge of the content and structure of the disciplinary and grievance procedures, the very existence of which influences acceptable behaviour, not only of employees, but managers too.

It is the organisation's responsibility to ensure that the contents and structures of the disciplinary and grievance procedures are widely known, and it is the individual's responsibility to behave within the rules. Breaches of the rules are often ignored by managers, especially if the offences are minor, but in such circumstances managers can appear to be condoning misbehaviour which, as a result, ultimately may become part of custom and practice, and managers may not wish this to happen. Managers should be aware of the dangers when they ignore minor incidents of misbehaviour, since if they are seen to be condoned, they will occur more frequently. If the manager then attempts to halt the behaviour through the use of the disciplinary procedure, the disciplined employee would have a justifiable complaint of unfairness, since similar acts committed by others went unpunished.

If we examine the content and the sequential nature of the structures of disciplinary and grievance procedures, we can see that they are designed to resolve problems fairly and as quickly as possible. When managers adhere to the structures, everyone who is subject to the procedures is being treated in exactly the same way, and no one can complain that they were treated in a selective and thereby unfair manner.

It has been suggested that when they first join the organisation, perhaps during the induction process, employees should be trained to understand the disciplinary and grievance procedures, on the grounds that knowledge of the rules and expected standards of behaviour would help to regulate their behaviour from an early stage in their employment. In fact, few organisations do this, and as we know, not all organisations have a formal induction system. Most organisations include complete copies of the procedures in the 'employee handbook' which is given to everyone when they first join.

Disciplinary rules and procedures

Organisations should be sure of the philosophy that underpins their disciplinary procedures. The organisation should ask itself, 'What is the disciplinary procedure for?' Is it there to protect the organisation? To punish undesirable behaviour? To act as a deterrent to undesirable behaviour? To control and regulate employees' behaviour? It may, of course, be all or any of these things, but which does the organisation require it to be? The threat of punishment, for example, may be seen as a deterrent, but punishment itself may be seen by certain types of manager as a source of satisfaction, in which punishment has been imposed upon a member of staff whom he or she dislikes. More than merely punitive, which of itself is relatively meaningless, the disciplinary procedure should be perceived as a positive and constructive instrument of management that should achieve something, such as the correction of an employee's behaviour and an assurance of desirable behaviour in the future, preferably by mutual agreement.

Organisations should make clear to their employees the kinds of sanction that particular items of behaviour would warrant. What, for example, are to be classed as 'minor offences' that attract little punishment? Sometimes the very fact that a warning has been entered onto an individual's personnel file may be regarded by that person as punishment. Moving up the scale of seriousness, what types of offence are to be classed as 'misconduct', and further up still, 'gross misconduct'? The nature of offences is changing. Inducing stress or pressure and bullying are now regarded as dismissable offences.

The rules that organisations incorporate into their disciplinary procedures are of several types. Internal rules are those that are specified by the organisation and are normally spelled out clearly, such as: 'it is an offence to arrive for work after, or leave work before, the contracted times laid down, unless such arrival and departure has prior managerial approval'. Specific rules of this nature have been identified by the organisation as those which would regulate behaviour. Usually they deal with obvious offences, such as:

- lateness;

- 'clocking in' an employee who has not yet arrived for work;

- wilful damage to the property of the organisation or another employee;

- failure to carry out a reasonable instruction given by a senior member of staff;

- aggressive behaviour or violence;

- stealing;

- drug and alcohol abuse.

More general internal rules may include negligence, insubordination and interfering with others, etc. Unlike the items on the above list, such rules cannot be specified precisely, since the offences they are dealing with may be regarded as subjective issues. An item of behaviour, for example, may be perceived by one person as negligent, but not seen in the same way by another. Also, the list of things over which one could be negligent is infinite, and cannot therefore be written down.

Also, where an individual's work performance falls below an acceptable minimum standard, action should be taken. Toleration of poor performance has the potential to legitimatise it. It is the manager's responsibility to ensure that the individual is aware of what is an acceptable standard of performance and is given an opportunity to meet the expectation. Normally in these circumstances, the manager will identify the reason/s for the shortfall and take remedial action, which could involve training, coaching or counselling. If poor performance continues, then the manager would be justified in invoking the disciplinary procedure.

Mandatory rules are those which the organisation is legally bound to include, such as the rules of health and safety at work and equal opportunities, although organisations may legislate internally against behaviour which is legal externally, such as smoking on the organisation's premises, harassment, rudeness to visitors or colleagues. Most disciplinary procedures are structured in four stages, as follows:

Stage 1   A verbal warning
Stage 2   A written warning
Stage 3   A final written warning
Stage 4   Dismissal

At every stage in the procedure, the alleged offending employee may if he or she so wishes be accompanied by a friend. Where the organisation is unionised, the 'friend' is usually a trade union representative.

It is recommended that managers issue a verbal warning only after they have carried out a thorough investigation into the employee's behaviour. This might mean interviewing the alleged offender in order to establish facts prior to carrying out the formal disciplinary interview. Indeed, this preamble may persuade the manager that rather than invoke the disciplinary procedure, he or she may assist the employee in finding a solution to a problem.

In one case, for example, the offence was persistent lateness on the part of an employee who had a good record. The manager's investigation discovered that the employee and his partner had recently parted company; he had three children to look after, which included getting them to school on time. After a little juggling with the morning working hours, the manager was able to organise the employee's working hours in a way that allowed him to attend to his children until he found someone who could do it for him.

If, however, a stage 1 verbal warning is issued, it should include reference to the offence for which the warning is given, the kind of behaviour that is expected in the future, and the possibility of stage 2 being invoked if the offence or a similar offence were to be repeated. Also, the employee should be advised that details of the verbal warning would remain on his or her personal file for a period of three months (which is the usual period for a first offence).

Stage 2 is invoked if the verbal warning given at stage 1 is ignored or if a similar offence is committed inside the three months. Stage 2 involves the issue of a written warning which should include details of the possible consequences of a repeated similar offence, and that the warning will remain on the person's file for six months, which is normal for stage 2.

Stage 3 involves a final written warning, including details of the offence, the kind of behaviour that is expected in the future and notice that a repeated offence could lead to dismissal. Normally this warning would be kept on the person's file for twelve months, or the individual may be suspended for a period without pay.

Stage 4 involves dismissal.

At every stage in the disciplinary procedure, an investigation into the circumstances of the offence should be carried out. For a first offence, the organisation may, at its discretion, invoke any of the three stages, depending upon the seriousness of the offence, for example if the organisation regards or has previously listed the type of offence as one of 'gross misconduct', for which the penalty is instant dismissal, or suspension on full pay pending the outcome of a thorough enquiry into the circumstances.

Grievance procedures

Grievance concerns the individual's rights in relation to the conditions of employment and treatment or relationships. Where, for example, an individual feels that he or she has been treated unfairly, that the organisation has failed to meet one of the terms and conditions of employment, or that other employees, such as managers, have for example treated him or her in a harassing or bullying way, then the employee may invoke the grievance procedure. Grievance procedures tend to be used most frequently in organisations where communication, interaction and the general internal relationship, both formal and informal, are poor. Typically, the grievance procedure is in three stages:

Stage 1   The employee, who may be accompanied by a friend, airs the grievance to the immediate manager/supervisor, and an attempt is made to resolve the issue.

Stage 2   This takes place if the issue was not resolved at stage 1, and usually involves a more senior manager. Again, the employee states the grievance and an attempt is made to resolve it.

Stage 3   This takes place if the issue was not resolved at the previous stages and usually involves the senior managers and the personnel/HR manager or director. The grievance receives a full hearing and a final attempt is made to resolve it.

Few grievances reach stage 3. Most are resolved at stage 1 and many at stage 2. In extreme circumstances, however, where the internal procedure has failed, special panels may be set up which may include the involvement of experienced external arbitrators, where appropriate, in attempts to resolve serious or complex grievances.

The purpose of grievance procedures is to allow employees to get dissatisfactions dealt with formally. They are often used when the nature of conflict or problem is with the manager–subordinate relationship, but they can be used across functions and on an organisational perspective. The law on written terms and conditions requires a note specifying to whom employees can apply to seek redress of a grievance, how the application should be made and what further steps they may take. They are intended to be fair, and fairly and consistently applied, with the onus upon the employee to show that the employer failed to act reasonably.

The grievance procedure itself should be clearly communicated to all employees. Employees should have the right to be represented and there should be a number of levels of appeal (see above). Also, when it is activated, each stage of the procedure should be completed within a pre-specified period of time.

Administering organisational justice

The procedures described here are the formal methods of regulating behaviour and administering internal justice. The stages described above include hearings which follow legalistic patterns of rules and procedures as one would find in an adverserial system of justice, in which the alleged offender is protected by the process. Both procedures focus on the individual, while 'collective' matters are dealt with through a disputes procedure.

It can be seen that disciplinary action is taken on the grounds of employees' conduct or capability. In the UK, there is no legal requirement for a disciplinary procedure, although where an organisation has one it is required to make reference to it in a statement of terms and conditions of employment; they should be explained to new employees and be available to them in written form. This should include the types of sanction that may be imposed, such as verbal and written warnings, suspension, dismissal and improvement targets.

Disciplinary procedures should be designed in accordance with recommendations included in recognised codes of practice, since if an internal issue, such as unfair dismissal for example, were to be referred externally to a tribunal or court, either may regard the dismissal as unfair if the procedure that was followed within the organisation failed to match the recommendations made in recognised codes of practice.

Where a manager fails to supervise adequately, undesirable behaviour may take place within work groups or teams, in which, for example, a team may informally 'discipline' one of its members because he or she has stepped outside the internal norms of the team. With the present trend for teamworking, care should be taken by managers to ensure that quasi-disciplinary or other punitive measures are not handed out indiscriminately by the team, since this could result in the recipients of such measures experiencing the effects of stress, even to the extent that they feel they have the right to terminate their contract, which could, in turn, result in a case of constructive unfair dismissal.

Employee well-being

The obvious situations are those that have a reputation for inducing stress, such as work that is unavoidably pressurised, or situations that are created by inept managers with inappropriate styles who bully and apply threatening and coercive measures.

Discrimination, on whatever grounds, may also cause stress. Treatment that is unfair, such as bypassing an obvious candidate for promotion and thereby failing to provide an equal opportunity, can make the individual feel that his or her work is undervalued or, indeed, that they themselves are undervalued. It may be that the manager has failed to notice a person's potential; either way, this will have an adverse impact on the person's well-being.

Conclusion

For many generations, it was perfectly legitimate for managers to exploit the knowledge, skills and physical and mental stamina of employees; to carry out discriminatory acts against people on the grounds of their sex or minority group status; and to dismiss employees once they were 'worn out', or if they became pregnant and, therefore, no longer of any use to the organisation, or merely because the manager carrying out the dismissal did not like the dismissed person.

Women and members of minority groups were routinely given low-status jobs on low pay and reduced conditions compared with those of white indigenous males, and not considered for promotion, simply because of their sex, skin colour, race or ethnic origin. Managers could exercise coercive tactics when special attendance or higher productivity were required, and generally to do as they pleased with their staff without the risk of any formal rebuke.

Unable to obtain redress through the law for the way they were treated, employees largely relied upon their trade unions to make representations on their behalf. In the early days, when workers banded together to use their solidarity to make representations to the organisation about the terms and conditions of their employment, they were said to have formed themselves into 'combinations of workers'. This started to happen in the late seventeenth and early eighteenth centuries, but those in government, who were allied to the owners of the organisations, acted swiftly to prohibit such combinations. After the first quarter of the eighteenth century, however, trade unions were given legal status and they proliferated in the subsequent years. The history of the trade unions is punctuated with legislated acts, but it was not until the early twentieth century that employees were recognised as an important element.

CHAPTER 9

Technology in society

Introduction

The main purpose of this chapter is to demonstrate the effects that the introduction of new technology may have upon the well-being of individual employees. Technology is defined in several ways, and in terms of well-being, arguments in favour as well those against it are presented. How particular new technologies have influenced societal and workplace changes is discussed, and it is hoped that some of the many myths that surround new technological ideas are exposed and laid to rest. Finally, the implications of the continuous and exponential rate of advancement in various fields allow the prediction of several obvious and, perhaps, some not so obvious visions of the future.

Technology as an agent of change

One approach to this complex and wide-ranging subject is to examine the degree to which it has affected us in worldwide terms. While the industrialised world clearly is responsible for the development of what we commonly call 'modern technology' and 'new technology', advancement in its wide variety of fields is not progressing or being introduced at an even pace across the globe. Millions of years ago, for example, when the first versions of what ultimately evolved to become *homo sapiens*, we ran in hordes and were migratory. We did what today's wild creatures do now; we hunted and gathered, found shelter and defended ourselves in the best way we could. Then, when we had exhausted the provisions of a particular area, we moved on to find another and repeated the process. This paradigm of the way we lived lasted for millions of years, and within that time we continued to evolve.

Explanations of ancient human social evolution vary, but the general belief is that our focus upon the need to survive was coupled with a need to develop, and that because human beings are rational creatures, we realised that we did not have to keep on the move to do so. It was when we learned to cultivate the ground that we stopped moving around and progressed from the *hunter-gatherer* stage to the *agrarian* stage. Settlements began to appear and we built our own shelters. Toffler (1980) identified three main paradigms, each of which is a set of conditions that determined the human lifestyle over the ages. He characterises human progress by describing three 'waves of change': first, the shift from hunter-gatherer to agrarian; second, from agrarian to industrial; and third, from industrial to post-industrial.

Hunter-gatherer to agrarian

Archaeological evidence supports the view that these paradigm shifts brought very significant changes to our lifestyles. The agrarian paradigm became a long and slow agricultural revolution from about 8000 BC, to the seventeenth and eighteenth centuries AD. At that time the populations were still mainly rural and mainly involved in agriculture, even though the settlements had become towns and cities.

Technology, which at this stage we can define as 'a way of doing things', was developing slowly and setting the rate of change. Archaeological evidence shows that there were tools, which were used for agriculture and building, domestic pots, containers and other vessels for eating and general use around the dwelling, and weapons, since we still had to defend ourselves. This was the real beginning of technology, and in fact more than a hint of the beginning of industry. Ideas were superseded by better ideas which brought new 'ways of doing things', or 'new technology'.

Agrarian to industrial

The Scientific Revolution of the sixteenth and seventeenth centuries revealed the early technological possibilities that gave birth to the Industrial Revolution, which is still in progress now in countries that have developed moderately. Such countries have predominantly manufacturing-based economies, utilising electro-mechanical technologies which are resource intensive, a pattern which is evident in eastern Europe and parts of Africa and South America, and there is still traditional industrial activity of this nature in parts of highly developed areas such as Europe and the United States. The employment of low-skilled people manufacturing standardised products characterises this kind of industrial activity. These areas are typical of those that produce most of the world's pollution and waste which are seriously damaging the world-wide environment, even to the extent that they now threaten the progress of natural evolution.

Industrial to information

In Europe, the United States, Japan, Singapore and other parts of Asia, therefore, there are two concurrent paradigms progressing at different rates: the 'industrial', which is now almost spent, and the so-called

'Information Age', which began in the 1950s and exploded in the 1980s and 1990s, and is now proceeding at an extraordinary rate of amplification and elaboration. In terms of technological innovation, the computer is the main medium. The pace was originally set in the United States and was quickly picked up by the other developed countries. Subsequent creative innovation continued in the United States and Europe, and in terms of market exploitation, the Microsoft Corporation is by far the most successful organisation. In Asia, however, innovative organisations have been quick to identify compatible relationships between one kind of new technology and another, and have made broad and deep inroads into Western markets with products and services. This ability to recognise, bring together and exploit compatible relationships between one kind of technology and another has become a technology in its own right. It has been said that Asia simply sits and waits for the products of the inventive West.

It is difficult to analyse the meaning of the changes that have occurred. Toffler refers to the transitory periods that carried us from one paradigm to the next as 'waves of change'. The first 'wave' moved across millions of years; the second occurred within a few hundred years, and the third is with us now, but so is the second, and there is still plenty of evidence of the first.

> The collision of wave fronts creates a raging ocean, full of clashing currents, eddies and maelstroms which conceal the deeper, more important historic ideas.

> Alvin Toffler (1980)

The rate of innovation has been far greater than the rate of actual change, and there are several reasons for this. The first is related to the exponential rate of advancement. When organisations introduce new process technology, they have to wait for a return on the capital they have invested. The capital employed is not limited to the purchase of the new hardware and software. Large-scale, costly internal changes to the structures of work systems usually accompany the introductory process, and work space and human resources have to be reorganised. These changes take place alongside the need to maintain the day-to-day effectiveness of the whole undertaking, all of which is costly. Inside the capital return period, further technological innovation takes place, but the organisation cannot adopt it until the return of capital has been secured. In some areas of new production and administrative technology, it is possible to incorporate minor advancements by modifying the original systems at a relatively low cost, but opportunities to do this are the exception.

The second reason is related to the difference between basic and applied science. In applied science, research work is carried out with a pre-specified application in mind, so that such scientists are able to deliver new technology when and to where it is required. In this respect, industrial and commercial managers have to become adept at identifying locations within their systems where innovation is required, and expressing clearly the nature of the change. In basic science, however, research is carried out for the sole purposes of advancing knowledge and understanding, and whether or not applications can be found often hangs in the air for a long time. Sometimes, people, which includes scientists, do things because they can, rather than because it has been specified by someone else as a requirement. Invention, therefore, rather than innovation is most often the result of basic research.

The third reason is related to social and political acceptability. Cloning and genetic modification are examples of this. Announcements of certain scientific breakthroughs often induce fear and suspicion among the general public, who, when the *possibility* is made known, assume that it is going to happen. Social tensions and conflict arise, and organisations become hesitant about going ahead with the related projects. When the cloned 'Dolly the Sheep' first appeared, everyone smiled, but when the prospect of cloning human beings arose, nobody smiled. In the UK, land belonging to farmers who had agreed to participate in experiments in genetically modified vegetation for use as food was invaded by protestors, the new crops were destroyed and the affected areas of their properties were wrecked.

People feel insecure about such dramatic change. They find their security in stability, and while sometimes much of their fear is attributable to lack of total understanding of the science involved, they have, in the light of horror stories about the outcomes of particular experiments, good ground for being suspicious and feeling insecure. In these circumstances, scientists and politicians have much to learn about how to communicate with the population about these issues. It takes years to build feelings of stability, but such feelings can be destroyed in a few seconds.

The fourth reason is related to the timing of the introduction of change. Everyone is a layman at most things, and it takes time for people to internalise all the implications of technological innovation, and those responsible for announcing the innovation and introducing it frequently fail to take account of this. As Toffler puts it: 'There is a shattering stress and disorientation that we induce in individuals by subjecting them to too much change in too short a time.'

Rate of advancement

Today, scientific breakthroughs are the milestones of progress, but back in the agrarian paradigm, someone must have fashioned an implement with which to till the soil. Later, further, improved implements were fashioned, and over the years the designs and types of materials were changed in the continuous search for efficiency. Since then the rate of change of advancement has been exponential, from its painfully slow beginnings to the present day's dazzling pace. This is not to imply, however, that the progressive paradigms have replaced each other in accordance with the *law of succession*; they have not. There is a strong element of continuity in most areas. In the advanced countries the early agrarian and industrial periods may have faded from view, but as we can see, agriculture and industry are still very much around us, and will remain in place for a long time to come; new technology has improved their efficiency, particularly with the use of chemicals and mechanisation, although this has reduced human resource demands significantly. Thirty years ago, agriculture drew upon more than 20 per cent of Western workforces, whereas now the figure is little more than 3 per cent and still reducing. The creation of unemployment is one of the arguments that does not favour the introduction of new technology.

Definitions of new technology

Technology was described above as 'a way of doing things' and new technology, therefore, as a 'new way of doing things'. But technology has been defined in other ways:

- workplace technology, i.e. how an organisation turns its inputs into outputs;

- the term is often used to describe computers, machinery and computerised manufacturing and administrative systems, including 'hardware' and 'software'.

The word itself comes from the Greek *techne*, meaning art, craft or skill. So-called hardware is not purposive. 'Techniques', on the other hand, are related to human or organisational goals. Arts, crafts and skills are human qualities and so, therefore, is technology. Technology is not something that is materialistically tangible, it is a quality that human beings possess; a quality that enables them to do things. Assisted by incessant curiosity and intelligent and creative progression of ideas, human beings invent things because they possess the technology to do so. When, therefore, we stand admiring a new computer or an innovative item of software, we are perceiving not technology but the products of technology. Seen in this way, technology is a way of doing things – a distinctively human way of doing things.

A clear example of this is seen when we look at the *purposes* of organisations which are to survive and develop. To survive and develop, organisations need to set themselves objectives, which have to be achieved by preset times, and they need to formulate strategies and policies that state the direction in which they intend to go and how they intend to achieve those objectives on the way. The survival and development of any organisation ultimately depends upon its ability to continue to be of use to its prime beneficiaries, and failure in that respect will lead to its demise.

These are rules that have not changed since the first organisation was formed, and they have almost reached 'cliché' status. The main purposes of organisations, therefore, are a constant factor and they will never change, but the technologies that organisations have employed as their means of achieving their objectives – their ways of doing things – have been changing continuously and always will be subject to change. Some organisations have withered away through inefficiency, ineffectiveness or redundancy, while others have survived by achieving their objectives. If organisations are going to survive, develop and succeed, therefore, they have to be willing to accept the changes that new technology brings with it. Indeed, all of the technological change that is introduced is provided by organisations.

To whom it may concern

It was said earlier that technology has not advanced at an even pace across the globe. There are areas of the world which are still firmly rooted in the second paradigm, and indeed in some cases, at the beginning of it. Those in these areas stare in awe across the divide between themselves and the advanced world, areas which have developed vast industries and public utilities to ensure their survival, further development, longer healthier lives and greater comfort. So while we bask in the luxuries that modern technology has made possible, there are massive areas of the world in which the greater parts of the populations do not even know when they are next going to eat. Even in the wealthy industrialised world, new technology is not available to all, but we return to that issue later.

Technology and lifestyle

Technology in the second half of the twentieth century came to be seen as a trigger for unemployment, and as the main cause of the deskilling and dehumanisation of work. In support of these factors, it was not difficult to find unemployed people claiming that they had 'been replaced by a computer', as a result of workplace changes in the form of computer-assisted or totally computerised manufacturing techniques. Technology, therefore, is still viewed by some with deep scepticism and suspicion, and in their perception with apparent good cause.

On the other hand, it is possible to develop arguments that contradict these negative views of technology. Firstly, it may be argued that the employment effects of the introduction of new technology are positive because it creates demands for new and improved products and services. Secondly, it can be shown that new technology has the effect of upgrading people's skills, rather than deskilling them, and that the outcome of this depends upon how the work is organised around the technology. Thirdly, it can be argued that technology can actually create employment, along with improvements to the quality of working life. Technology can contribute towards positive organisational development and change. Whatever one's personal view of all of this is, it has to be accepted by everyone that we now live in a technologically orientated society.

Our lives are shaped and conditioned by technological innovation. Most of the technology that we use today was unknown and barely imagined by our parents.

Exhibit 9.1 *That's one small step for man...*

In the 1930s in the UK, the *Sunday Graphic* newspaper ran a fun competition in which the winning prize was a trip for two on the first public flight to the Moon. On 16 July 1969, when Neil Armstrong stepped onto the Moon from the lunar module of Apollo 11 and made his well known and dramatic statement, the *Sunday Graphic* was long gone, but its editor (retired by then) and the winning couple were still alive! It will be interesting the see what this new millennium has to offer.

Present and future technology

Now that we understand the historical background, and the context in which modern technology is continuing to develop, we may set out to examine the effects that it is having upon the way we live and work. In particular, we highlight how new technology, especially information technology, shapes and reshapes our routines and alters the detail of how we perform tasks at home and at work. We also re-emphasise the effects of the exponential rate of advancement in recent times.

The roots of the word technology are known, and on the grounds that it is a human quality embracing knowledge and skills that enables us to do things, it is safe to say that new technology appears when we augment such qualities and, thereby, are enabled to do things in ways which are technically, economically, environmentally and/or in terms of safety more efficient and effective. From the beginning of the first shift in the paradigms of human lifestyles, technology always has changed the ways in which people live and work, so we should not be surprised when it changes our own lives.

The enchantment of technology

As we know, this advancement has been continuous for millions of years, but it is the *rate* as well as the *fact* of change that should concern us. From the beginning of the Industrial Revolution, which is like yesterday in terms of the time-span of human existence, technology in most organisations remained unchanged for many years; children inherited jobs from their parents, and craftsmen were able to pass their industrial genes down to their apprentices. Today, the fast and continuous rate of change means that individual workers are having to acquire new knowledge and develop new skills simply to continue effectively in their jobs. Many people are now on their third or even fourth career, either because they were unable to respond to the demands of new technology in their previous jobs, or because they did not have the will to adapt to the changes.

New technology provides us with new, and often surprising, ways of doing things; sometimes it enables us to do things that previously were impossible or too long term to be of any use. Sometimes we become so obsessed with the complexities of the technologies in which we are involved that it is difficult to keep our eye on the fact that our objectives have not changed and still need to be met. As Alfred P. Sloan[1] is reputed to have said when running General Motors, 'When you're up to your hips (or thereabouts!) in alligators, you tend to forget that the original objective was to drain the swamp!' (Sloan, 1954).

When Concorde was being developed in the UK and France, politicians and economists were concerned about the continuous cost increases which soared above the original estimates. This poor financial planning drew considerable media attention. Then when it first took to the air, people were awestricken by the beauty of its design, and the technological achievement in terms of its performance. Everyone wanted to fly in it. The interest was so high, that people hardly ever mentioned its purpose. They did not say that they were going to Beirut, they said that they were 'going on

---

Concorde'. When working in, or running a 'high tech' business, one's fascination with the technology itself can lead to the unwitting perception that the means of transport is more important than the reason for taking the journey.

A business still wishes to survive, develop further and make a profit. That has not changed, but the means we employ in our quest for the realisation of those goals have changed markedly, and new technology enables us to succeed in a more efficient and effective way and across a broader range of objectives. This means that technology has changed what we actually do – it has changed the nature of the tasks that make up our jobs.

One example of this is in written communication. Managers once spent the first hour or so of the working day reading letters that were written several days earlier, sorting them into 'important', 'urgent' or 'can wait' categories, and then briefing a secretary about how best to respond in each case. The secretary would take down the boss's 'dictation' and reappear later with letters for him or her to sign. Now, there is comparatively little conventional mail, and we find ourselves reading fax messages and e-mails instead, some of which might have been sent the night before, or this morning – even a minute ago. Speeding up communications like that allows the manager time to be more of a manager and less of a paper-pusher, although many still cannot demonstrate that they have learned this lesson. Such innovation speeds up the business rate of an organisation, but it also changes our habits and routines at work. It also changes our use of the language; the phraseology of e-mails and text messages, for example, is very similar to the abbreviated style with which we write our holiday postcards. This in turn has affected the way we speak and write in formal situations.

Where are we now?

Most areas of the industrialised world are between the second and third waves of change. But the exponential nature of technological advancement means that we are on the threshold of the greatest change of all time. This will include social upheaval and a restructuring of the class system, and it seems that we are sleepwalking through the whole thing. Many believe that the 'third wave' has already arrived for the following reasons:

1. Traditional industry – the remains of the Industrial Revolution – is declining rapidly.

2. The rapid growth of the information infrastructure continues.

3. Large proportions of many populations express serious disquiet over 'third wave' products; for example, parents are worried about the possibility of physical and mental damage that might be caused to their children because of their extensive use of computers, the Internet and mobile phones.

4. Political parties now find themselves making decisions and pronouncements about issues that their predecessors would have found shocking and frightening.

5. Special government funded bodies have been set up to monitor and advise upon the ethics and other implications of new possibilities, such as, in the UK, the human embryo, etc.

6. 'Internet fraud' has created a new diversification for criminals and a new source of satisfying the needs of perverts, particularly paedophiles.

Evidence of the forthcoming third wave is mounting rapidly, and this gives rise to the question of how we shall cope with it. The first and obvious step is to waken from our sleepwalk and accept that change is occurring. Secondly, we have to ensure that we develop for ourselves the knowledge and skills that will enable us to cope with and take advantage of third wave products and services. And finally, we have to remain flexible and prepared to adapt to change, since the willingness to accept and embrace change is the most essential ingredient to self-survival and success, especially since change will continue.

The class system

The importance of the traditional class system has been dwindling for many years. In some areas of the world it is based upon land ownership, heredity and accident of birth, while in others, it is money and high corporate or political status that has located people on the social hierarchy. As technology is becoming more and more complex, divisions have begun to appear between those who are highly technologically skilled and knowledgeable and those who are less so. The degree to which individuals are limited in their technologically creative and exploitative knowledge and skills will determine where they will sit in the new hierarchical order. Inevitably, where people will be hierarchically located within the organisation will determine their social positions. A hierarchy of technological capability has become visible:

Hierarchy of technological capability			
1	Top-level creative	1A	Top-level user
2	Medium-level creative	2A	Medium-level user
3	Moderate-level creative	3A	Moderate-level user
4	Low-level creative	4A	Low-level user

The creative innovators are in the vanguard of technological advancement, but the ability to understand, use and exploit what they create is also vital. There are always more users than providers of technology.

Effects of technology on people

In terms of the effect that new technology has upon employment, perceptions vary. Some say that it creates unemployment because it reduces the demand for human resources:

- automation makes people so highly efficient that the need for some positions is eliminated;

- automation is deliberately designed to eliminate jobs. Many trade unions are still less than enthusiastic about automation, despite the fact that it usually allows people to work in safer, cleaner and healthier conditions, while removing the boredom of repetitive tasks;

- some trade unions have insisted on agreements with managers that prohibit laying off workers or transferring them to lower paid positions.

It has also been postulated that companies that can afford to invest in high-tech are in a better position to do business profitably:

- we shall, therefore, see shakeouts in which many smaller companies that cannot afford such investment will be releasing employees;

- while some people are replaced by machines, others work with machines to get the job done;

- many people today work side by side with robots, each doing what each does best.

The hidden dangers of Internet use

The Internet, once little more than a dream, has since the 1990s very quickly become an integral part of normal life. The number of families and individuals who use the Internet for pleasure purposes, shopping, banking, education and a host of other services is high and increasing daily. Business organisations rely on Internet connections to do just about everything imaginable. Its use has become commonplace as the venue for, *inter alia*, interviewing prospective employees, creating a 'virtual shopfront', a 'one-stop' access point for purchasing capital equipment and raw materials, and access to information that enables companies to keep abreast of the competition. In addition, the advent of so-called 'dot com' companies has arrived, although more than half of them disappear within a year of commencing, largely because they expected the Internet to do their work for them; the Internet is just the means of transport – you have to do your own selling!

So what effect is such frequent usage having upon people's social and psychological well-being? A recent study shed light on this issue after an analysis had been carried out on the effects upon almost 2,000 people during the first two years of their Internet use. Most used it primarily to communicate with others. The more people used it in their households:

- the less they communicated with members of their families;

- the smaller was their circle of friends and acquaintances;

- the lonelier they felt in their lives;

- the more symptoms of psychological depression they displayed.

These findings clearly suggest that Internet use is not without serious psychological consequences. We need to be concerned about both the physical and psychological damage that may result. After all, the time we spend on line with others must displace the richer, social interaction that comes from face-to-face contact with others. Time spent on the Internet must also displace activities that would preserve and foster a healthier lifestyle, such as participation in sport and other physical activity. In terms of our health, it is noteworthy that 40 per cent of children under the age of eleven years, who spend time using the Internet, playing games on screens and watching television, are overweight, and that half of these overweight children are classified as obese.

By association, it is clear that over-reliance on Internet technology in the workplace may have a hidden physical and psychological cost to employees. It is one that might be overcome, however, by balancing the more solitary aspects of work with more opportunities for richer, social encounters. Today's managers must pay closer attention to the potential costs of isolating individuals by keeping them shackled to their computers, especially when they are concurrently screaming out for teamwork and cooperation.

Conclusion

Technology is not new – it has been with us from time immemorial. It is the nature of technology that is new in the sense that technology is a way of doing things. Technology has been developing in human society for millions of years. At first, the rate of development that caused us to change our lifestyles was, by modern comparison, slow, naive and cumbersome, but after the Scientific Revolution of the sixteenth and seventeenth centuries, the rate of change became exponential, an entirely different paradigm emerged and the Industrial Revolution was born. Now, advancements appear at a phenomenal pace. No single individual can possibly keep abreast of all new developments and people tend to become versed in the technologies that have changed our domestic lifestyles and the nature of work.

The use of new technology can enhance the likelihood of an organisation's survival and further development, but care should be exercised about how it is introduced and the effects that it may have upon the well-being of individuals who, through lack of understanding, feel threatened and are made to feel insecure and unstable in their positions.

We in the Western, industrialised communities have a responsibility for the survival of people in the undeveloped world. It will be several generations before they will be able to make use of what we have now, and thus ensure at least their survival.

A final word of caution about the over-use of the instruments that new technology has introduced into our lives. People at work, as well as those at home, can suffer from physical and psychological illnesses through spending too much time in front of a computer screen. Many children have developed the habit of going straight to the computer when they arrive home from school. As a result, they become socially isolated, depressed, lonely in their lives and physically challenged when exertion is required of them.

Managers too need to put the use of technology into perspective. Pretending that they are managing 'teams' while concurrently shackling their staff individually to computers may have a dramatic adverse effect on the amount of interest and satisfaction they find in their jobs.

References

Sloan, A.P. (1954) *My Years with General Motors*. New York: Doubleday.

Toffler, A. (1971) *Future Shock*. London: Pan.

CHAPTER 10

Managing organisational change

Introduction

Nobody would argue with the suggestion that one of the most important managerial skills that will be required in the twenty-first century is the ability to manage change effectively. While managing change always has been an essential managerial skill, it has to be accepted that it is a skill that is being used more frequently than ever before. In the past, the pace of change was comparatively moderate, and changes were made slowly and usually with great caution, but in today's organisations change occurs rapidly, and its exponential rate has turned it into a continuous process, so that change has become an integral part of organisational life. For a variety of reasons, organisations are forced to make changes, which implies that the alternative is their demise. People who wish to succeed, and wish their organisations to succeed, therefore, have to be willing to accept and adapt to change.

The nature of change

Here we will explore the nature of the external pressures that organisations face today, and to which they usually have to respond by implementing internal changes. We will also examine the range of changes that are internally stimulated, and draw distinctions between types and dimensions of change in terms of the degree to which change is *superficial* or *deep, continuous* or *discontinuous,* and *long term* or *short term.* Managers and employees alike have come to expect that change will occur, and it is its nature that concerns them, rather than the disturbance that change causes or the repetition of the process.

External pressures

The main external pressures for change arise from government intervention, which comes chiefly in the form of new legislation; from the economy, which may cause rises and falls in market demands and the availability of skills; from social trends, in which changes in life-styles, fashions and environmental interests pressurise the organisation into making changes; and from technology, which can mean changes to internal 'hard' and 'soft' systems in which the organisation is a technological user, and product technology, in which the organisation as an innovator has to make changes to accommodate the new product or service. Various acronyms have been used as aide-memoires for these phenomena, one of which is PEST:

P   Political intervention
E   Economic conditions
S   Social trends
T   Technological innovation

Political intervention includes law, codes of practice, civil and human rights, and changes in government policies which may, for example, introduce international moves such as applying sanctions against selected states.

Economic conditions include the condition of the national, regional and local economies, high/low unemployment, rising/falling market demands, changes in overseas economies, the organisation's own financial health.

Social trends include demands for new techno-products (more versatile mobile phones, etc.), shifts in fashions and lifestyles affecting clothing and household goods and changes in social values bringing pressure from environmentalists, including local pressures relating to pollution and international pressures regarding global warming, and so forth.

Technological innovation covers the introduction of more efficient working processes and *product innovation*, in which the organisation as the innovator may attempt to enter the market with a new product, which again may imply changes to the work system. Also, innovations by competitors in the form of modified or entirely new products, or the use of new, innovative materials, may put pressure upon the organisation to bring in competing versions.

Internally stimulated changes

An acronym that might be used as an aide-memoire to internally stimulated changes is PRICES:

P   Problems with current systems demanding change
R   Relocation of plant
I   Innovation in current work systems
C   Culture change process
E   Economically triggered changes
S   Service levels to customers

Problems with systems

Typically, administrative and production work systems do not last for ever. Largely owing to the cumulative effect of minor continuous internal changes, parts of the administrative system become ineffective and alternative ways of doing things have to be found. In the production system traditional plant, for example in manufacturing, eventually becomes unusable, and when we attempt to purchase replacements we find that all that is available is the capital equipment supplier's modified version of what we need. Such changes are usually designed to reduce the cost of operation and maintenance. Employees, of course, have to be trained in the operation of newly designed machines.

Relocation

Communication and transport have become particularly important in recent years, and industrial and commercial companies often find that there are savings to be made by moving closer to their clients and customers, the proximity also presenting the opportunity to improve delivery times. Where internal changes demand new and/or high technology skills, it is often found that those skills are most frequently found in other areas, such as on modern business parks, high technology centres such as 'Silicon Valley', or areas in which the educational centres have a good reputation for producing knowledge and skills that are needed now and will be needed in the future. In the UK and other European countries, newly developed industrial sites almost always offer companies some kind of financial incentive to move in.

Innovation in current work systems

This refers to the introduction of new technology which, when it is on an organisation-wide level, brings with it the need for a total reorganisation of the structure and the reallocation of responsibilities (see Chapter 9).

Culture change process

As continuous changes occur, people adapt to them in their own way, and if we ignore the culture during the adaptation process, it will change – perhaps for the better, perhaps not. Managers should plan, organise and manage the culture, and regardless of the reason for change, the cultural implications should always be taken into account at the planning stage.

Economically triggered changes

At particular stages in the organisation's life, it is a good idea to audit the costs of administration and production to see if savings can be made. This is not done in the light of changes triggered by other causes, such as new technology or culture; it is done because with time, costs always increase, which of course narrows profit margins. The outcome of such an audit will usually carry with it recommendations for changes that would produce the cost savings that are needed to re-establish the margins.

Service levels to customers

The raising of customer service levels is externally prompted when customers demand better service such as faster deliveries of goods, or more importantly a quality of product that is closer to their needs than the current provision. In such cases making the necessary changes becomes a matter of urgency. Internally, however, and purely of its own volition, the supplying organisation may generate its own ideas for raising levels of service.

Continuous change

The need to update work systems, fierce competition in a global economy, changes in management systems and techniques and the introduction of new technology are cited as the most frequently found explanations that senior managers give for making changes. Top managers of course are keenly interested in external perceptions of the organisation, and tend to make statements which are designed to explain and justify the large, dramatic changes that their organisations are implementing. But change can be subtle too.

Continuous change occurs when minor alterations are made to work methods, the occasional new machine is introduced, and there is staff turnover and other human resource movements such as promotions, transfers and minor intrasectional realignments – all these cause cultural and behavioural changes that seem inconsequential at the time. These changes go almost unnoticed because they occur on a daily basis. What might be referred to as the 'growing child syndrome' is analogous to this kind of change:

> Parents are with their child every day and do not notice the tiny, imperceptible developmental changes that take place. On the other hand, a distant aunt, who has not visited you for five or six years, may look at the child and say, 'Oh my, hasn't she grown!'

Similarly, we may look back five or six years at the way things were in the organisation and realise the significance of the difference that the cumulative effect of these minor changes has had – sometimes it seems as if we are not working for the same organisation. Continuous change does not normally have an adverse effect upon the day-to-day well-being of employees, especially when they have hardly noticed that it has happened.

Discontinuous change

Discontinuous change, however, may have a dramatic effect on employee well-being. It occurs when sudden, organisation-wide upheavals take place in the form of what one might regard as 'overnight' change, such as a rapid, large scale reorganisation of a plant to accommodate further technological advance, or the introduction of special work systems to make way for a new product, and/or a new management structure for economic or administrative purposes. When this happens, employees feel a strong sense of job insecurity. Their motivation, commitment and performance reduce, and as a consequence the organisation's profitability suffers.

Managing change

The chief preoccupations of managers when they are planning and implementing change are usually related to the cost and technical aspects of the change process. It is true that this can be a complex and testing set of disciplines in which mistakes can be costly, but the key factor, and certainly the most essential ingredient to a successful change process, is an understanding of the way in which the human resource should be taken through it.

It has to be borne in mind that employees, particularly the long-serving ones, have developed very deeply-rooted sets of assumptions about how things are and how they should be. Such assumptions, which refer to job security, how things are done and what would be 'good' or 'bad' for the company, what the company is for, and so forth, are often held unconsciously, and only surface when they are threatened, but even when they are not threatened, they are still powerful determinants of attitudes and behaviour. One example of the effect of this species of unconscious assumption became evident in the UK when the publicly controlled utilities were privatised, in which the employees of the newly founded 'companies' were the same people who had been employed in the public 'authorities' for many years. Many were oblivious to the need for the organisation to ensure its own survival and the 'job-for-life' syndrome persisted long after the change in corporate status.

Those employees did not want to let go of the culture they had worked in for so long, and managerial awareness of this led them to decide upon a conscious and rational approach to culture change over the medium to long term, rather than the well-known 'unfreeze–change–refreeze' process. Ultimately, the improvement of managerial skills in introducing and then maintaining a planned change, coupled with the natural turnover of staff, created positive results in terms of culture. The old-style attitude of 'dealing with the *public*' was eventually replaced with a genuine and effective *customer* focus.

Resistance to change

When making changes, special consideration should be given to long-serving employees. Experience shows that as a general rule the more mature employees are, the more fiercely they are likely to resist change. Young people tend to welcome change and see it as a challenge, but older people derive security from the work habits and routines that they have developed over many years. Their skills have served them well in terms of their performance, but they feel abandoned and redundant when their previously valued abilities are no longer needed by the organisation. Such employees have experienced stability for many years; they draw comfort from the confidence they have in themselves to perform well, they have always felt secure in their positions. They resist change for many reasons as it may mean:

- a threat to their stability and may make their jobs redundant;

- a change of routines, which can be frustrating;

- being moved into jobs they may not understand;

- a change in status;

- a change in pay structure and other rewards;

- having to work in a new area with previously unknown colleagues;

- having to work for a new and unknown boss;

- having to work for a boss who is known, but not generally liked;

- a change in working hours;

- changing to a job that has insufficient challenge.

There are two main ways in which mature people see new technology. The first is to reject the whole idea of change because they lack the inclination to become involved, or because they fear that they will fail to understand it. The second is more interesting and may depend upon the rate at which the technology is introduced.

Exhibit 10.1

Older people who drive cars are often criticised by younger drivers for their failure to comprehend the technology at their disposal in a modern car. And yet the product technology that is now widespread in the automobile industry has been introduced gradually, some of it over many years, which means that older people have had a far greater amount of time to acquire an understanding and adapt to it. In many cases, therefore, more mature people are considerably more adept at driving modern cars than are their younger counterparts.

It may be that the introduction of new technology in the workplace is understood by the more mature employees far more readily than by the younger ones, and managers should not jump to the conclusion that older people are not ready to adapt to and accept change. It may depend upon the rate at which the technology is introduced. In any case, the willingness to accept and the ability to adapt to change are relative factors, regardless of age. Attitudes towards innovation are influenced by long held values, beliefs and emotional factors. It was said above that older people are more likely to resist change, but there are always exceptions to the general rule and managers should find the time and patience to spot those exceptions; after all, there is always room for experience.

Fear of change

People fear change. Making changes, particularly by introducing technology that alters work systems and the design of jobs, should be managed with honesty and understanding. Such changes alter the culture of the organisation which, if handled without appropriate sensitivity, may become hostile and ineffective, which may result in the loss of flexibility for, or acceptance of, the change one is making. Fear and suspicion are aroused, and motivation, commitment and job satisfaction suffer. Conversely, well-managed changes may result in a benign, cooperative and optimistic culture, in which the climate is pleasant and the managerial style encouraging and supportive, leading to raised levels of achievement, commitment and job satisfaction. One approach to allaying employees' fears about impending change is to follow a set of ground rules of which all managers should be aware.

Tell the employees

It is true that this may be affected by necessary secrecy for marketing reasons, or if there are possible predators around, but this should only affect the timing of when they are told. Today's managers are keen to elicit employee commitment and involvement in the affairs of the organisation, and planning a significant and/or discontinuous change should be seen as an opportunity in this respect.

Consult the employees

Employees have brains. By restricting their attention exclusively to the jobs they do, the organisation is using only a tiny proportion of their cerebral potential. For example, they work at or closer to the interface of production than do the middle and senior managers, and they possess knowledge in the finest detail of how things work. By consulting them over changes, they may respond with good ideas or even better ideas than the managers or their consultants produced in the first place. Furthermore, they may tell you that there are inadvisable elements in what you are proposing to do. After all, why employ, say, a couple of thousand brains and then use only those at or near the top?

Involve the employees

When they are consulted, employees believe that their views are valued, they become drawn into the prospective change process and they develop a sense of ownership of the change, which leads naturally to their commitment and motivation for a successful outcome.

Counsel the employees

There are no hard and fast rules about the timing of this, but when it is felt that the time is right, employees should be advised of their future status in the organisation. If there are going to be redundancies, the affected employees should be told as soon as possible, along with the relevant dates and details of the compensation they will receive.

This will give them an extended opportunity to find alternative employment.

Sometimes the company wishes to reduce the size of the workforce for economic reasons, and at other times people have to leave because the change indicates that their skills are no longer required. Techniques related to workforce reduction may prove to be useful in these circumstances. One may, for example, ask for voluntary redundancies or early retirement to be taken. There may, however, be problems with this in that when the organisation asks for voluntary redundancies, or offers early retirement, employees whom you wish to keep often come forward to volunteer. Much depends upon the timing and the separation deal the organisation is prepared to offer. Also, employees should not be made redundant until their trainability in new skills has been fully explored.

Motivate the employees

Employees who are to remain with the organisation should be told that this is the case. Managers should counsel the remaining employees and talk to them about their future role in the changed organisation. In cases where a change of role is involved, details of the new job in terms of its title, the terms and conditions and so forth should be thoroughly discussed, along with the timing and details of any training they may need. When this is done, people begin to feel secure again, they start seeking further information about the nature of the change, and their commitment and motivation starts to return.

Rally the employees

When the dust has settled, and everyone is aware of their positions in the new work situation, it is time to get people together in informal meetings to plan future working methods. It is possible that employees who are to work together in the future may never have worked together before, and the very fact that you are giving them the opportunity to meet and socialise for the first time sets up a bonding process. Additionally, such meetings will give employees the opportunity to meet and begin to relate to their new managers, and any problems that may be identified in this respect can be dealt with in the non-threatening environment of the informal meeting.

Rate of change

We have seen examples of the effects that the speed at which changes are introduced can have upon employees. In the middle of the twentieth century, academics and practising managers found it helpful to analyse organisations and explore their management and administrative structures. These were the first serious attempts to acquire a deep and technical understanding of organisations, and they produced some insightful and interesting perceptions. For example, Burns and Stalker (1961) located organisations on a dimension that ranged from *mechanistic* at one end to *organic* at the other. A significant proportion of their book, *The Management of Innovation*, was written in the marketing context, in which a mechanistic organisation was one that served the demands of a stable market, and in which an organic organisation served a market in which the demands were continuously changing. The researchers were concerned with the rate of change in the business environment of the organisation, rather than in its technology, although of course any significant environmental changes in demand might influence internal technological change.

Mechanistic organisations

Where an organisation has been meeting the same market demands for its products by supplying mostly the same customers in regularly repeated quantities for many years, and it appears to the organisation

---

that the market will neither rapidly nor greatly expand and that they have no reason to suppose that customers' tastes will change or that competitors will invade their field, then, say the researchers, the result will be a highly structured organisation, with centralised policies, rigid hierarchical ranks, strict administrative routines and tightly drawn boundaries between the departments. This, they say, describes the mechanistic organisation.

Organic organisations

Where customer demands are ever-changing, the organisation's speed and sensitivity to response becomes the essence of success, and a mechanistic administrative system and management structure would seriously inhibit its ability to remain in the market. This kind of situation, said the researchers, demands a flattened hierarchy, colleague relationships rather than boss–subordinate relationships as the predominant mode, short-lived and flexible administrative routines and shifting departmental boundaries. It has to be remembered that while their book was published in 1961, much of the research that led to it was written in the 1950s. One wonders if this is where HRM *really* began?

In this perception of organisations, it is worth reminding the reader that this was not a dichotomous description, but a dimension:

Mechanistic..Organic

With time, some organisations could be seen to be moving along the dimension, usually away from mechanistic and towards organic as technology advanced. Other, large and diverse organisations, can be located simultaneously on several points (see Exhibit 10.2).

In this context, Burns and Stalker were analysing the internal organisational form in terms of its appropriateness to its market. They saw the organisation as an open system. In such a perception, the success of the organisation is dependent upon the nature of internal human relationships, the arrangement of which was designed to reach high levels of cooperation, commitment and flexibility in pursuit of the corporate objectives. Organisations, of course, may or may not be appropriately designed to respond adequately to the problems posed by their external environment. Clearly, there is no 'one best way' to design and manage any organisation, since internally it needs to be capable of responding to external demands, the nature of which varies from one organisation to another and continues to change.

Exhibit 10.2

Examples of organisations that are seen to oscillate along the dimension might include a company manufacturing cash registers. Until the late 1950s, most shops had cash tills bolted to the serving counter. These were large, heavy, mechanical machines made of steel and brass, beautifully designed with chased surfaces. They were operated by pressing down on levers, an action that simultaneously opened the cash drawer and raised a selection of price tabs into a glass box on the top of the machine. The tabs revealed the total cost to the customer. The machine was not on line to anything, and it was not a calculator; the shop assistant had to calculate the total separately before pressing the levers. These machines were superseded by electrically operated devices, and a little later, calculating versions were produced. Today, such machines can be seen in antique shop windows, and shops and supermarkets use much more advanced equipment. Modern machines not only calculate from bar codes what the customer has to pay, they also print cheques, are able to monitor the stocks of the store and advise the purchasers of when fresh supplies will be needed.

Many readers will be aware of the developments that have been described in the above example, but how many will have thought about the implications that such development holds for the companies that manufacture products that are designed to supersede their earlier counterparts? In Exhibit 10.2, for example, what kind of people were involved in designing, making and assembling cash tills up to the 1950s? What knowledge did they need and what were their qualifications and skills? From which social stratum of the community did they come? Obviously, where such companies employed mechanical engineers, they now needed electrical and electronic experts. These employees also needed to be innovative in their approach to the technical and aethestic designs of the machines. The processes and systems through which the new products were manufactured also needed to be re-engineered, which resulted in employing fewer people, but people of a high technical calibre.

This in turn significantly altered the culture of the workplace, and companies had to learn what steps they needed to take to ensure the retention of these valuable employees. After the changes brought about by the introduction of the new technology, companies found that they were highly – if not totally – dependent upon the knowledge, skills and innovative abilities of their employees for their success and profitability. Today it can be seen that organisations that experienced such changes in the final quarter of the twentieth century are now embarking upon a new generation of change, in which what were referred to then as the 'high-tech' skills of employees are becoming redundant in the face of technology that is even further advanced. As this change process continues, organisations have to decide which employees they can retrain and retain, and which they have to let go.

These developments have already signalled an end to the 'long-term job', and therefore for organic organisations to offer careers to people is, in many cases, imprudent. It may prove wiser for organisations, when engaging highly skilled staff in the first place, to make them aware of the continuous internal technological changes and how those changes may affect the duration of their employment. To some degree, this situation is ameliorated by the intellect and attitudes of the employees themselves, who most often are well aware of the fluid nature of the technologies they have adopted as the bases for their careers. Such people are well able to develop themselves along appropriate lines, keeping themselves abreast of new technological developments, and in many cases are themselves the innovators. In such cases, the organisation may decide to offer advice and assistance by providing information about the technological direction in which things are likely to proceed, and offering training to fill in any gaps in knowledge and understanding that may appear in the future.

Change and stress

Organisational change that is mishandled will induce stress among many of the employees. Those who are stressed through the fear of change may start looking around for alternative employment, and usually the very people you would like to retain are those who choose to leave. Many employees have already experienced how their organisation manages change, and have become cynical about it. They are adversely affected by too much change in too short a period of time, they become overloaded with the change-related information, and their fear of failure coupled with experience of previous managerial failure to effect change efficiently and effectively makes them apathetic, disinterested and fatigued.

It has been known for organisational managers to plan change in a clandestine way, and when the plans are complete and they think the time for change has arrived they launch it, often to the shock and dismay of the employees. It is often the case that during the clandestine period, confidentiality of the plans has been breached and rumour has spread. Fear spreads quickly, especially when it is fear of the unknown.

Obviously, in such circumstances, staff turnover rises sharply, and some valuable people are lost, but the employees who remain become stressed through insecurity and they feel under-valued because the managers have chosen not to consult them. Senior managers who do this kind of thing are living in dreamland. While some believe that how the company is managed should not interest the employees, in that 'it is none of their business', others may have pleasureable but naive expectations about how the employees will react to the news that things are going to change. Because they have been involved in planning the change for so long, they have become engrossed in its positive side, and find it hard to accept that as far as their employees are concerned, it may have a downside. The change-related fears and frustrations mentioned above are just as natural a reaction to change as are approval and eager anticipation. Employees will always welcome pleasant surprises, but tend to become stressed by shocks.

In particular circumstances, however, there is a justifiable case for witholding information about forthcoming planned change. For example, an organisation that intends to be 'first to market' with a new product may not succeed if the employees are consulted from the start, since information usually finds its way beyond the boundaries of the organisation. The answer here is to tell the employees as soon as it is recognised that the time element would make it impossible for a competitor to undermine the launch of the new product.

In addition to reorganisation stimulated by human resource management, which brings about leaner flatter structures, the introduction of new technology is accompanied by changes to methods of working which naturally indicate changes to the actual tasks that employees have to perform. In Chapter 9 we saw examples of how new technology can change the way we carry out workplace tasks, which obviously means training people in new skills. The main fear experienced in this context is that of failure to understand and acquire the skills that would enable them to operate effectively within the new technological environment.

Conclusion

It is clear that the effective and successful management of change, particularly when introducing new technology, is dependent upon the cooperation of a committed, motivated and flexible workforce, which includes active, mutual support between and among managers. Any system is only as good as the people who operate it. Organisations *per se* do not make changes, it is the people who work internally who do that.

The human resource, therefore, is the key factor, and if managers wish to secure a clean, effective and successful change, they need to elicit employees' commitment to, acceptance of and involvement in the changes that are to take place. Even then the path towards the introduction of new technology is not an easy one to follow; such things are never simple and straightforward. With some justification, many managers regard the change from one technology to another as a difficult prospect, but if the human resource is managed appropriately, much of the technologically-related difficulty will diminish.

When the change is complete and everyone is in their new positions, checks need to be made to ensure that everyone understands what they are doing; not only for the sake of efficiency and effectiveness, but for the well-being of individuals. Perceptions of change are very much subject to the element of individual difference, and managers have to accept that employees' perceptions of the changes they have made will vary from one employee to the next.

Managing change is a complex business and many texts have been written about it. There is no one best way to handle the process, since it is organisationally specific. Very often, fears that cause stress among employees are usually driven by rumours about the kinds of change that are coming, and are therefore fears of the unknown. In this chapter we have provided a set of ground rules, but these should be interpreted to complement the nature of the organisation in which the changes are to take place. Broad rules are fine, but since all organisations are unique, detailed rules about how to bring about change will never pass into the common law of management.

References

Burns, T. and Stalker, G.M. (1961) *The Management of Innovation.* London: Tavistock.

References

Adams, J.S. (1961) 'Toward an understanding of inequity', in R. Likert (ed.), *New Patterns of Management*. Maidenhead: McGraw-Hill.

Arnold, J., Robertson, I.T. and Cooper, C.L. (1997) *Work Psychology*. Pitman: London.

Blake, R.R. and Mouton, J.S. (1964) *The Managerial Grid*. Houston, TX: Gulf.

Brech, E.F.L. (1975) *The Principles and Practice of Management*, 3rd edn. London: Longman.

Burns, T. and Stalker, G.M. (1966) *The Management of Innovation*. London: Tavistock.

Cannon, W.B. (1929) *Bodily Changes in Pain, Hunger, Fear and Rage*, 2nd edn. New York: Appleton-Century-Crofts.

Cooper, C.L., Cooper, R.D. and Eaker, L.H. (1988) *Living with Stress*. Harmondsworth: Penguin.

Cooper, R. (1998) 'Sentimental value', in *People Management*. London: Institute of Personnel and Development.

Currie, D. (1990) *Stress in the National Health Service, Southampton* (a report for Southampton Business School). Southampton: Southampton Institute.

Drucker, P. (1955) *The Practice of Management*. London: Heinemann.

Fox, A. (1966) *Industrial Sociology and Industrial Relations*. Royal Commission on Trade Unions and Employers' Associations Research Paper No. 3. London: HMSO.

Friedman, M. and Rosenman, R.H. (1974) *Type A Behaviour and Your Heart*. New York: Knopf.

Garrison, K.R. and Muchinsky, P.M. (1994) 'Attitudinal and biographical predictors of incidental absenteeism', *Journal of Applied Psychology*, June, pp. 385-9.

Herzberg, F.W., Mausner, B. and Snyderman, B. (1957) *The Motivation to Work*. New York: Wiley.

Holmes, T.H. and Rahe, R.H. (1967) 'The social readjustment rating scale', *Journal of Psychosomatic Research*, vol. 11, pp. 213–18.

ICF Inc. (1995) *Valuing Older Workers: A Study of Costs and Productivity*. A report prepared for the American Association of Retired Persons.

Kacmar, K.M. and Ferris, G.R. (1990) 'Theoretical and methodological considerations in the age–job satisfaction relationship', *Journal of Applied Psychology*, April, pp. 201–7.

Katz, D. and Kahn, R.L. (1978) *The Social Psychology of Organisations*, 2nd edn. Chichester: Wiley.

Kelly, R.M. (1991) *The Gendered Economy: Women, Careers and Success*. London: Sage.

Lawrence, P.R. and Lorsch, J.W. (1969) *Organisation and Environment*. Homewood, IL: Irwin.

Likert, R. (ed.) (1961) *New Patterns of Management*. Maidenhead: McGraw-Hill.

McGregor, D. (1960) *The Human Side of Enterprise*. New York: McGraw-Hill.

Maslow, A.H. (1987) 'A theory of growth motivation', in A.H. Maslow, *Motivation and Personality*. New York: Harper & Row.

Mayo, E. (1933) *The Human Problems of an Industrial Civilization*. New York: Macmillan.

Mintzberg, H. (1979) *The Structuring of Organisations*. Englewood Cliffs, NJ: Prentice Hall.

Mullins, L.J. (1993) *Management and Organisational Behaviour*, 3rd edn. London: Pitman.

Perrow, C. (1967) *Organisational Analysis – A Sociological View*. London: Tavistock.

Quinn, R.P., Staines, G.L. and McCullough, M.R. (1994) *Job Satisfaction: Is there a Trend?*, Document 2900-00195. Washington DC: US Government Printing Office.

Selye, H. (1974) *Stress without Distress*. Philadelphia: J.P. Lippincott.

Sloan, A.P. (1954) *My Years with General Motors*. New York: Doubleday.

Taylor, F.W. (1911) *The Principles of Scientific Management*. Harper & Bros.; (1947) *Scientific Management*. New York: Harper & Row.

Thurstone, L.L. and Chave, E.J. (1933) *The Measurement of Attitudes*. Chicago, IL: University of Chicago Press.

Toffler, A. (1971) *Future Shock*. London: Pan.

Trist, E.L., Higgin, G., Pollock, H.E. and Murray, H.A. (1963) *Organisational Choice*. London: Tavistock.

Vroom, V.H. (1970) *Management and Motivation*. Harmondsworth: Penguin.

Woodward, J. (1980) *Industrial Organisation – Theory and Practice*, 2nd edn. Oxford: Oxford University Press.

Index

abilities and disabilities, 137

absenteeism, xvi, 4, 11, 17, 54, 62, 78, 153

acceptable discrimination, 141

acceptable minimum standard, 204

accept/adapt to change, 229, 238

acceptance of diversity, 154

actions and/or omissions, 133, 183

added value, 10, 21, 138

administering organisational justice, 208

advanced industrialised nations, 132

adversarial system, 208

African countries, 131

age discrimination, 149, 181

Age Positive, 138, 182

agriculture and industry, 212

alcohol, 3, 5, 39, 45, 64, 204

alienation, 15, 17, 109, 153

Amsterdam Treaty 1997, 193

ancient indigenous peoples, 132

annual health checks, 53, 58, 62

annualised hours schemes, 99

Apollo 11, 220

Asian industry, 83

attitudes, 19, 50, 57, 106, 111, 124, 130, 150, 167

  authoritarian, 101

  changing, 171

  measuring, 167, 171

  prejudiced, 179

  survey, 171, 177

authority, 75, 92, 109, 111

automation, 225

autonomy, 111

Bacon, Francis, 113

balance of probabilities, 200

bed-to-work trap, 31

behaviour, 50

behavioural

  changes, 234

  effects of stress, 39

  inclinations, 159

  patterns, 118

  sciences, 122, 123

behaviourism, 162

benefits, 122
    and facilities, 2
    and services, 190

blurred hierarchy, 124

breaches of rules, 202

Britain and the US, 83

bullying, 62, 154, 177, 209

bureaucracy, 85

business case
    for employee well-being, 1, 5, 57, 61, 82
    for equal opportunities, 130

Cammel Laird shipyard, 186

career opportunities, 13, 78

categories of stress, 27

causal link – stress, 199

change, 18, 46, 69, 124, 148
    accept and adapt to, 229, 238
    and stress, 245
    culture, 233, 238
    fear of, 238, 246
    in status, 237
    internally stimulated, 231
    nature of, 230
    resistance to, 236

Chartered Institute of Personnel and Development, 182

cheating at work, 16

chronic stress, 28, 34, 39

civil and human rights, 195, 230

class system, 224

coaching and counselling, 14, 93, 173, 205

Code of Practice on Risk Assessment, 61

collision of wave fronts, 214

combinations of workers, 210

commitment, 3, 11, 14, 17, 20, 49, 71, 87, 88, 92, 101, 126
    'model', 85

common law of management, 248

company 'agony aunt', 47

compensation (court actions), 54

compensatory awards (amounts), 25, 197

computer terminals – shackled to, 96, 227

computer – the main medium, 214
    assisted manufacturing techniques, 219
    manufacturing, 219

Concorde, 221

conscious discrimination, 134

constructive unfair dismissal, 209

consultation, 239

content theories (of motivation), 110, 117, 166

contingency theory, 85

continuous change, 46, 230, 234
    deadlines, 50

contract of employment, 97

control and compliance model, 85, 89, 124

coping vs expression, 164

coping with stress, 44, 50

core and peripheral workers, 100

corporate affairs – employee involvement, 92

corporate objectives, 60, 243

counselling, 48, 50, 64, 66, 71, 145, 239

counsellor (manager as), 47, 93

creative innovators, 225

culture, 35, 53, 57, 66, 73, 81, 97, 122, 124, 130, 145, 150, 179, 201, 233–4, 244

curve of intended work performance, 41

customer care, 71

customer-facing employees, 176

daydreaming, 17, 173

decision-making, 52, 80, 89, 144

dehumanisation of work, 219

delayering, 18, 77, 89, 123

deliberate discrimination, 134

depression, 39, 226

deskilling, 219

developing staff, 13, 60

disability, 137, 141, 146, 152, 191
  definition, 192

Disability Discrimination Act 1995 (UK), 137, 192

Disabled Persons (Employment) Acts 1944 and 1958, 191

discipline, 54, 68, 93
  procedural stages, 201–5

discontinuous change, 230

discrimination, 130
  age, 181
  conscious, 134
  direct, 183, 188, 190
  disability, 191

impact on well-being, 153, 209

indirect, 183, 188, 190

legitimate, 133

marital status, 184

policy, 151

race, 190

sex, 183, 184, 187

societal, 131

unconscious, 134

discriminatory factors, 151

dismissal, 190, 205

disputes procedure, 208

Dolly the Sheep, 215

downsizing, 18, 70, 77, 89, 123

drug and alcohol abuse, 39, 64, 204

duty of care, 199

early retirement, 240

economic conditions, 231

education, 60

e-mails, 222

emotional concerns, 3

emotional intelligence, 19

emotions, 20–1

employee assistance programmes, 2, 48, 64, 66, 190, 200

employee development, 88
  handbook, 203
  relations, 24, 65
  retention, 11, 244
  survival strategies, 15
  well-being, 1, 4, 11, 22, 57, 60, 68, 70, 73, 82, 84, 101, 105, 123, 126, 131, 177, 209, 235

employment
  and health, 60
  contract, 200
  legislation, 98
  market, 100
  policies, 59
  relationship, 91
  tribunals, 54, 197, 201, 209
Employment Act 1989, 185
Employment Protection Act 1975, 185
Employment Protection (Consolidation) Act 1978, 185
empowerment, 89, 107, 123
environmental factors, 26
equal opportunities, 59, 111, 130, 138, 143–4, 193
  policy, 129, 148, 150
  policy statement, 151
Equal Pay Act 1970, 185
Equal Pay (Amendment) Regulations 1973, 185
equal treatment, 129, 143–4
equality and fairness, 137, 142, 143
equity-inequity theory, 119
equivalent work, 186
esteem needs, 112, 121
ethnic origin, 141
European Union, 193, 194
European Directive on Equal Treatment, 182
European Employment Strategy, 193
eustress, 38

expectancy theory, 119, 167
exponential rate of change, 18, 214, 220, 222
external
  environment, 243
  pressures, 230
extrinsic and intrinsic job factors, 106, 108, 113, 117
extrinsic and intrinsic stressors, 42, 43, 55

fairness, 129, 137, 142, 144, 154
  at work, 194
Family Friendliness, 194
fathers – new legal rights, 143
fax and e-mails, 222
fearful perception – stress situations, 247
female employment, 193
fiddling, 16
fight or flight reaction, 36, 38
financial, 48, 121
flat structures, 70, 77, 88, 123, 172, 246
  criticism, 78
flexible workforce, 247
flexible working, 98, 100
flight to the Moon, 220
food policy (staff restaurant), 53
four categories of welfare, 3
functional
  flexibility, 98
  specialists, 78

general adaptation syndrome (GAS), 35, 37

genetic modification, 215, 216

genuine occupational qualification (GOQ), 196

genuinely material factor (GMF), 187

global competition, 81, 172

global economy, 131, 234

global market, 18, 69

global competition, 81, 172

'going on Concorde', 221

goodwill, 97, 178

government intervention, 230

grievance procedure, 54, 68, 93, 200, 201–2

   stages of, 207

gross misconduct, 201, 206

group exercises, 174

groups (social), 96

'growing child syndrome', 234

habit-forming work cycle, 15

Harvard Business School, 95

Hawthorn studies, 85, 95, 105

headcount philosophy, 94

health and safety, 57, 60, 111, 126, 173

Health of the Nation Report, 63

health of the organisation, 57, 182

healthy
   and safe working environment, 200
   eating, 53
   lifestyle initiatives, 52, 63, 227

workplace, 1, 45, 53, 57, 60

heroes, 49

hidden dangers of Internet use, 226

hierarchical order, 124, 141

hierarchy of needs, 20, 112, 114

hierarchy of technological capability, 224

'high-tech' skills, 244

higher-order needs, 20, 114, 116, 166

HIV/AIDS, 2, 5, 63

hostile atmosphere, 74, 122

HR (Human Resource), 9, 66, 84, 88, 247

   movements, 234

   strategy, 172

HRM (Human Resource Management), 4, 6, 13, 20, 77, 83–103, 130, 157, 246

human function curve, 41

human relations approach, 95, 103, 122, 126

human relations model, 85, 88

Human Rights Act 1999, 185

humour – a coping device, 16

hunters and gatherers, 212

'hygiene' factors, 115

illegal recruitment advertisements, 188

independent legislative action, 193

indirect discrimination, 183, 188, 190

individual differences, 30, 50, 55, 111, 137, 247

induction, 93, 202

industrial genes, 221

Industrial Revolution, 85, 142, 213, 221, 223, 227

Industrial Welfare Society, 4

industrial work paradigm, 85, 126, 212

Information Age, 214

information technology, 78, 220

inherent prejudice, 135

innovation
    current work systems, 233
    product, 231

integration of policies, 130

intellectual well-being, 3

internal justice system (IJS), 182, 201

internal legislation, 182

internal politics, 102

Internet, 223, 226

interpersonal perception, 161

interviews, 150, 226

intrapreneurship, 21

intrinsic job factors, 108

intrinsic stressors, 43

involvement, 90, 101, 105, 109, 114, 239
    and commitment, 106, 126

ivory tower attitude, 177

job
    description, 188
    enlargement, 98, 123
    enrichment, 123
    evaluation, 186
    insecurity, 13, 235, 245

involvement, 60, 62, 111, 117, 122
    redesign, 123
    requisition, 188
    satisfaction, 60, 62, 97, 98, 105, 109, 117, 120, 122
    security, 14, 62, 70, 90, 97, 111, 235

job-for-life syndrome, 236

job-person unit, 43, 116

King, Martin Luther, 195

lateral non-reporting relationships, 77

law of succession, 217

leadership, 93, 124
    skills, 10
    styles, 9, 63, 73, 165
    training, 10

leaner, flatter structure, 77, 89, 91, 246

legislation
    aspects of employee well-being, 181
    compliance, 92, 144
    legitimate discrimination, 133, 137
    minimum standards, 68, 130

Lever Bros, 2

lifestyle, 50, 52, 159
    advice on, 52–3
    paradigms of, 212

line and staff management, 78, 80

litigation, 196
    and stress, 25, 54, 61, 198
    cost, 25

court decisions, 68
media reporting, 25, 198
long hours culture, 31
long-serving employees, 235–6
long-term change, 230
'look after your heart', 64
Lord Chancellor, 148
Lord Mayor, 148
loss of earnings, 199
lost productivity, 24, 178
low skilled people, 213
low status jobs, 210
low tolerance for pressure, 42
lower-order needs, 20, 116, 166
lunchtime drinking, 5, 45

macho management, 62
male–female balance, 134, 141, 194, 195
management
    and leadership, 9
    and workforce – blurred
        distinction, 78, 89
    by objectives, 85
    development, 18
    systems and techniques, 83, 234
    theory and practice, 83, 105
management gurus, 83
manager–employee relations, 65, 78, 174, 208
managerial control, 17
    and non-managerial staff, 89
    attitudes, 174
    command structure, 83

managerial grid, 175
    perceptions, 94
    style, 62, 66, 72, 177
managers as unique individuals, 174
    as a counsellor, 47
    assumptions, 139
    naive expectations, 246
    perceptions of employees, 5
managing
    change, 235
    diversity, 60, 129, 138
    individual differences, 157
    lifestyle, 52
    organisational change, 229
    stress, 44
mandatory equal opportunities
    policies, 131
mandatory rules, 205
manufacturing-based economies, 213
marital status, 144, 149, 184
material welfare, 4
maternity rights, 143
matrix process, 78, 80
measuring attitudes, 167, 171
mechanistic
    administrative system, 242
    organisations, 241
medically qualified staff, 64
meditation and relaxation, 55
mental and physical well-being, 1, 58, 59, 68, 183
    and physical absence, 17
    and physiological changes, 38
    balance sheet, 119
    breakdown, 41
    illness – stigma, 34

mental effect of stress, 34, 45

methods of working, 96, 246

Microsoft Corporation, 214

minor ailments – stress related, 40

minor offences, 203

minor operational decisions, 96, 123

minority groups, 129, 131, 132, 138, 143, 152, 167, 210

misconduct, 203

mobile phones, 223

modern-day Luddites, 17

modern technology, 212, 220

monitor employee well-being, 58

monitor employees' attitudes, 168

monotony and powerlessness, 15

motivation, 19, 60, 91, 105, 162, 240
    and commitment, 3, 20, 235
    and morale, 97, 106
    content theories, 166
    process theories, 166
    satisfaction and performance, 235
    theorists, 112, 115, 119, 166

motivation and performance, 8, 20, 88

motivation–hygiene theory, 112, 115

motor car industry, 123

multiskilling, 89, 91, 98, 101, 123, 172

mutual trust, 10, 124

mutuality of interest, 6, 88

Nagasaki and Hiroshima, 47

National Disability Council (for England, Wales and Scotland), 192

natural ability, 10
    evolution, 213
    leadership, 9

negative views of technology, 219

new immigrants, 132, 145,

new technology, 69, 212
    definitions of, 217
    introduction of, 247

non-cash rewards, 59, 122

Northern Ireland Disability Council, 192

numerical flexibility, 98

occupational support schemes, 2, 48, 64, 66, 200

'one small step for man', 220

organic organisations, 241–2, 244

organisational
    climate, 73
    development (OD), 122, 123
    effectiveness, 125
    objectives, 218
    perspective, the, 68
    structure, 70, 74

out-of-character behaviour, 40, 45

overnight change, 235

pace of change, 229

panic attacks, 52

paradigm shifts, 212
    industrial and post-industrial, 212
    of human lifestyle, 212, 220

part-time work, 141, 194

patterns of attendance (at work), 58

pay, 111

equality, 144
pension, 2, 111, 122, 190
pension scheme, 111
salaries and wages, 111
value of staff's work, 81, 91, 178, 209
peer relationships, 111
perceptions, 159
and attitudes, 167
influence on motivation, 162
of change, 247
of people, 161
of stress, 50
of the work of others, 161
of work situations, 161
selective, 160
performance = ability × motivation, 8, 20, 41, 90
performance, 74
and job satisfaction, 120
appraisal, 4
record, 48
related pay, 99
standards, 42, 58
peripheral work, 15, 100, 102
and commitment, 101
person specification, 188
personality
characteristics, 161
development, 158, 167
factors, 159
personnel management, 84
department, 49, 93
persuasive information, 173
PEST, 230

physical
activity, 52, 64, 65, 227
and mental damage, 223
differences, 137
effects of stress, 35, 45, 50
injury, 60
safety, 60
violence, 132
well-being, 3, 58, 59, 68
work environment, 106, 111, 141
working conditions, 96, 105, 137
physiological needs, 20, 112
pleasureable outcomes, 118, 246
plight of stressed employees, 63
pluralistic perspectives, 86
policies on discrimination, 129
political
acceptability, 215
correctness, 147, 171
incorrectness, 147
interventions, 230
parties, 223
pollution and waste, 213
poor performance – toleration of, 204
positive and negative emotions, 21
positive discrimination, 134, 145, 149, 195
positive stress, 37
post traumatic stress disorders, 28, 34, 48
potential appraisal, 4
power and control, 124
predicting in-job performance, 189
prejudices, 134, 143, 179

present and future technology, 220

pressure
    and performance, 41
    and stress, 7, 58
    and well-being, 6
    to discriminate, 134

PRICES, 231

primary emotions, 20

prime benficiaries, 218

private health scheme, 190

problem-solving, 80, 89
    decision-making unit, 10, 89
    groups, 10

problems at home, 50

problems with systems, 232

process technology, 214

process theories of work motivation,
    110, 117, 166

product technology, 231

productivity losses, 62, 178

project managers, 80

promise of a reward – motivator, 121

promotion, 21, 78, 102, 108, 118,
    133, 143, 144, 187, 234

psychological
    contract, 18, 97, 98, 201
    damage, 226
    depression, 226
    differences, 137, 157
    illnesses, 34, 40
    injury, 199
    kicks, 15, 114
    needs, 113
    reward, 121

'pull yourself together…', 63

punitive measures:
    groups, 209
    procedural, 203

PYTBULLS, 63, 72

Quaker Cadbury families, 2

quality of working life, 219

questionnaires, 150

race, 149, 191
    preconceptions, 132, 143
    relations, 150

Race Relations Act 1976, 190

racial discrimination, 190

rate of change, 214, 241

'real world' of management, 102

reasonable instruction, 204

recent immigrants, 132

recognising stress symptoms, 34, 45,
    46

recreational facilities, 2

recruitment and selection, 93, 187
    advertisement, 151, 188
    catchment area, 145
    disabled, 138
    processes, 134

recruitment market, 5, 12

reduced performance, 23–4, 42

reducing staff numbers, 89, 240

reductionist stance, 94

redundancy, 2, 18, 21, 47, 70, 102,
    152, 172, 190, 239

redundant skills, 236, 244

register of disabled people, 191

religion (discrimination), 143, 149, 181

relocation, 232

Remington and Sons, 142

reputation as an employer, 12, 25, 182

resistance – to stress, 35, 36

respect and courtesy, 124, 176

response bias, 171

responsibility, 75
    as a status symbol, 110
    at home, 142
    in job, 109, 111, 116, 142

retention of employees, 82

retirement, 2, 30, 240

retrain and retain, 244

return on capital, 215

reverse discrimination, 145, 149, 195

reward
    as an outcome, 121
    flexibility, 99

rights and privileges, 97

rightsizing, 18, 70, 77, 89, 123

risk assessment, 61, 200

Rover Cars in the UK, 90

Rowntree, 2

rudeness – to visitors, colleagues, 205

sabotage, 17

safety needs (motivation), 20, 112

satisfaction, 101, 105, 117
    and fulfilment, 106
    and performance, 122

satisfaction and dissatisfaction, 115

scepticism and suspicion, 219

Scientific Management, 83, 85, 103

scientific revolution, 213, 227

scrutinising selection decisions, 150

second-class citizens, 131

second paradigm, 218

selection
    and promotion systems, 133, 143
    decisions, 93
    process, 152
    tests, 152

selective perception, 160

self-actualisation, 20, 112, 114

self-confidence, 8, 63

self-development, 14

self-esteem, 113

self-generated work, 49

self-perception – and the job, 113

self-preservation, 102

self-report questionnaires, 40

semantic differential scale, 40, 168

sense of ownership, 239

service levels (to customers), 233

sex
    and marital status, 149, 183
    discrimination, 149, 187, 210
    essential qualification, 196

Sex Discrimination Act 1975, 185, 187

sexual health, 2

shackled to computers, 96, 227

short-term change, 230

sickness absence, 4, 11, 24, 45, 62, 68, 122

significant life changes, 32

Silicon Valley, 232

situational differences, 137

skin colour, 138

smoke-free work areas, 53

smoking, 3, 5, 39, 50, 205

social
  acceptability, 215
  adjustment scale, 33
  and psychological well-being, 226
  hierarchy, 224
  organisation, 96
  skills, 63
  structures, 224
  trends, 231

Social Security Act 1989, 185

socialisation, 135, 158, 167, 179

socially isolated, 99, 101

societal discrimination, 131

socio-economic strata, 244

source of power, 86

sources and causes of stress, 31

spans of control, 124

specific statement – equal
  opportunities, 151

stable employees, 237

stable market, 241

staff
  representative groups, 86
  restaurant, 53, 177
  retention, 82
  turnover, 68, 122, 150, 234, 245

status of the job, 110

stealing, 204

sting of injustice, 153

strategic management role, 75

strategies on discrimination, 129
  for the long term, 69, 71

stress, 7, 13, 21, 23, 91, 131, 177
  and change, 32
  and disorientation, 216
  and individual difference, 30
  and personality, 27
  as a commuter, 26
  audit, 31
  avoidance techniques, 51, 52, 65
  behavioural effects, 39
  causes, 53
  cost of, 24, 54, 61
  degrees of severity, 31
  measurement scale, 40, 55
  mill, 26
  natural reaction, 7, 26
  reduction strategies, 39, 45, 62
  self-induced, 27, 30
  sources and causes, 23, 31, 53,
  surveys, 54, 73
  symptoms, 45, 46, 52, 55
  types of, 27

stress-related sickness absence, 24, 54

stressful jobs, 43

structure
  and culture, 75, 77
  components of, 75
  flatter, wider, 88, 123
  mechanisms and dimensions, 74
  primary purposes, 75
  the importance of, 57, 77
  visible design, 89

suicide, 7

Sunday Graphic newspaper, 220

superficial and 'deep' change, 230

supervision – the technical aspects of, 116

survival and development (organisational), 70

suspension on full pay, 206

system of justice (internal), 182, 201

system theory, 85

systems of payment, 59, 62

talent war, 101

Taylorism, 85

team membership behaviour, 96, 165

teamworking, 80, 95, 209

technical organisation, 96

technological
    change, 19, 218, 244
    innovation, 214, 231

technology
    a human quality, 217, 220
    a way of doing things, 213
    and lifestyle, 219
    as an agent of change, 211
    complexities of, 221
    in society, 211
    the enchantment of, 221

telecommuting, 99, 101

terms and conditions of employment, 105, 106, 111, 144, 208

Theories X and Y, 72, 174

theory of growth motivation (Maslow), 112

third world poverty, 132

three main paradigms, 212

Thurstone scale, 169
    example of, 170

Trade Union and Employment Rights Act 1993, 185

trade unions, 86, 91, 98, 205, 210, 225

traditional industrial activity, 223

training, 8, 93
    and counselling, 205
    and development, 60
    and promotion decisions, 143, 144
    for change, 173
    opportunities, 143, 187, 189

'transferred down' staff, 71

transient stress, 27, 38

Treaty of Rome, 193

trust, 21
    and goodwill, 18

two concurrent paradigms, 213

two-dimensional theory (motivation)
    Type A and B personalities, 29

typewriter – debut, 142

UK National Health Service, 63

UK Civil Service, 184, 189

unconscious discrimination, 134

under- and over-utilisation, 62, 153

unemployment, 82

unfair disadvantage, 133, 137, 149, 151

unfair dismissal, 209

unfair selection for redundancy, 152

unfair treatment, 137, 151, 153, 202, 209

'unfreeze–change–refreeze', 236

unique value systems, 159

unitary frame of reference, 85

unitary perspective, 86

upgrading people's skills, 219

US and European markets, 83

'us and them', 6, 77

US civil rights legislation, 144

value added, 21

value of the work effort, 81, 91, 178, 209

valued abilities, 59, 236

values and beliefs, 73, 135, 159, 161, 179

verbal and written warnings, 205

virtual shop front, 226

voluntary redundancies, 240

wages and salaries, 94, 116

waves of change, 212, 214, 222

welfare role of personnel, 60

Western Electric Company, 95

wider, flattened organisations, 70, 77

wilful damage, 204

women
    and minority groups, 12, 141
    prejudices against, 141

work
    and individual differences, 58
    and non-work relationships, 74, 75
    groups, 96
    measurement, 96
    methods, 96, 246
    motivation, 110
    of equal value, 186
working climate, 66
    conditions, 96, 108, 116
    time, 111
    time flexibility, 98
    time regulations, 3

zero hours contracts, 99